SEVENTY YEARS
of
CINEMA

SEVENTY YEARS

of

CINEMA

by

PETER COWIE

CASTLE BOOKS ★ NEW YORK

This Edition Published by Arrangement with A. S. Barnes & Co., Inc.

SBN 498-06635-5

Printed in the United States of America

For My Parents

Acknowledgments

I am indebted to the Information Department and Book Library of the British Film Institute for their courtesy and help during the research for this book. Also to Allen Eyles and Anthony Slide for looking over the manuscript and correcting many errors.

The following individuals have kindly loaned stills to the author: Roy Armes, Ivan Butler, Saul Kahan, Tom Vallance, and especially Roger Manvell and Joel W. Finler. Other photographs have been provided by the following companies and organizations: British Lion, La Cinémathèque Française, Columbia Pictures, Compton Films, Connoisseur Films, Contemporary Films (London), Europa Film (Stockholm), Gala Films, Hungarofilm, Metro-Goldwyn-Mayer, Miracle Films, Paramount, Polish National Film Archive, The Rank Organisation, Sandrews (Stockholm), Svensk Filmindustri (Stockholm), Twentieth Century-Fox, United Artists, Warner Brothers, and Warner-Pathé (London).

Contents

Introduction

This volume does not pretend to be a comprehensive history of the cinema. I have tried to give some signposts to the significant developments in the film as an art and as a sophisticated medium of entertainment. The reviews pay tribute to the films responsible for such trends; the movies that, either at the time of their release or later, have opened new paths and set a standard for others to follow.

Most of the celebrated pictures are described, from *The Great Train Robbery* and *The Birth of a Nation* to *Persona* and *Bonnie and Clyde,* but there are also some works which to my mind have been unjustly neglected and which have a worthy place in the complex pattern of world film production.

The preponderance of material on the cinema of the last twenty-five years reflects not so much an increase in output as a growing recognition of the *range* of film expression in many different countries since the war. The chronological method will, I hope, emphasize the density of the cinema's history as well as its brevity.

In addition to the reviews, there is also a check list of other major features produced during the period, a list of outstanding short and documentary films, and a short guide to facts and events in each year.

All films discussed (with one or two exceptions) appear under the year in which they were released in their country of origin. P.D.C.

London, June 1968

SEVENTY YEARS
of
CINEMA

Pre-history

Books as large as this one have been devoted entirely to the confused pre-history of the cinema; some authorities have even traced the medium back to 1645, when Athanasius Kircher projected printed pictures (on glass) on to a screen. Certainly the problems of definition (what is the difference between a film and a series of pictures projected at speed?), of geography (several pioneers were working in various countries more or less simultaneously), and of copyright make it a thorny subject to tackle in a few sentences. However, some skeletal chronology of the final stages can be attempted, as follows:

Celluloid had been in existence since the 1860s. A French anatomist, *Etienne-Jules Marey,* developed the "fusil photographique," an elongated, blunderbuss-shaped antecedent of the movie camera of today. During the eighties, he also manufactured film strips. *Eadweard Muybridge,* an Englishman resident in California, was fascinated by the movement at speed of animals and people, and he took thousands of closely-linked photographs to analyze this. When projected in sequence, these obviously did (and still do) look like a stuttering motion picture film.

Between 1885 and 1887, *Louis Aimé Augustin Le-Prince* apparently projected moving pictures in a New York workshop, by means of a single-lens camera *cum* projector. A tablet in Leeds (England) commemorates him as making a camera and projector in 1888 and taking pictures in that year on Leeds Bridge.

In October, 1889, *Thomas Edison* is said to have screened moving pictures in a New Jersey laboratory. Edison relied heavily on his assistant, William K. L. Dickson, and made no significant advances on his own. But he was a skillful business man who knew how to exploit rights and patents. In August 1891 he was granted a patent for his perforated film camera, and in 1894 he patented his Kinetoscope, which employed celluloid for commercial purposes.

Mention should also be made of *Emile Reynaud,* whose elaborate Praxinoscope attracted thousands of Parisians to the Musée Grévin during the nineties.

1895

February: R. W. Paul supposedly projects some moving films in Hatton Garden, London.

February: The Lumière brothers are given a French patent for their 20 frames-per-second camera *cum* projector.

March 22: The Lumière brothers show their first film, *La Sortie des Usines Lumière à Lyon-Montplaisir,* to a private audience.

March 30: In England, Birt Acres uses his Kinetic Lantern to record the University Boat Race.

September: Moving pictures are presented by Thomas Arnat at the Cotton States Exposition in Atlanta.

November: Max Skladanowsky screens the first films *in public,* in Berlin.

December 28: The first public showing of films in Paris, by the Lumière brothers. Titles include *L'Arrivée d'un Train en Gare de la Ciotat, L'Arroseur Arrosé* (the first "fiction" film), and *Le Goûter de Bébé* (Baby's Breakfast).

1895: A frame from the Lumière brothers' early film, L'ARRIVÉE D'UN TRAIN EN GARE DE LA CIOTAT.

1896

UNE PARTIE DE CARTES. France.

The first film by Georges Méliès, who himself played one of the card players, in his own garden at Montreuil-sous-Bois. While Lumière has been the spiritual mentor of such "realistic" directors as Flaherty, Grierson, Rossellini, De Sica, Reisz, and Cassavetes, Georges Méliès has incited the romantic and the illusionist in film-makers like Buñuel, Carné, Welles, Bergman, and Truffaut. As the late Georges Sadoul emphasized, Lumière may have founded the *cinematograph*, but Méliès established the *cinema*, and those are two very different things. All Méliès's films depended on a degree of fantasy and trickery for their impact. He ran the Robert Houdin theatre in Paris from 1888 onwards, and the extensive workshop there proved invaluable for the development of all manner of apparatus.

Méliès was a born performer. Throughout his career he played the central role in all his films. Indeed he did everything connected with their production: the script, the direction, the décor, the special effects, even the basic photography.

THE EMPIRE STATE EXPRESS. United States. An excellent railroad picture, made for Biograph.

1896: Facts of Interest

In Britain, J.D. Walker and E.G. Turner exploit the Edison Kinetoscope and phonograph. R.W. Paul films the Derby horserace and screens it to an audience the same night. G.A. Smith was also a prominent member of the British school. He was a portrait photographer who used films as accompaniment to his lectures. By April, 1897, he had sold his first film, made with a home-built camera.

Promio, a cameraman working under Louis Lumière, shot a tracking film of the Grand Canal in Venice, from a gondola, the first work of its kind.

Max Skladanowsky visits Stockholm and makes some films, probably the earliest pictures shot in Sweden.

On April 23, the Lumière brothers give a public performance of their films at Koster and Bial's Music Hall, New York.

Lillian Gish, Buster Keaton, and King Vidor are born.

1897

Facts of Interest

Georges Méliès builds his own studios and produces around 60 shorts.

Louis Lumière is responsible for between 300 and 400 shorts.

1898

TEARING DOWN THE SPANISH FLAG. United States.

A brief but important propaganda gesture filmed in a single studio room by Albert Smith and J. Stuart Blackton, founders of the Vitagraph Company.

THE CORSICAN BROTHERS. Britain. Director: G. A. Smith.

Based on a stage play; contains a "transparent" ghost thanks to double exposure.

1898: Facts of Interest

Gaumont—British is founded.
The first films are shot in Japan.
René Clair, Sergei M. Eisenstein, and Preston Sturges are born.

1899

THE DREYFUS AFFAIR (L'Affaire Dreyfus). France. Director: George Méliès.

Demonstrations greeted the screening, and this film was banned in France. It told the story of the case in twelve scenes, and is one of the few films by Méliès that is related in earnest, bereft of gags or artifice. Méliès was as committed as any artist could be, and took a brave stand on the whole business.

1899: Facts of Interest

The first British studio is built in New Southgate, outside London, by R. W. Paul, after a quarrel with Edison had cut off the supply of films from America.

Australia makes her first film, *The Early Christian Martyrs*.

An extract from "King John" is the first Shakespeare work to be set on film.

Jean Cocteau and Alfred Hitchcock are born.

1900

GRANDMA'S READING GLASS. Britain. Director: G. A. Smith.

This film is now regarded as having pioneered the use of sequence (the same scene broken into close-ups, medium shots, and so on).

ON A RUNAWAY MOTOR-CAR THROUGH PICCADILLY CIRCUS. Britain. Director: R. W. Paul.

The travelling, or tracking, shot is employed subjectively and dramatically for the first time.

1900: Facts of Interest

Luis Buñuel is born in Spain.

1901

THE INDIARUBBER HEAD (L'homme à la Tête de Caoutchouc). France. Director: George Méliès.

In this brief but devastating film, Méliès's flair for spectacle is obvious. We see a table outside the studio. Méliès appears and places a platform, from which a head protrudes, on top of the table. It is the head of the director himself (although Méliès remains by its side in the picture); it jigs around, chattering away quite happily to its imaginary audience. Méliès summons an assistant to press a pair of blowers nearby, and the head suddenly starts to swell. Eventually, when the assistant pumps too zealously, the head can expand no longer and explodes instead. Like many of the silent shorts, *An Indiarubber Head* turns on a single gag, but the construction of this film is extraordinarily mature. Méliès is in absolute control of the operation, and there is a delightful moment when he "manipulates" his audience's susceptibilities by "shrinking" the head a little and beaming at the camera.

ATTACK ON A CHINA MISSION. Britain. Director: J. Williamson.

Filmed in the director's own garden. An early example of the "faked incident" picture, showing Boxers storming the house.

HISTOIRE D'UN CRIME. France. Director: Ferdinand Zecca.

Inspired by the wax figures in the Musée Grévin, and the first film by Zecca.

1901: Facts of Interest

Edwin S. Porter becomes a cameraman for Edison. Walt Disney is born.

1901: Georges Méliès plays in his own THE INDIARUBBER HEAD.

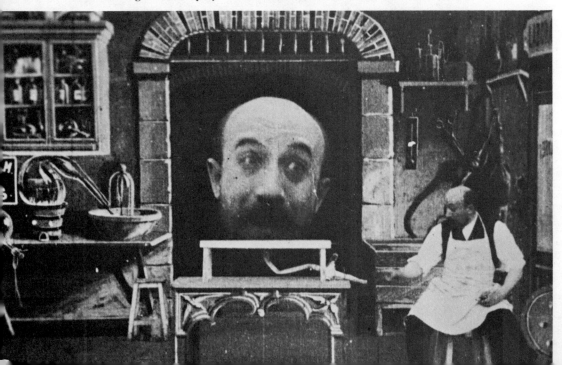

1902

A TRIP TO THE MOON (Le Voyage dans la Lune). France. Director: Georges Méliès.

In 1932, Méliès wrote: "For 20 years I made fantasy films of all kinds and my principal aim was to find for each film original gags, a big central effect, and a climax at the end." His invention was prodigious, and he completed approximately 450 films between 1896 and 1908. *A Trip to the Moon,* inspired by the novels of Jules Verne and H. G. Wells, cost some 10,000 francs to produce, and was about three times as long as other films of the period. Méliès designed the enormous cannon that launched the explorers on their way, and he also made the extraordinary masks worn by the Selenites, who scurry along like human lobsters in their underground palaces (they were played by acrobats from the Folies-Bergère). The whole film is a splendid and enthusiastic dream.

Checklist of other important films

MARY JANE'S MISHAP. Britain. G. A. Smith. A cautionary tale about a girl who dies in an explosion and then returns as a ghost to haunt those who are being warned against repeating her stupidity.

LES VICTIMES DE L' ALCOOLISME. France. Director: Ferdinand Zecca. A five-part movie based on Zola's *L'Assommoir (The Gin Shop).*

1902: Facts of Interest

The Electric Theatre in Los Angeles becomes the first regular commercial cinema.
Max Ophüls, William Wyler, and Vittorio De Sica are born.

1903

THE GREAT TRAIN ROBBERY. United States. Director: Edwin S. Porter. With Max Aaronson, Marie Murray, George Barnes, Frank Hanaway. Production: Edison. One reel.

Edwin S. Porter made *The Great Train Robbery* in the autumn of 1903. It consisted of 14 scenes, although the last of these, a close-up of an outlaw aiming his gun into the camera, was produced merely as a shock effect, and according to the distributor involved could be projected at the beginning of the film if necessary! Not only did *The Great Train Robbery* tell a *story* of dramatic impact, but it hinted excitingly at the possibilities of parallel montage which Griffith was to use so purposefully. The *movement*, as well as the narrative, was carried over from one scene to another. This was particularly impressive in the sequences showing the robbery itself (from a train in full flight) and the escape of the bandits on horseback through the mountains. Porter continued to make important movies, but *The Great Train Robbery* established the pattern of the American adventure film for at least two decades. It can also be described as the archetype of the Westerns that were to pour out of Hollywood in future years. The bandit leader was played by Max Aaronson, later to be known as Max Anderson and then "Broncho" Billy, the prolific star and director of Westerns.

Checklist of other important films

A DARING DAYLIGHT BURGLARY. Britain. Director: Frank Mottershaw. A short account of a robbery that had many affinities to the Porter film described above.

THE RUNAWAY MATCH. United States. Director: Alfred Collins. A precocious film in which all kinds of camera movements and positions are exploited to advantage.

1903: Facts of Interest

First Japanese cinema opens—in Tokyo.
First all-Dutch film, *The Adventure of a French Gentleman without Trousers.*

A frame from Edwin S. Porter's THE GREAT TRAIN ROBBERY. 1903.

1904

LE VOYAGE A TRAVERS L'IMPOSSIBLE. France.
Director: George Méliès.

The sun, not the moon, is the object of Méliès's explorations here, which begin in the Swiss mountains as some scientists prepare for a journey through space. Forty scenes in various locales.

1904: Facts of Interest

Italian film production begins with two shorts: *Manoeuvres of the Alpine Troops in the Colle della Ranzola,* and an account of the Susa-Moncenisio motor race.

1905

RESCUED BY ROVER. Britain. Directors: Lewin Fitzhamon and Cecil Hepworth. With Sebastian Smith, Mrs. Smith, Cecil Hepworth, Mrs. Hepworth, and "Baby" Hepworth.

"The British school," wrote the late Georges Sadoul, "saved the cinema from the eternal glass house of the early studios." Operating on poor resources, the British directors were much more liable to follow Lumière than Méliès. Their first major achievement in the fiction film was *Rescued by Rover,* in which a stolen child is recovered through the astuteness of the family dog. Hepworth's talent lay in his narrative style. Even today, one is never conscious of any breaks between sequences, so simple and persuasive is the logic of the story. The shots of Rover dashing through the streets are brilliantly linked, and there is an effective contrast between the shabby attic where the child is hidden, and the comfortable home of the Hepworths. In its compositions, too, *Rescued by Rover* is often inspired. The old gypsy takes a swig from a bottle of spirits in her curiously-lit room and looks uncannily like a Rembrandt image or an inhabitant of Chaplin's *Easy Street* (see *1917*). The film was made for £7.13s.9d., and nearly 400 prints were sold.

FALSELY ACCUSED. Britain. Producer: Cecil Hepworth.

An ambitious and complex story of theft in the City of London, constructed along the lines of a feature film.

1905: Facts of Interest

The first "nickelodeon" opens in Pittsburgh in November.
Max Linder starts appearing in films.
Greta Garbo is born.

1905: RESCUED BY ROVER, directed by Cecil Hepworth.

1906

THE 400 TRICKS OF THE DEVIL (Les Quatre Cents Farces du Diable). France. Director: Georges Méliès.

A parade of virtually all Méliès's technical tricks, a kind of morality fable full of ghosts and metamorphoses. No director since has succeeded so well as Méliès in realizing the schoolboy's flights of imagination. His films are like a collection of fairy tales, never patronizing and never vulgar.

THE DREAM OF A RAREBIT FIEND. U.S.A. Director: Edwin S. Porter.

A fantasy tale based on a man's nightmares, with special effects and dissolves between shots playing an important part.

1906: Facts of Interest

Edison builds a studio in the Bronx for $100,000.
Biograph also establishes studios in New York City.
The first documentary record of the Olympic Games is made, in Greece.
John Huston, Billy Wilder, and Luchino Visconti are born.
In Britain, Charles Urban and G. A. Smith launch a color film process known as Kinemacolor.

1907

RESCUED FROM AN EAGLE'S NEST. United States. Director: Edwin S. Porter.

This melodrama, which suffered from being shot in the studios to too large a degree, is famous because it featured D. W. Griffith in his first screen appearance. An eagle snatches a baby away from outside his home, while Griffith is away felling timber. The hysterical mother brings him the message, and the rescue operation begins. Griffith is lowered by rope down a cliff face and then has to battle with the eagle before being hauled to safety with his child, his face bloody but smiling. There are too many crude backcloths and false effects (the "paper" eagle, for instance), and the only merit of the film is its omission of captions, which adds to the suspense and the level of audience involvement.

1907: Facts of Interest

Formation of Essanay by George Spoor and "Broncho Billy" Anderson.

Thomas Ince appears in the cast of *Seven Ages,* directed by Edwin S. Porter.

Svenska Biografteatern, the principal Swedish production company, is founded.

Alexander Drankov opens Russia's first film studio, and in Britain Will Barker builds a stage on the site of the future Ealing Studios.

Fred Zinnemann is born.

1908

Checklist of important films

THE ASSASSINATION OF THE DUKE OF GUISE (L'Assassinat du Duc de Guise). Directors: Le Bargy and Calmettes. France. The first important costume film about the nobility, with music by Saint-Saens.

THE LAST DAYS OF POMPEII. Italy. Director: Luigi Maggi. Based on the novel by Sir Bulwer Lytton. Massive historical reconstruction.

1908: Facts of Interest

D. W. Griffith, engaged by Biograph as an actor, becomes a director too, and shoots the first of his 450-odd films, *The Adventures of Dolly*. In August, in *For Love of Gold*, he uses the close-up for the first time.

Emile Cohl makes the first cartoons in France, *Fantasmagorie* among them.

The "Pathé-Journal" in France becomes the world's first regular newsreel.

Jacques Tati is born.

1909

EDGAR ALLAN POE. United States. Director: D. W. Griffith.

The artificial light and shadowplay are subtle in this film, inspired by Poe's story, "The Raven."

1909: Facts of Interest

Lt. Shackleton's record of the expedition to the South Pole is the first really successful documentary.

Griffith shoots 138 films.

Mary Pickford makes her début in *The Violin Maker of Cremona*.

35 mm becomes the internationally-accepted film size (introduced and developed by Thomas Edison).

Charles Magnusson joins Svenska Bio as production manager, and the Swedish cinema proper is born.

Winsor McCay's brilliant cartoon, *Gertie the Dinosaur*, is the first animated film produced in the U.S.A.

1910

SIMPLE CHARITY. United States. Director: D. W. Griffith.

One of Mary Pickford's earliest appearances. A plea for the better treatment of old folk.

1910: Facts of Interest

The first "Broncho Billy" film is released on July 30. Tom Mix appears for the first time on the screen in a documentary, *Ranch Life in the Great South West*.

1911

THE LONEDALE OPERATOR. United States. Director: D. W. Griffith.

Cross-cutting between scenes reaches its most advanced stage here with the hero hurrying to the rescue of Blanche Sweet in a railroad depot.

MAX, VICTIM OF QUINQUINA (Max et le Quinquina).

Max Linder playing the drunkard with a polish and an individual style remarkable for the period.

1911: Facts of Interest

Mack Sennett joins with Kessel to form Keystone, and directs his first film, *Comrades*.

1912

THE CONQUEST OF THE POLE (A la Conquête du Pôle). France. Director: Georges Méliès.

Although the trick monsters and special effects that Méliès used constantly must have shocked his audiences at the time, they are always tempered with a good-natured wit. Near the beginning of *The Conquest of the Pole*, there is an amusing interlude when some sturdy suffragettes try to steal the Professor's thunder by launching their own "aeroscaphe," which refuses to leave the ground, despite all the balloons atop the vehicle. Later, we see one of these women fall from a balloon and hurtle downwards to "explode" on the sharp roofs of Paris.

The film starts with Professor Maboul (Georges Méliès) demonstrating a model of his fantastic aeroplane. Then comes the assembly and the launching. When the Arctic is reached the flying machine descends, but too abruptly, and it disintegrates. Méliès's master stroke is his abominable snowman, which rises from the depths of a lake, with stalactites for his moustache. He smokes a pipe and looks fairly benevolent until like the Cyclops he starts eating the explorers. Rescuers arrive just in time from another aircraft, and as the Professor and his crew leave the Pole, all the seals and penguins in the neighborhood flap farewell. *The Conquest of the Pole* seems a very fluid film, full of movement and action. In fact, Méliès creates this illusion by means of moving backgrounds, and the camera stays rigid. This film, like several others in the director's catalogue, was tinted, and the colors used to enchanting effect. It is the last major film by the great French pioneer, who was slowly to fade from the scene and be forgotten until 1928, when he was recognized selling fancy goods in the Gare de Montparnasse.

Checklist of other important films

THE MASSACRE. United States. Director: D. W. Griffith. An advanced, intelligent, and fast-moving Western.

LES MISERABLES. France. Director: A. Capellani. Based on the novel by Victor Hugo; an exceptionally long film, in four parts. There were 120 copies sold within a few months.

THE MUSKETEERS OF PIG ALLEY. United States. Director: D. W. Griffith. Remarkable camerawork distinguishes this Griffith movie.

THE NEW YORK HAT. United States. Director: D. W. Griffith. From a script by Anita Loos, starring Mary Pickford and Lionel Barrymore. Close-ups already predominate in this film.

QUEEN ELIZABETH (La Reine Elisabeth). France. Sarah Bernhardt in a peculiar and alarming demonstration of the incompatibility of stage and screen. Adolph Zukor paid 20,000 dollars for the rights.

A SOLDIER'S HONOR. United States. A remarkably inventive and well-color-tinted Western from Thomas Ince.

1912: Facts of Interest

There are 717 films produced in Italy, probably the most advanced national cinema at this time.
Lillian Gish makes her début in Griffith's *An Unseen Enemy*.
Victor Sjöström and Mauritz Stiller direct their first films.
William Fox establishes the Fox Company.
The first film studio is built in Hungary.
The British Board of Film Censors is set up.
Michelangelo Antonioni is born.

1912: *A design for Georges Méliès's* THE CONQUEST OF THE POLE.

1913

INGEBORG HOLM. Sweden. Script and Direction: Victor Sjöström, from the play by Nils Krook. Photography: Henrik Jaenzon. Players: Hilda Borgström, Eric Lindholm, Georg Grönroos, William Larsson, Aron Lindgren, Richard Lund. Production: Svenska Bio. Five reels.

Victor Sjöström joined Svenska Bio in 1912, after fourteen years of acting and directing in the theatre. *Ingeborg Holm* was his eighth film, and was photographed for the major part out of doors, as was the custom in Swedish cinema. Its social relevance was acute. Loopholes in the Poor Law regulations enabled speculators in forced labor to buy children from destitute women. When the film opens, Ingeborg is still happily married, with her infant sons and daughter. The father is a successful shopkeeper, and the family lives comfortably. But Holm dies after a sudden heart attack. There are debts to be faced, and the widow is driven implacably into the hands of the authorities. She is lodged in the Poor House, and has to part with her children one by one. Then she hears that her daughter is ill, and in desperation she escapes and makes her way to the house where the girl has been lodged. But she is found and brought back to the hospice. Sjöström shows her as a woman white-haired before her time, caressing her apron or a piece of wood as if it were her baby. There is a stern anger in Sjöström's approach to his subject. He uses scenes of hardship and sentimentality to convince his audience of the injustice of the system, and the natural surroundings of the city and its neighboring woods imply that this is an authentic situation and that Ingeborg Holm is literally deranged by social conditions.

Checklist of other important films

THE BATTLE OF GETTYSBURG. United States. Director: Thomas Ince. Fine battle scenes.

FROM THE MANGER TO THE CROSS. United States. Director: Sidney Olcott. An early Biblical epic, made on location in Palestine for the Kalem Company.

HAMLET. Britain. Director: Hay Plumb. With Johnston Forbes Robertson.

THE MYSTERIOUS X (Det Hemmelighedsfulde X). Denmark. Director: Benjamin Christensen. A mature and technically dazzling film by the least known of the cinema's great directors.

QUO VADIS? Italy. Director: Enrico Guazzoni. One of the elaborate and tolerably well acted spectaculars in which the Italians excelled in these early years, influencing many American producers in the process.

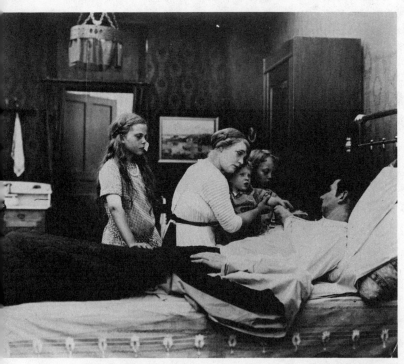

The family take leave of their breadwinner in INGEBORG HOLM.

THE STUDENT OF PRAGUE (Der Student von Prag). Germany. Director: D. Stellan Rye. A variation on the Faust theme, suggesting the path the German cinema was to take in the next decade.

1913: Facts of Interest

Serials are launched in both France and the United States.

Hollywood is given as a name to a small village in the outer suburbs of Los Angeles.

Warner Features Company is founded by Harry M. Warner.

Percy Nash builds the first studio at Elstree (England).

1914

CABIRIA. Italy. Director: Piero Fosco (otherwise known as Giovanni Pastrone).

The one genuinely influential Italian film of the early years. An epic, set during the Punic Wars, which covered Hannibal's crossing of the Alps and the spectacular siege of Syracuse. Camera movements (panning and tracking shots) made the vast sets and plaster models look very impressive, and there was a rousing music score by Idebrando Pizzetti. Shooting took seven months, and the cast included Italia Almirante, Umberto Mazzato, Raffaele di Napoli, Lydia Quaranta, and Ignazio Lupi. The captions were written by Gabriele D'Annunzio.

Checklist of other important films

FANTOMAS. France. Director Louis Feuillade. One of the first masterly serials on French crime.

A FOOL THERE WAS. United States. Director: Frank Powell. Theda Bara (an anagram of Arab Death!) is the female vampire who sucks vitality from her male victims. Powell himself had appeared in several films by Griffith.

JUDITH OF BETHULIA. United States. Griffith's first historical spectacular and his last film for Bio-

1914: Spectacular elements to the fore in CABIRIA.

graph. A four-reeler divided into four distinct segments like *Intolerance* (see *1916*).

THE PERILS OF PAULINE. United States. The twenty-episode serial featuring Pearl White.

1914: Facts of Interest

Chaplin completes his first film, *Making a Living*, at Keystone.
Cecil B. DeMille makes the first of his 73 films, under the title *The Squaw Man*.

1914: From the most famous serial of them all, THE PERILS OF PAULINE.

1915

THE BIRTH OF A NATION. United States. Script: D. W. Griffith, assisted by Frank Woods, from the novel and play, *The Clansman,* by Thomas Dixon, with additional material from the same author's *The Leopard's Spots.* Direction: Griffith. Photography: G. W. Bitzer. Music score: Joseph Carl Breil and D. W. Griffith. Players: Lillian Gish, Mae Marsh, Henry Walthall, Miriam Cooper, Mary Alden, Ralph Lewis, George Siegmann, Walter Long. Production: Epoch Producing Corporation / Reliance-Majestic / Mutual. Twelve reels (approximately 165 mins.).

The Birth of a Nation is the outstanding film of its era, made without leading stars on a budget of about $110,000 and shot, incredibly with just one camera, by Billy Bitzer. Its vast fresco covers the advent of the Civil War, the long years of the War itself, and the subsequent rise to power of Negro factions in the south. The first ninety minutes of the film are barely dated at all, save for some embarrassing captions. The inevitability of the War clouds the friendship between the Stonemans (from Pennsylvania) and the Camerons (from South Carolina). Their relationship gradually embodies Griffith's hatred of war, his regret at the spectacle of a nation torn by prejudice and topographical differences. The assembly of the two armies, the battle strategy at Atlanta and Petersburg, and the assassination of Lincoln are reconstructed meticulously, with dashes of humor flecking even the most heart-wringing sequences (the young Cameron sisters giggling uncontrollably as they hide in the cellars from a marauding troop of guerillas in Piedmont).

Griffith's style is mellifluous and assured. In the previous five years he had initiated and perfected one technical advance after another: close-up, the fast overhead travelling shot, the split screen, the masked screen, wide panoramas. Now they are blended unostentatiously into the narrative, taking third place to historical accuracy and emotional emphasis. In the second half of the film, his review of race relations borders on the hysterical, with the Radical, Stone-

man, emerging as villain of the piece, and one feels that he seriously underestimated the sensibilities of his audience. But the current of images is impressive nonetheless, and the editing is extraordinarily sophisticated for the period. In the last ten minutes, as the Ku Klux Klan races to the rescue of Dr. Cameron, Griffith cuts hither and thither between half-a-dozen situations, creating a pitch of tension that still leaves an audience breathless at the end.

THE VAMPIRES (Les Vampires). France. Script

D. W. Griffith.

The savagery of war condemned by Griffith. This still shows Robert Harron in HEARTS OF THE WORLD (see 1919).

and Direction: Louis Feuillade. Photography: Manichoux. Players: Musidora, Edouard Mathé, Marcel Levesque, Jean Aymé, Louis Leubas. Production: Film Gaumont. (360 mins.)

Feuillade's interest in criminal practice reached its apogee in *Les Vampires,* a ten-part serial released during 1915 and 1916. The Vampires are a gang of jewel thieves who are seemingly indestructible and whose network includes malevolent chambermaids, distinguished gentlemen of affairs, and the eponymous Irma Vep (Musidora), a kind of Mata-Hari who manages to secure one position after another in the fortresses of virtue—bank clerk, stage actress, hotel telephonist. The gang is hunted down by an earnest young newspaper editor and a reformed criminal named Mazamette, who directs winks at the audience and relishes each new development of the intrigue. But the Vampires also encounter a rival organization, run by a suave, immaculately dressed villain enamoured of Irma Vep.

Feuillade's vision of the Paris of prewar days, with its dusky streets and tumbled rooftops, is sufficiently intelligent and perceptive to allow the film to proceed beyond the naïve. Even though the stratagems of the Vampires are preposterous, they are so cleverly engineered, and take place so unpredictably in drab, familiar streets, that, like anarchy, they provide their own justification.

Not for nothing did Feuillade make 170 comedies between 1910 and 1925: his characters are always ready to laugh at their own pomposity. Musidora, sheathed from head to foot in black, tactile crepe, communicates quivering disdain through her eye-slits as she is captured by the rival gang (Feuillade is really the first director to conceive of the female villain). The style, despite the mostly immobile camera, never lapses into theatricality. One feels one is gazing through a window at the surrealistic turn of events, whether it be at a room-load of cocktail guests prostrated by gas, or at Irma Vep's descending a multi-storeyed building by drainpipe. *Caligari* is still five years ahead, but in *Les Vampires* Feuillade's use of shadow and silhouette is astonishingly advanced.

THE CHAMPION. U.S.A. Script and Director: Charles Chaplin. Photography: Rollie Totheroh. Players: Charles Chaplin, Bud Jamison, Edna Purviance, Leo White, Ben Turpin. Production: Essanay. Two reels.

SHANGHAIED. United States. Script and Direction: Charles Chaplin. Photography: Rollie Totheroh. Players: Charles Chaplin, Edna Purviance, Wesley

Charlie as an unorthodox boxing champion. This still is from CITY LIGHTS (see 1931), with Eddie Kane as referee and Hank Mann as Chaplin's opponent.

Ruggles, John Rand, Billy Armstrong, Paddy Mc-Guire, Leo White. Production: Essanay. Two reels.

Chaplin made some thirty five films with Keystone before moving to Essanay in 1915. Here he was able to develop his own style of humor away from the powerful framework of Sennett slapstick. *The Champion* and *Shanghaied* are characteristic of this period, although a significant note of pathos was introduced in *The Tramp* (also 1915). In *Shanghaied* Charlie is dragged aboard a ship and is soon summoning all his resourcefulness in keeping stable in the heaving saloon while he tries to serve meals. Charlie's skill as a juggler and an acrobat comes to the fore here, but so too does his eagerness to launch a vicious and surreptitious attack at those who annoy him. Unlike other silent comics, Charlie is never willing to make a sacrifice without ensuring that he has an audience, and in *The Champion* he delights in the mass of spectators clustered round the ringside. The ring is indeed too small to hold him, and Charlie uses every possible

maneuver within the confined space to flummox his lantern-jawed opponent, even performing an elegant catwalk on the lower rope as his rival is temporarily floored. It is already plain that Chaplin's cinema revolves around The Little Fellow, and that the camera is there not to explore but merely to record behavior. In the climactic fight scene, there are just two camera setups, with hectic cutting between crowd and ring.

Checklist of other important films

TILLIE'S PUNCTURED ROMANCE. United States. Mack Sennett's six-reel burlesque on the Cinderella theme that proved a model for many later comedies and starred Chaplin with Marie Dressler.

1915: Facts of Interest

Universal City is opened by Carl Laemmle, and produces over 250 films in its first year of operations.

1915: Irma Vep (Musidora), "sheathed from head to foot in black, tactile crepe," in LES VAMPIRES.

The Technicolor Corporation is founded.
Triangle Pictures Corporation is established by Ince, Griffith, and Sennett.

Gloria Swanson receives her first billing, on *The Fable of Elvira and Farina and the Mealticket*. Orson Welles is born.

1916

INTOLERANCE. United States. Script: none. (The film was improvised from Griffith's own invention. No scenario actually existed.) Direction: D. W. Griffith. Photography: G. W. Bitzer. Music score: Joseph Carl Breil and Griffith. Players: Mae Marsh, Fred Turner, Robert Harron, Sam de Grasse (*Modern Story*); Howard Gaye, Lillian Langdon, Olga Grey, Bessie Love (*Judean Story*); Margery Wilson, Eugene Pallette, Spottiswoode Aiken, Ruth Handforth (*Medieval French Story*); Constance Talmadge, Elmer Clifton, Alfred Paget, Seena Owen, Carl Stockdale (*Babylonian Story*). Production: Wark Producing Corporation. Fourteen reels. (220 mins.)

Enthused by the tremendous success of *Birth of a Nation* (which was to gross some $18 million in a short time), Griffith devoted two years to the pro-

duction of *Intolerance*. This was a much more complicated and ambitious film, and has never enjoyed quite the same public acclaim as its predecessor. It consists of four stories, on the theme of intolerance and "love's struggle throughout the ages"—the conflict of Christ with Rome and the Pharisees, the massacre of St. Bartholomew in France, the downfall of Babylon, and the clash between capitalists and workers in contemporary America. Griffith cross-cuts between these stories constantly (there are even short flashbacks within each episode), carefully husbanding his effects so that all four stories come simultaneously to a climax. In this respect Griffith was to exert a major influence on the Soviet directors of the twenties. But, fifty years later, it is the sheer prodigal-

1916: INTOLERANCE: from the Modern Story.

INTOLERANCE: *Griffith's use of close-up (Mae Marsh).*

ity of the film that endures. The crowd scenes in the Nebuchadnezzar sequence had over 16,000 extras on the screen at one time; a single costume, for the "Princess Beloved," cost $8,000. All this was accomplished without a shooting script (for reasons of secrecy), or any sketches for the sets. Like all Griffith's work, *Intolerance* has a didactic ring that makes the captions seem pompous. But it lives up to the director's dictum that "Art is always revolutionary, always explosive and sensational."

THE PAWNSHOP. United States. Script and Direction: Charles Chaplin. Photography: William C. Foster and Rollie Totheroh. Players: Edna Purviance, John Rand, Henry Bergman, Albert Austin, Eric Campbell, Charles Chaplin. Production: Mutual Corporation. Two reels.

The time he spent with Mutual was the happiest phase of Chaplin's career, and in the twelve two-reelers he made for the Corporation he developed nearly all the comic business that appears in his later work. As the head clerk in a pawnship (run, significantly, by "The Wandering Jew"), he dusts his bowler before slipping it into an empty birdcage and starting a fracas with a fellow employee. His movements are lightning-fast, and there is something in his agility that corresponds to Chaplin's own image of American life (in his Autobiography he speaks of the "alacrity" of everyone in New York when he first arrived). Charlie, though rarely malicious, is always

Charlie Chaplin feigning innocence in THE PAWNSHOP.

45

a formidable opponent, and after bamboozling the other clerk with a ladder and pelting him with dough (supplied, in all innocence, by Edna), he proceeds to disembowel an alarm clock brought into the shop by a hopeful client ("It's known as little Ben and I've had it ever since it was a wrist watch"), and only the intervention of the proprietor stays him from pouring acid into someone's goldfish bowl. So Charlie is already established as an irritant in the midst of blockheads, encouraging people to fight him and never hesitating to cheat or humiliate those less nimble than himself.

Checklist of other important films

THE ARYAN. United States. A Western, written by a screenwriter of stature (C. Gardner Sullivan), featuring and directed by William S. Hart.

THE BATTLE OF THE SOMME. Britain. Directors: Geoffrey Malins and J. B. McDowell. The first extensive documentary on World War One.

CARMEN OF THE KLONDYKE. United States. Director: Reginald Barker. A superior serial of the period, which was to run in seven parts, starring Clara Williams.

THE GREAT PROBLEM. United States. Rex Ingram's début as a director.

HELL'S HINGES. United States. Starring William S. Hart. A landmark among early Westerns, with its strong moral tone and its sinister, dangerous township.

1916: Facts of Interest

Chaplin signs for Mutual at a record salary of $650,000 a year.
"Goldwyn Picture Co." is established by Samuel Goldfish and Archibald Selwyn.
Alexander Korda makes his first films in Hungary.
Harold Lloyd starts filming Lonesome Luke one-reelers.

1917

EASY STREET. United States. Script and Direction: Charles Chaplin. Photography: William C. Foster and Rollie Totheroh. Players: Edna Purviance, Albert Austin, Eric Campbell, James T. Kelley, Henry Bergman, John Rand, Charlotte Mineau, Frank J. Coleman, Charles Chaplin. Production: Mutual. Two reels.

Chaplin's comedy is never meaningless slapstick for its own sake. It always appeals to the conscience, to the strain of humanity that so many of us try to conceal within ourselves. Charlie is the eternal outsider, forever peering in at a unified society that time and time again proves cold and brutal. In *Easy Street* he is a down-at-heels romantic, creeping into the Hope Mission where Edna is playing the piano. But in the next sequence he foolishly joins the police force just as a massive fight is in progress on Easy Street. Charlie is soon embroiled with the bully of the area (Eric Campbell), and shrewdly gasses him in a street lamp. This is the most violent of the Mutual films; Campbell behaves like an ancestor of King Kong, tossing men around like skittles, and recovers to chase Charlie through one squalid rooming house after another. Chaplin has said that he tried to strike a mood for each new comedy, and throughout *Easy Street* he emphasises the poverty and the raw struggle for life in the slums, possibly remembered from his own childhood at Kennington.

THE IMMIGRANT. United States. Script and Direction: Charles Chaplin. Photography: William C. Foster and Rollie Totheroh. Players: Edna Purviance, Albert Austin, Henry Bergman, Stanley Sanford, Eric Campbell, James T. Kelley, John Rand, Frank J. Cole-

The characteristic look of envy as a hungry Charlie sits beside Mack Swain in HIS TRYSTING PLACE (1914).

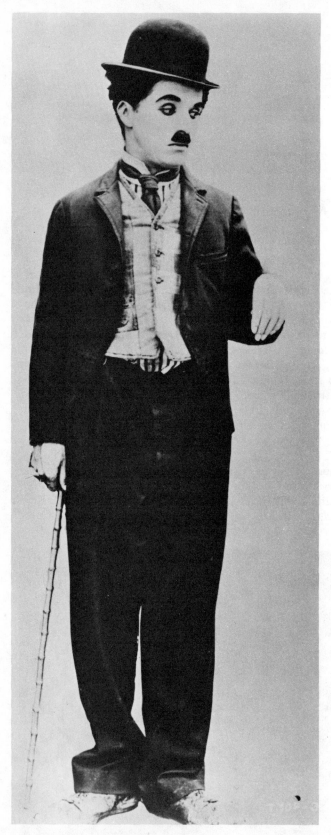

Charles Chaplin in his finest period.

man, Charles Chaplin. Production: Mutual. Two reels.

In his autobiography, Chaplin recalls what an ordeal it was for him to enter a restaurant on arrival in the States, on account of his slow speech and English accent. There is a long scene in *The Immigrant* that must derive from these experiences, with a ferocious waiter (played by Eric Campbell, the best heavy Chaplin ever met) making a contrast with the orchestra that plays so blandly in the background. Few captions are needed in this little masterpiece of irony. It starts with Charlie on board a crowded ship outside New York, leaning over the side as though seasick but instead turning round suddenly with a fish for his pains. On arrival "in the Land of Liberty," he is roped in and labelled with the other passengers before going ashore and venturing into a restaurant. One admires Charlie's mettle, even in a foreign country: having paid his check with the tip left by a kindly artist, he promptly asks his benefactor for a two-dollar loan—with which he marries Edna.

Checklist of other important films

THE ADVENTURER. United States. Director: Charles Chaplin. Charlie as Convict No. 23, "The Eel," escapes from prison guards and bursts for an intoxicating few minutes into high society.

THE BUTCHER BOY. United States. Director: Roscoe "Fatty" Arbuckle. Buster Keaton's first appearance on film.

JUDEX. France. Another colossal serial from Louis Feuillade; although this time—as a result partly of official protest—the leading character is a righter of wrongs, who fights and overcomes Favraux, the criminal banker.

A POOR LITTLE RICH GIRL. United States. Director: Maurice Tourneur. The fey beauty of Mary Pickford at its most beguiling in this adaptation of Eleanor Gates's novel.

TERJE VIGEN. Sweden. Ibsen's poem about the intrepid fisherman who pierces the Napoleonic blockade and finds only tragedy on his return from prison was the source of this extraordinary film by Victor Sjöström, imbued with his characteristic feeling for landscape and the elements.

1917: Facts of Interest

John Ford directs his first film—*The Tornado*.
Paramount Pictures is established in the United States; and UFA is started in Germany.
Mary Pickford is rated the most popular star in America, half a million votes ahead of Alice Joyce and the rest.

1918

THE OUTLAW AND HIS WIFE (Berg-Ejvind och hans hustru). Sweden. Script: Sam Ask and Victor Sjöström, from the novel by Johan Sigurjonsson. Direction: Sjöström. Photography: J. Julius. Players: Sjöström, Edith Erastoff, John Ekman, Niles Aréhn, Jenny Tschernichin-Larsson. Production: Svenska Bio. (2781 metres).

That relentless Destiny that was to haunt the French cinema in the thirties can already be discerned in one of Victor Sjöström's most intense and ambitious films, *The Outlaw and his Wife*. The tale of Berg-Ejvind, who is proscribed for stealing a sheep to feed his starving family and who, despite the love of Halla (Edith Erastoff), finds a miserable end in the mountains, is related with a dour efficiency and earnestness. There is a Puritan attitude inherent in the sacrifice of Berg-Ejvind's infant daughter, when the authorities come to arrest the outlaw. The union of the two fugitives is not recognized by society, and so their child, the personification of their happiness, and of their sin, must perish.

But, apart from his assured use of flashbacks, Sjöström was the first Swedish director to realize the importance of landscape in the cinema. The solitude and predicament of Berg-Ejvind and his wife speak through the images, with the clouds and the mountains expressing a life of rigor and simplicity. Alone in these natural tracts, human beings take on a dignity that has infused later Swedish films like *The Bread of Love* (see *1953*) and *The Seventh Seal* (see *1957*). The death of the outlaws, enveloped and frozen stiff by the snow, is one of the most wrenching in all cinema.

THOMAS GRAAL'S FIRST CHILD (Thomas Graals bästa barn). Sweden. Script: Harald B. Harald (Gustaf Molander and Mauritz Stiller). Direction: Stiller. Photography: Henrik Jaenzon. Players: Victor Sjöström, Karin Molander, Jenny Tschernichin-Larsson, Torsten Winge, Alex Nilsson. Production: Svenska Bio. (1737 metres.)

Mauritz Stiller's supreme talent for directing his players has only recently been rediscovered. There is a spirited mischievousness about the performances of Victor Sjöström and Karin Molander in *Thomas Graal's First Child* that makes other acting of the period seem academic and ponderous. The film swarms with visual gags, never overstated to the point of farce. Graal and Bessie are about to be married (their tempestuous courtship had been described by Stiller in *Thomas Graal's Best Film*), and Sjöström's exuberance is tested to the limit when he loses the ring at the altar. The wedding reception, with excited children drinking champagne, is as brilliantly composed as the famous scene in *Greed* (see *1924*). In the car the couple begin to argue whether their firstborn should be a boy or a girl. The dispute reaches drastic proportions and much of the honeymoon is spent with both parties in high dudgeon, eating in separate rooms and slamming doors abruptly. But a common enemy unites them again, and Stiller sustains the comedy with a series of deft and ironic interludes of the type that Myrna Loy and William Powell, and Clark Gable and Claudette Colbert, were to revel in decades later. One is readily engaged by Sjöström and Karin Molander. They always have a sarcastic retort waiting up their sleeve; and, for all their eagerness to escape on flights of fancy, they are homelovers at heart. The film is not weighed down with the plethora of captions common in 1918, but what preserves it so well half a century later is the universal humor inherent in the domestic relationship and its erotic byplay. *Thomas Graal's First Child* is a model of tight construction and steady, scintillating rhythm.

Checklist of other important films

CARMEN. Germany. The first film of stature from Ernst Lubitsch, with Pola Negri as the Spanish minx.

LA DIXIÈME SYMPHONIE. France. Abel Gance,

49

1918: "The importance of landscape" in THE OUTLAW AND HIS WIFE.

one of the most lively and revered of French directors, made his mark with this experimental and poetic drama about an orphan married to a famous composer.

HEARTS OF THE WORLD. Britain. Director: D. W. Griffith. The most moving of all the war films made during 1914–1918.

THE SINKING OF THE LUSITANIA. United States. Director: Winsor McCay. The first feature-length cartoon. McCay had already made pioneer strides in animation with his *Gertie the Dinosaur* shorts from 1909 onwards.

STELLA MARIS. United States. Director: William J. Locke. Mary Pickford as both cripple and slave girl in perhaps her most unusual film.

TIH MINH. France. Another twelve-episode serial by Louis Feuillade, concerning an Annamite girl involved in a number of gross crimes on the French Riviera.

Short films and Documentaries

A DOG'S LIFE. United States. Chaplin's first film for First National, in which Charlie the tramp is compared to the dog who has to struggle for survival and endure the hefty kicks of society. "I was beginning to think of comedy in a structural sense," he recalls, "and to become conscious of its architectural form. Each sequence implied the next sequence, all of them relating to the whole."

SHOULDER ARMS. United States. At a time when everyone was afraid of commenting on the war, Chaplin produced a witty and incisive satire of life in the trenches—and it proved a box-office success too.

1918: Facts of Interest

Ingmar Bergman is born.
There are 840 films completed in the United States.

1919

BROKEN BLOSSOMS. United States. Script and Direction: D. W. Griffith, based on "The Chink and the Child" in Thomas Burke's *Limehouse Nights*. Photography: G. W. Bitzer. Special Effects: Hendrick Sartov. Music score: Louis F. Gottschalk and D. W. Griffith. Players: Lillian Gish, Richard Barthelmess, Donald Crisp, Arthur Howard, Edward Peil, George Beranger. Production: Adolph Zukor/United Artists. Six reels. (87 mins.)

Chaplin, Fairbanks, Griffith, and Mary Pickford formed United Artists in order to avoid the system of block booking that disfigured the distribution side of the industry. *Broken Blossoms* was the first film to be produced for the new corporation, and it proved to be Griffith's last major success. Its picture of London's Limehouse is reminiscent of Dickens at his most graphic level. Each set houses a wealth of detail, and the early scenes, in "a great Chinese treaty port," are filled with the velvety, almost phosphorescent lighting effects later hailed as revolutionary in the films of Josef von Sternberg. Richard Barthelmess is the soul of sensitivity and contemplation as "The Yellow Man." He is entranced by Lucy (Lillian Gish), who lives in bivering fear of her foster father, Battling Burrows (Donald Crisp), "a gorilla of the jungles of East London." Although the captions are as naïve and pompous as any in Griffith's work, several scenes are quite remarkably brutal and naturalistic—the ring-battle between Burrows and his rival, or Lucy's desperate attempts to escape from the closet as her father smashes down the door with an axe. Large close-ups are used sparingly and to great effect. There is a spate of unannounced flashbacks near the beginning of the film that must have been startling in 1919; and, in the original version, beams of coloured light were thrown on the screen during the projection of the film, to add emotional weight to certain moments. *Broken Blossoms* is Griffith's most restrained and poignant film, taking its mood from the saturnine devotion of "The Yellow Man."

SIR ARNE'S TREASURE (Herr Arnes pengar). Sweden. Script: Gustaf Molander and Mauritz Stiller, from the novel by Selma Lagerlöf. Direction: Stiller. Photography: J. Julius. Art Direction: Harry Dahlström and Alexander Bakó. Players: Richard Lund, Mary Johnson, Concordia Selander, Wanda Rothgardt, Axel Nilsson, Stina Berg, Erik Stocklassa, Hjalmar Selander. Production: Svenska Bio. (6000 feet.)

Stiller's masterpiece endures so well because, unlike the majority of expressionist films, it is swiftly narrated, and because it possesses a rare unity of style, embracing desolate landscapes and crowded interiors. Set in the eighteenth century, the film describes the escape of three Scottish mercenaries led by Sir Arne (Richard Lund) from a castle where they have been imprisoned by King Johan III. They plunge through the implacable winter weather, but find that the coast

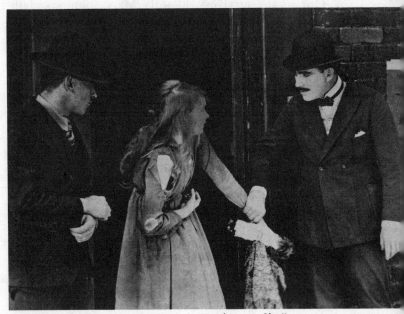

1919: "Griffith's most restrained and poignant film"—
BROKEN BLOSSOMS.

1919: The mercenary and his victim (Richard Lund and Mary Johnson) in SIR ARNE'S TREASURE.

has been surrounded by ice. They are trapped, and in panic they loot and pillage the mansion of Sir Arne. One of the survivors, Elsalill (Mary Johnson), falls in love with Sir Archie. But he has no compunction in using her as a human shield when confronted by the local guardsmen, and Elsalill's bier is borne across the snow in a winding *cortège* that has rightly become one of the most celebrated shots of the silent cinema.

A mood of desperation pervades *Sir Arne's Treasure,* and the mesh of conflicting desires holds the film in a taut, dramatic form. Stiller knows instinctively when to accelerate the tempo (in the firing of the mansion, for example) and when to dwell on scenes of ritualistic significance (the old lady's vision of the knives being whetted in the snow). Nature, as so often in Swedish films, plays her inexorable role, lashing the mercenaries with blizzard after blizzard and yielding only when the tragedy is complete, so that the ice melts and the waves return. *Sir Arne's Treasure* has the stature of a Nordic saga, and Stiller's understanding of the subtleties of human psychology lifts it out of time.

Checklist of other important features

BLIND HUSBANDS. United States. Dastardly behavior at a resort in the Dolomites, with Erich von Stroheim acting, designing, directing, and writing his first film.

J'ACCUSE. France. The first, and rather overrated, pacifist film by Abel Gance. It was accused of being anti-militaristic when it showed the wholesale slaughter of the Flanders campaign.

TRUE HEART SUSIE. United States. Director: D. W. Griffith. Lillian Gish and Robert Harron as the simple-hearted dreamers, whose moments of great joy and enthusiasm are recounted with pastoral affection by Griffith. The short "thought" flashbacks here are a sign of Griffith's complete mastery of the medium.

1919: Facts of Interest

United Artists Corporation founded by Chaplin, Griffith, Fairbanks, and Mary Pickford.
Lenin nationalizes the cinema in the U.S.S.R.
Svensk Filmindustri is founded in Sweden, and is still today the largest production company there.

1920

THE CABINET OF DOCTOR CALIGARI (Das Kabinett des Dr. Caligari). Germany. Script: Carl Mayer and Hans Janowitz. Direction: Robert Wiene. Photography: Willi Hameister. Art Direction: Walter Reimann, Hermann Warm, and Walter Röhrig. Players: Werner Krauss, Conrad Veidt, Lil Dagover, Friedrich Feher, H. H. von Twardowski. Production: Decla-Bioskop/Erich Pommer. (81 mins.)

This morbid, haunting fable inaugurates the German expressionist cinema of the twenties. In the tiny, huddled town where Dr. Caligari exhibits his somnambulist monster Cesare, the distorted perspectives themselves have a menacing existence. The twisting passages and triangular windows reflect the vision of a madman, but of whom—the Doctor, or the young narrator who is dragged off to the cells at the end, or even the audience? It is a tribute to the subtlety of the scenario that one still questions the ultimate logic of the film. Sanity is revealed as being merely relative: the Doctor is either an island of sanity in a sea of madness, or a lunatic worming his way into an innocent community.

Everything, and yet at the same time nothing, seems symbolic in these abstract décors, where the characters shift in hideous harmony with the objects around them. The acting by Conrad Veidt and Werner Krauss is superbly formalized. Caligari is one of the cinema's immortal figures, demented and obsequious, apprehensive and inscrutable, loathsome and authoritative. *The Cabinet of Doctor Caligari* is based on expressionist principles, but the world it creates is established on an unearthly, persuasive order that enables it to survive many another film of its time.

EROTIKON. Sweden. Script: Mauritz Stiller and Arthur Nordéen. Direction: Stiller. Photography: Henrik Jaenzon. Art Direction: Stiller. Players: Anders de Wahl, Tora Teje, Karin Molander, Vilhelm Bryde, Lars Hanson, Torsten Hammerén, Carina Ari, Martin Oscar, Stina Berg. Production: Svensk Filmindustri. (5800 feet.)

The sophisticated comedy film was developed primarily by Ernst Lubitsch, Mauritz Stiller, and Cecil B. DeMille. *Erotikon* is regarded by many critics as being the summit of Stiller's career. Certainly it is his most exotic film. A ballet was composed specially for one scene at the Stockholm Opera so that Stiller, with his unfailing sense of dramatic irony, could reflect in this presentation ("Queen of the Shah"), the extravagant deceptions and pomposities of high society. Like his other comedies, *Erotikon* derives its humor from the mutual distrust among the leading characters. The wife, Irene (Tora Teje), of an absent-minded Professor of Entomology, is courted by a young sculptor and by a self-important Baron. Stiller does not so much disapprove of the "depraved" upper classes; rather he endorses their sly disregard for decorum. Casting contemporary modesty to the winds, Marthe, the old Professor's niece, smokes a cigarette while lying full length on a couch with her calves amply displayed. The elegant, brittle fencing between the sexes is characteristic of the period, and of a similar tendency on the stage in the works of Shaw, Somerset Maugham, and Frederick Lonsdale.

THE GOLEM (Der Golem). Germany. Script: Paul Wegener. Direction: Wegener, Carl Boese, Henrik Galeen. Photography: Karl Freund, Guido Seeber. Art Direction: Hans Poelzig. Players: Paul Wegener, Albert Steinrisck, Lyda Salmanova, Ernst Deutsch, Lothar Müthel. Production: Projektions A.G. Union. (97 mins.)

Paul Wegener had worked as an actor under Max Reinhardt. But his greatest film, *The Golem*, constantly veers away from the expressionist tradition, and its stylistic affectations are comparatively few. It was shot in 1920 (Wegener himself had first tackled the subject five years earlier). The Golem is the sacred monster, fashioned from clay, who can rise to help the Jews in times of need. The Ghetto in medieval Prague swarms to life in Hans Poelzig's designs. The buildings and the laboratories have a latent dy-

1920: "The German expressionist cinema of the twenties." **THE CABINET OF DOCTOR CALIGARI.**

1920: A group from Mauritz Stiller's **EROTIKON.**

namism; an impression emphasized by the incandescent lighting, which sculpts faces out of the shadows that proliferate in this hermetic community. Wegener's own portrayal of the Golem also has an impassive strength; he is a watchful monster handicapped by his very composition, powerless when the amulet is torn from his chest by a curious child outside the Ghetto.

Threaded into the legend is a love affair between Florian, one of the Emperor's courtiers, and the sloe-eyed Jewish girl, Miriam. For all its ardor and frankness, this romance is too naïve. Its ludicrousness makes even more striking the control and ingenuity of Wegener's direction in other scenes—for example, the massive images that Rabbi Low "projects" on the walls of the court to illustrate the tribulations of the Jewish people. Astrology and superstition flourish in such an environment, and even the vulpine head of Astaroth swimming in space does not tax the film's plausibility. But practical issues are never forgotten: the Golem chops wood as dispassionately as he drags Miriam through the streets. And the Imperial decree against the Jews, delivered by the swaggering Aryan on horseback, was surely a chilling premonition of things to come in Germany.

Checklist of other important features

DR. JEKYLL AND MR. HYDE. United States. Director: John S. Robertson. John Barrymore as Stevenson's dangerous, unpredictable doctor; the stress in this version is on gruesome effects.

THE LAST OF THE MOHICANS. United States. Directors: Maurice Tourneur and Clarence Brown. A splendidly realized version of the James Fenimore Cooper novel, with the Fort William Henry massacre standing up today as one of the finest sequences in the early American cinema.

THE MARK OF ZORRO. United States. Director: Fred Niblo. A finely photographed, swashbuckling romance set in nineteenth-century Spanish California, with Douglas Fairbanks as the knight errant.

WAY DOWN EAST. United States. Griffith's tragic study of a New England family, with Lillian Gish as the girl lured into a mock marriage. Two great scenes: the blizzard, and the desperate journey on the breaking ice.

WHY CHANGE YOUR WIFE? United States. One of Cecil B. DeMille's satirical comedies at the expense of American customs. Starring Gloria Swanson and Bebe Daniels.

1920: Facts of Interest

Concentration of the American film industry in Hollywood: 50 studios with 25,000 employees now.
Federico Fellini born.

1921

FOOLISH WIVES. United States. Script and Direction: Erich von Stroheim. Photography: Ben Reynolds and William Daniels. Art Direction: Stroheim and Richard Day. Players: Erich von Stroheim, Maude George, Mae Busch, Cesare Gravina, Malvine Polo, George Christians, Dale Fuller. Production: Universal. (120 mins.)

Born in Vienna in 1885, Stroheim came to the U.S.A. circa 1906, and towards the end of World War I he became typecast as a Prussian officer in films. He showed extraordinary aplomb in his first effort as director, *Blind Husbands* (see *1919*), and for the next ten years no one, not even the more complacent Lubitsch, could rival his derisive view of high society. *Foolish Wives* cost approximately $1.3 million and took a year to shoot. It is set in Monaco, where Princess Olga and Princess Vera live with a spurious Russian count named Karamzin (Stroheim). When

the American ambassador and his wife arrive on the Riviera, Karamzin seizes the opportunity of insinuating himself into the woman's favor, and attempts to seduce her when they take shelter after being caught in a storm. The portrait of despicable vanity given by Stroheim here is right to the last detail. Karamzin is self-satisfied, and a charlatan; in one of the silent cinema's most famous scenes, he weeps crocodile tears with the aid of a finger bowl in order to ward off the complaints of a chambermaid he has made pregnant. He gambles brazenly with other people's money; and at the very end he jumps from the balcony of a burning villa *before* the ambassador's wife. Visually, the film is full of sensual violence and expressionist symbolism (the strips of light that convert the counterfeiter's apartment into a gilded cage of vice). Jealousy and resentment are the underlying emotions of Stroheim's cinema; and there is one shot in *Foolish Wives,* as the camera closes in on the maid's black eyes while she grows more and more demented, that contains them both to a terrifying degree.

THY SOUL SHALL BEAR WITNESS (Körkarlen). Sweden. Script and Direction: Victor Sjöström, from the novel by Selma Lagerlöf. Photography: Julius Jaenzon. Art Direction: Alexander Bakó and Axel Esbensen. Players: Victor Sjöström, Hilda Borgström, Tore Svennberg, Astrid Holm, Concordia Selander, Lisa Lundholm, Tor Weijden, Nils Aréhn, John Ekman. Production: Svenska Bio. (60 mins.)

Few critics in Sweden felt that it was possible for Sjöström to make a film of Selma Lagerlöf's allegory on good and evil, *Körkarlen.* Ironically, it is the breathtaking technique of *Thy Soul Shall Bear Witness* that endures, and the psychological conflict between the flesh and the spirit that has become dated. The film is a protest against moral degradation (like all Sjöström's work), a passionate exhortation to examine past sins and to adhere to rigid principles of

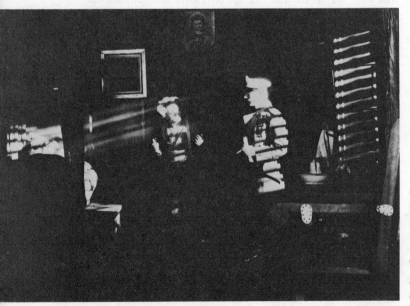

1921: *"The strips of light that convert the counterfeiter's apartment into a gilded cage of vice"—FOOLISH WIVES.*

conduct. David Holm (Sjöström) is the coarse-grained, jocular tramp who is knocked unconscious during a brawl in a cemetery. As the clock strikes midnight, the phantom carriage appears, with Death as its driver, come to claim his victim. Meanwhile, flashbacks tell of Holm's drunken past and the collapse of his marriage. The construction of these flashbacks is complex, and in fact about four-fifths of the film takes place in the graveyard itself. Sometimes as many as four images are superimposed on one frame. The first action of the wagoner, as he comes to carry off the wealthy man who has committed suicide, is startlingly ingenious: there seems to exist a very real separation between soul and body. Touches of brilliance overcome the handicap of the silent medium. When Holm is summoned from his physical envelope to join the coachman, he puts his hands to his *ears*, not his eyes. As Bergman will do over three decades later, Sjöström contrasts scenes of tranquillity and happiness (Holm's memories of lakeside frolics with his children), with moments of uncanny menace—when Holm tries to stop his wife from taking poison, Death, the coachman, answers with a shrug, "I have no power over the Living."

JOHAN. Sweden. Script: Arthur Nordéen and Mauritz Stiller, from the novel by Juhani Aho. Direction: Stiller. Photography: Henrik Jaenzon. Players: Mathias Taube, Jenny Hasselqvist, Hildegard Harring, Urho Somersalmi, Lilly Borg. Production: Svenska Bio. (1900 metres.)

The lovers in JOHAN (1921).

1921: Victor Sjöström (right) in his own masterpiece,
THY SOUL SHALL BEAR WITNESS.

Stiller is remembered principally as a director of light comedies, but *Johan* demonstrated without doubt—if any still remained after *Sir Arne's Treasure* (see *1919*)—that Stiller could express the Scandinavian way of life as well (and as moralistically) as Sjöström. Marit, the wife of the farmer Johan, is lured into temptation by Vallavan, a visitor to the area. Vallavan, like so many "strangers" in the Swedish cinema, is the embodiment of romance, of the hopes and fears that the bitter climate and the endless drudgery have suppressed in the country folk. Deep in her psyche, Marit resents the staid conventions of her life; she dislikes the exalted position of Johan's mother as the

aged mistress of the farm. When the lovers decide to escape, Stiller's command of film language is gloriously revealed. Vallavan's boat is soon involved in a vertiginous trip through some rapids, and Marit's emotional confusion and remorse at deserting her husband are imaginatively suggested by the waves lashing the tiny boat. The journey down the river is a whirling descent into chaos and misadventure, just as the huge dam about to be blown up at Selangar is a metaphor for Marit's own smothered passion. There is a certain lack of harmony in *Johan,* a not altogether successful matching of satire and high drama, but Stiller's vision of bucolic life and attitudes is sophisticated and intuitive beyond his time.

Checklist of other important features

L'ATLANTIDE. France. A vastly expensive film, shot on location in the Sahara and featuring Stacia Napierkowska as the mysterious queen of the desert. Feyder's first full-length film and a commercial triumph.

BE MY WIFE. United States. Max Linder, the impeccable suitor, posing as a scarecrow, piano instructor, and gallant fighter, in order to achieve his ends.

ELDORADO. France. Director: Marcel L'Herbier. A melodrama set in and around a shabby nightclub in France that is typical of L'Herbier's work in the twenties. He later (1943) founded IDHEC, the famous French film school.

THE FOUR HORSEMEN OF THE APOCALYPSE. United States. Director: Rex Ingram. Rudolph Valentino won his spurs in this super-production set in Argentina and Europe, as two wings of a family live to hate each other through the 1914–1918 war.

THE KID. United States. Chaplin's first full-length film, in which he abandons much of the knockabout farce of his earlier work in favor of pathos and naturalism. Jackie Coogan plays "The Kid."

TOL'ABLE DAVID. United States. Director: Henry King. A melodramatic, but also finely descriptive film about life in rural America, with Richard Barthelmess as the vigorous son of a man killed by three outlaws.

Short films and Documentaries

THE GOAT. United States. Directors: Buster Keaton and Malcolm St. Clair. Buster, "the wrong man," is wanted for murder, and the chase scenes are as uproarious as ever. Keaton the mimic and acrobat is in peerless form here.

THE PALEFACE. United States. Directors: Buster Keaton and Eddie Cline. Lepidopterist Keaton finds himself surrounded by hostile Indians, but joins them in their fight against the oil magnates and concludes the proceedings with a two-year kiss for his beloved.

1921: Facts of Interest

Peter Ustinov, Henri Colpi, Jack Clayton, Chris Marker, Andrzej Munk, Grigori Chukhrai are born.

1922

NOSFERATU, Eine Symphonie des Grauens. Germany. Script: Henrik Galeen, from the novel *Dracula* by Bram Stoker. Direction: F. W. Murnau. Photography: Fritz Arno Wagner. Music score: Hans Erdmann. Players: Max Schreck, Alexander Granach, Gustav von Wangenheim, Greta Schröder, G. H. Schnell, Ruth Landshoff, John Gottowt. Production: Prana Film, Berlin. (70 mins.)

1922: The vampire in Murnau's NOSFERATU.

F. W. Murnau is considered by many scholars as the best German film director. In 1922 he was thirty-three, and he had already made nine features, most of which have now disappeared. *Nosferatu* is loosely based on Bram Stoker's novel *Dracula*. Nosferatu himself is a dead man come horribly to life in his Carpathian castle, and when he pursues a young clerk over the sea to Bremen, he demonstrates a virulent power, laying waste to the ship's crew and spreading death among the townsfolk on his arrival. But he sucks the blood of his female victim for too long and, as daybreak comes, Nosferatu melts abruptly away.

Murnau's feat is to convey through the limited means at his disposal a real sense of hostile imbalance. There are passages when the images jerk forward one after the other as in a nightmare, or when strips of negative are used to create an hallucinatory effect. And yet despite all this, the texture of *Nosferatu* is boldly naturalistic: compare its sunstruck but chilly streets with the stylized décor of *The Cabinet of Doctor Caligari* (see *1920*). Murnau was already testing the potentialities of deep-focus photography and, furthermore, the less artificial elements of expressionism, such as the monstrous shadow when the vampire's fingers stretch forward and slide across the landing. Real locations were also used, instead of the studios that were at the time thought indispensable to German directors.

WITCHCRAFT THROUGH THE AGES (Häxan). Sweden. Script and Direction: Benjamin Christensen. Photography: Johan Ankerstjerne. Editing: Richard Louw. Art Direction: Holst-Jorgensen. Players: Maren Pedersen, Clara Pontopiddan, Elith Pio, Oscar Stribolt, Tora Teje, Benjamin Christensen, Johs Andersen. Production: Svenska Bio. (120 mins.)

The director of this quasi-documentary on witchcraft was a Dane, Benjamin Christensen, who had already in 1913 proved himself to be an *auteur* of uncommon imagination and with a pictorial flair far ahead of his time. *Häxan* is the only film of his vintage period that is extant. In many respects it is more

makes a not altogether dignified journey from Gascony to Paris, and soon insults Porthos, Athos, and Aramis in turn. In the duels and chases that ensue, he displays the nimbleness and the traces of anarchic behavior that had characterized much of his work for Pathé before the war. The musketeers are surrounded by modern luxuries such as sausages, telephones, and even a motor bike for facilitating quick escapes. In the end, Linder decimates the Court soldiery before returning the precious brooch and frustrating the vicious Cardinal. Linder's gags inspired some of the more sprightly incidents in later films by Chaplin, The Marx Brothers, Laurel and Hardy, and Pierre Etaix. It was tragic that he committed suicide in 1925.

Checklist of other important features

LA FEMME DE NULLE PART. France. Louis Delluc, one of the principal theoreticians of French cinema in the silent period, probably reached his height with this perfectly wrought story of persuasion and lost youth, as a middle-aged woman returns to her old house.

1922: Max Linder as "Dart-in-Again" in
THE THREE MUST-GET-THERES.

Teutonic than the average German film of the twenties, deriving much of its visual style from medieval painters—Dürer, Bosch, Cranach, Breughel—while its spirit is unmistakably Nordic. There is an air of superstition and fatalism that extends even to Christensen's comments on contemporary cases of witchcraft. Immorality and evil behavior bring their foul rewards, claims the film, and in a series of terrifying scenes one observes the results—deformed old women (recruited, incidentally, from a hospice in Copenhagen), intolerant clergymen, obscene and barbaric experiments. Christensen's technique is immaculate, and the establishment of period detail is meticulous. But his later films are mostly unknown. He worked rather fruitlessly first in Germany and then in Hollywood before returning to Denmark and dying in 1959.

THE THREE MUST-GET-THERES. United States. Script and Direction: Max Linder. Players: Linder, Frank Cooke, Caroline Rankin, Bull Montana, Harry Mann, Jobyna Ralston, Jack Richardson, Charles Mezzetti, Clarence Wertz. Production: Max Linder. (Five reels.)

Max Linder had started his career in vaudeville, learning to fence and appearing in nightclubs in his spare time. Between 1907 and 1914 he made over 300 short comedies in France, and came to America in 1916. But it was only during his second visit to Hollywood in 1919 that he began to make really successful comedies there. His agility and tenacity are seen to splendid effect in *The Three Must-Get-Theres*, an affectionate parody of the Douglas Fairbanks film of "The Three Musketeers." As "Dart-in-Again," Linder

Short films and Documentaries

NANOOK OF THE NORTH. United States. Director: Robert J. Flaherty. During the years 1914–1916, Robert Flaherty edited some film footage he had shot in Labrador and Baffin Land into a long study of the "happy-go-lucky" Eskimos, but the negative was destroyed by fire, and so it was not until 1919–1920 that he was able to film what is now known as *Nanook of the North*. Nanook (meaning "Bear") is the head of an Eskimo family. Hunting walrus, seal, or polar bear is as routine to him as his daily work is to a city businessman. Flaherty stresses the simplicity of this existence—the day that starts with the search for breakfast and ends with the impromptu building of an igloo. But underlying the film's jovial tone is a sense of respect for the Eskimos' heroic will to survive. As documentary, *Nanook of the North* set a new standard because of its unselfconscious realization, due not merely to the innocent behavior on Nanook and his family before the cameras, but also to Flaherty's own profound knowledge of Eskimo life and susceptibilities. It is an instructive film on the ethnological level, and it is a warm and amusing human drama too. Nanook comes to symbolize a way of facing the world, of taking it by the scruff of the neck and wringing existence from it with a laugh.

COPS. United States. Directors: Buster Keaton and Eddie Kline. Keaton, still under the influence of Sennett, baffles the local police force with boisterous invention.

1922: Facts of Interest

W. H. Hays now in charge of censorship of production in the United States.

Greta Garbo makes her screen début in Erik Petschler's *Luffar-Petter*.

The first film school is started—in Yugoslavia.

Alain Resnais (*Hiroshima Mon Amour*) is born.

1922: From NANOOK OF THE NORTH.

1923

SAFETY LAST. United States. Script: Harold Lloyd and Hal Roach. Direction: Fred Newmayer and Sam Taylor. Photography: Walter Lundon. Editing: Fred L. Guiol. Players: Harold Lloyd, Mildred Davies, Bill Strothers, Noah Young, W.B. Clarke. Production: Hal Roach Associates. (Six reels).

To survive the silent film era, a comedian had to have a readily identifiable personality, looks, and qualities that distinguished him from his rivals. Harold Lloyd began to make one-reelers for Rolin and Pathé in January 1916 and from then until 1938 he was almost continuously at work. In his best comedies he played the ambitious country hick with an ingratiating grin beneath his black spectacles and his gleaming hair. In *Safety Last* he is as springy as a terrier, thirsting for promotion in the city store, always on the doorstep hours before time and an irritant to the head floorwalker with his self-satisfied air. When his sweetheart follows him from Great Bend, however, Harold is rather desperate to earn money. Together with his pal Bill he offers to scale the DeVore skyscraper for a thousand dollars to attract publicity to the store. But Bill is involved with an irate policeman, and Lloyd begins the long climb himself. It is undoubtedly one of the funniest sequences in the cinema. As he moves higher and higher above the crowds, the hazards proliferate. He is assailed by pigeons; his foot is entangled in the spring of the gigantic store clock; a mouse decides to investigate his trousers. "We made pictures as we went along," recalls Lloyd. "Even in *Safety Last* we made the climb first. Then we went back and worked out how to build up to the climb; we knew the general idea of the country boy coming to the city, but not its detailed resolution." This method gave Lloyd's comedy a wonderful sense of impending disaster, of a climax round the corner that was sure to produce even greater laughs.

THE COVERED WAGON. United States. Script: Jack Cunningham, based on a novel by Emerson Hough. Direction: James Cruze. Photography: Karl Brown. Editing: Dorothy Arzner. Players: Ernest Torrence, Tully Marshall, J. Warren Kerrigan, Lois Wilson, Alan Hale. Production: Famous Players Lasky. (9200 ft.)

Today, the more than a hundred films directed by James Cruze have vanished from memory, except for *The Covered Wagon*. Cruze had been an actor in the cinema since 1908, and his first assignment as director was *Too Many Millions* in 1918. Although its plot line appears rather ponderous now, *The Covered Wagon* was surely the most accurate of the early Westerns. Cruze's thirst for realism prompted him to commission some fifty experts to research into the story and to establish the costumes and locations. Eventually the exteriors were shot in Snake Valley, Nevada, more than eighty miles from the nearest railroad station. The great trek westward by the pioneers is the theme of *The Covered Wagon*. Some aim for Oregon, some for California. The journey quickly thins out the wagon train. Hardship, homesickness, clashes with the Indians, and snow all take their toll.

One of the most famous scenes is the fording of the river. "It's most important of all to get the babies across," says an old timer, "They'll be the real pioneers." This unselfish attitude colored much of the film, and the undertow of patriotism was probably as much responsible as the spectacular elements for the huge commercial success of *The Covered Wagon*. It ran fifty-nine weeks at the Criterion Theatre, New York, eclipsing even *The Birth of a Nation* records. It was, after all, the first of an endless line of pioneer sagas, whereby the eighteenth century proved as rich a ground for film-makers as the nineteenth century; and Karl Brown's photography, particularly his night work, made a significant contribution to the value of the film.

GUNNAR HEDE'S SAGA (Gunner Hedes Saga). Sweden. Script and Direction: Mauritz Stiller from the novel *En Herrgardssägen* by Selma Lagerlöf. Photography: J. Julius. Art Director: Axel Esbensen.

Players: Einar Hansson, Pauline Brunius, Mary Johnson, Stina Berg, Adolf Olchansky, Thecla Ahlander, Gösta Hillberg, Hugo Björne. Production: Svensk Filmindustri. (4337 ft.)

Stiller came as near as any director can do to creating a visual poem in *Gunnar Hede's Saga*. It is unlike anything else he undertook, and it stands apart from contemporary films by its weird power and fervency. Nils is a shy, musically-inclined young hero, who leaves his home and travels up to Lapland, inspired by his father's exploits there. But when Nils himself tries to follow the same trek southwards, disaster strikes. His herd of reindeer stampedes, and he is knocked unconscious. When at last he reaches home, he is suffering from severe amnesia, and languishes in the old manor until the sound of a girl's violin restores his memory. The story, however, is negligible, for the film is an ode. The characters seem lit with spiritual grace and charm. Delirium merges with reality after Nils's experience, contrasting poignantly with the violent journey as the reindeer stream over the ice and snow. Dreams and flashbacks abound—Ingrid's vision of the "Lady of Grief" in a coach drawn by black bears is outstanding among them. *Gunnar Hede's Saga* combines elements of the epic and the introspective film; it is essentially a mood piece, with each image setting up a resonance beyond its immediate meaning, each cunning dissolve luring one farther into a strange, luminary world.

Checklist of other important features

CRAINQUEBILLE. France. Director: Jacques Feyder. This film about the poor areas of Paris, based on a novel by Anatole France, was really far ahead of its time and brought a new degree of realism into French cinema.

THE HUNCHBACK OF NOTRE DAME. United States. Director: Wallace Worsley. Arguably Lon Chaney's most striking and vivid characterization, supported by some extraordinary mob scenes.

THE PILGRIM. United States. Chaplin as a convict who becomes a suave clergyman, discomfited by the appearance of an old cell mate. Much knockabout, without perhaps the subtlety of *The Kid*.

SIEGFRIED. Germany. The first of Fritz Lang's two-part interpretation of the Nibelungen Saga, in which a dynamic Siegfried slaughters the dragon (a brilliant piece of trick photography) and indulges

1923: *"The great trek Westwards" in THE COVERED WAGON.*

his lust for immortality. There is also an impressive dream sequence conceived by Walther Ruttmann.

THE WHEEL (La Roue). France. Abel Gance spent five years on this turbulent film, in which three men are madly in love with the same girl, and his work cast a powerful influence over the avant-garde movement of the twenties. Jean Cocteau claimed: "There is the cinema before *La Roue,* and the cinema after *La Roue,* just as there is painting before and after Picasso."

A WOMAN OF PARIS. United States. Chaplin's first melodrama, starring Edna Purviance, but not Charlie, in a tale of female suffering and masculine "villainy" (Adolphe Menjou).

Short films and Documentaries

GRASS. Directors: Merian C. Cooper and Ernest B. Schoedsack. Outstanding documentary about an Iranian nomad tribe.

SEVEN YEARS' BAD LUCK. United States. Max Linder improvising in the face of misfortune and offering a timeless lesson in the art of avoiding ticket collectors on trains.

1923: *GUNNAR HEDE'S SAGA—"a visual poem."*

1923: Facts of Interest

Kenji Mizoguchi makes the first of his eighty-eight films.

1924

GREED. United States. Script and Direction: Erich von Stroheim, from the novel *McTeague* by Frank Norris. Photography: Ben Reynolds, William Daniels. Editing: Rex Ingram. June Mathis. Art Direction: Cedric Gibbons. Players: Gibson Gowland, ZaSu Pitts, Jean Hersholt, Tempe Piggott, Dale Fuller, Chester Conklin, Sylvia Ashton, Hughie Mack. Production: M-G-M (Sam Goldwyn, Irving Thalberg). (132 mins.)

Although it was reduced to half its length, *Greed* still looms larger than any other American film of the early twenties. Stroheim describes the life of Mc-Teague, a shaggy, rustic hero unrepresentative of his times, in a series of great tableaux and climactic incidents. The film is geared to a high pitch of crisis from start to finish. McTeague moves from a gold-mine in California to a dentistry practice on Polk Street, San Francisco. He has been shielded by his mother from fleshly temptations, and falls madly in love with Trina, introduced to him by his close friend Marcus. The wedding night amounts almost to rape, so blundering is McTeague's approach, and this is the first and capital cause of the rift between them. Trina becomes a miser. She scorns her husband for his slow wits. They wrangle incessantly, and the marriage disintegrates. (Big chunks of film are clearly missing here, and Trina's transformation from demure bride to avaricious harridan is very nearly ridiculous.) Finally, McTeague murders her in a night of rage, and plunges into Death Valley with her gold, to escape the police. Marcus, seeking revenge, pursues him. Both men are trapped without water, sustained only by mutual hatred and desire for the money. McTeague finds himself handcuffed to Marcus after he has beaten him to death, and he lets his faithful pet canary fly away, in the bitter knowledge that it is doomed, like him, to struggle only a little longer. Stroheim would have approved of Ophüls's dictum —"Details, details, details!" He took enormous pains to ensure that individual scenes were crammed with realistic accessories. In the wedding sequence, Stro-

1924: The wedding reception in GREED.

heim's jaundiced eye discerns a funeral *cortège* outside the window; and the celebrations are pervaded with an atmosphere of orgiastic indulgence that whets the greed of Marcus. The day at the Oakland Amusement Park is full of kinetic movement, and time and again the absence of sound is more than counterbalanced by the monstrous close-ups and the expressions of rage, fear, and sadism that inhabit McTeague's features. The photography has an incandescent quality that heightens the spill of gold between Trina's hands, the murder scene in the Kindergarten, and the parched brightness of the desert. It is the intensity and the brutal naturalism of *Greed* that make it a tragedy on a titanic scale.

THE LAST LAUGH (Der Letzte Mann). Germany. Script: Carl Mayer. Direction: F. W. Murnau. Photog-

65

1924: The aging porter in THE LAST LAUGH.

raphy: Karl Freund. Art Direction: Robert Herlth, Walter Röhrig. Players: Emil Jannings, Mady Delschaft, Max Hiller, Emile Kurz, Hans Unterkirchen, Olaf Storm. Production: UFA. (71 mins.)

Naturalism was popular among writers and artists of the twenties (*vide* the novels of Theodore Dreiser), and its influence can be seen in the films of Murnau as well as in those of Stroheim. *The Last Laugh* records the slow, inevitable decline of an elderly porter (Emil Jannings) in the Atlantic Hotel. At the start of the film he is resplendent in his uniform (a token of high class life), greeting guests with dignity and aplomb. But then he is told by the manager that he is to be replaced. He is stripped of his uniform and made to care for the lavatories downstairs, to the concern of his family and the delight of his neighbors. A ludicrous final sequence (dictated by UFA) shows the old man becoming rich overnight. There are no captions used in *The Last Laugh;* the story is told in a series of discreet and evocative camera movements. At one point Karl Freund even strapped the camera to his chest and reeled around to simulate the old man's drunkenness. The sparkling reflections of the revolving door in the foyer predominate in the visual scheme, and symbolize life's roundabout, which offers good fortune one moment and misery the next. The door is also a barrier, separating the porter from the bustle of the world, just as the heavy doors of the lavatory close behind him after his demotion, as though he were being imprisoned *in tenebris*. Contrasts between rich and poor are popular at this period, and Murnau makes frequent use of cross-cutting to comment on the social scene in Germany. (One famous pair of shots shows Jannings sipping soup in the lavatory while a wealthy woman consumes oysters upstairs.) But *The Last Laugh* abides as a film not because of these familiar similes but because of its fluent protest against a society that witnesses such disgrace.

1924: From John Ford's first major film, THE IRON HORSE.

THE IRON HORSE. United States. Script: Charles Kenyon and John Russell. Direction: John Ford. Photography: George Schneiderman and Burnett Guffey. Music score: Erno Rapee. Players: George O'Brien, Madge Bellamy, Judge Charles E. Bull, William Walling, Fred Kohler, Cyril Chadwick. Production: Fox. (160 mins.)

John Ford, born of Irish stock, arrived in Hollywood in 1913 and directed his first picture four years later. But not until 1924 did he show his inimitable gift for portraying the old West, with a respect for its "wide, open spaces," and for the human contacts that somehow flourished under primitive conditions. His uncle was a laborer on the Union Pacific when it was built and *The Iron Horse* takes the construction of a transcontinental railroad as its theme. Idealism in Ford's work has often been identified with this Westward journey—in *Wagonmaster* (see *1950*), for example, or *The Searchers*. There is also a degree of private suspense in *The Iron Horse*, for Davy Brandon is searching for his father's murderer; but the most lasting scenes are those involving the railroad itself. Ford fixes his camera to the front of a locomotive so that the moving riders alongside make dynamic patterns across the screen. A buffalo charge is brilliantly handled, as is the massive battle at the end. *The Iron Horse* is the longest of Ford's 132 films and in effect contains many climaxes, perhaps none more vibrant than the "meeting" between the Union Pacific and the Central Pacific groups at Promontory Point, Utah, on May 10, 1869; and Ford allegedly used the original trains "Jupiter" and "116." With its cast of 5000, the film is essentially episodic, and one can find countless portents of Ford's later fancies—the domestic witticisms, the hardy, crusty characters, and the lyrical compositions (campfire scenes, or Indians silhouetted against the horizon).

SHERLOCK JUNIOR. United States. Script: Jean C. Havez, Joseph A. Mitchell, Clyde Bruckman. Di-

1924: Keaton fancies himself in evening dress in SHERLOCK JUNIOR.

rector: Buster Keaton. Photography: Elgin Lessley, Byron Houck. Art Direction: Fred Gabourie. Players: Buster Keaton, Kathryn McGuire, Joe Keaton, Ward Crane, Jane Connelly, Erwin Connelly. Production: Metro Pictures Corporation. (10 reels.)

By 1924 Keaton was in full spate, as productive as any of the great silent comedians and experimenting with the medium much more than Chaplin. *Sherlock Junior* misses the tightly packed humor of a short like *The Goat* (see *1921*), but it is as inventive—situation-wise—as anything Buster did. He plays a cinema cleaner-cum-projectionist who, after failing as an amateur sleuth, falls to dreaming in the projection booth. He enters the world of the screen romance he is showing, and this splendid idea enables Keaton to defy logic for the next half hour. He shifts from one incongruous set of circumstances to another, stepping from an African jungle into a desert, from a seascape into a snowbank, and so on. In his fantasy he is attended by a manservant who drives him round on the handlebars of a motor bike. Here is the film's one great sequence. Buster, unaware that his "driver" has vanished, plunges over hill and highway as obstacles bow before his confused but trusting gaze. (These acrobatics apparently overturned two cameras and demolished a car.) It's beyond dispute that Keaton used his pliable physique with more expediency than any of his rival comedians. He was a genuine tumbler, leaping nimbly from danger to danger, with a Houdini-like flair for slipping away from cops, companions, and anything hostile. Keaton has now been rehabilitated, perhaps overrated, by a postwar generation. Is it because his sceptical view of a machine age is so attractive now, or because his blank-faced sophistication endures better than Lloyd's eager ambition and Chaplin's Victorian tramp?

Checklist of other important features

AMERICA. United States. Griffith's last film of importance, a spectacular about the Revolution enlivened by some remarkable war scenes.

MIKAEL. Germany. Director: Carl Th. Dreyer. A somewhat leaden, but finally very moving, study of friendship that marks a significant stage in the career of one of the world's greatest directors.

THE NAVIGATOR. United States. Directors: Buster Keaton, Donald Crisp, and Jean C. Havez. Keaton struggles for survival with his girlfriend in a sea of technological devices. Vintage comedy.

PARIS QUI DORT. France. Only twenty-five years old when he made this film, René Clair demonstrates his avant-gardist sympathies in a curious imbroglio, where a mad scientist sends the whole of Paris to sleep.

THE SAGA OF GÖSTA BERLING (Gösta Berlings saga). Sweden. Director: Mauritz Stiller. A two-part epic of Swedish country life, in some degree both apogee and swan song of the "golden age" in Swedish films.

THE THIEF OF BAGDAD. United States. Director: Raoul Walsh. Douglas Fairbanks produced and starred in this Arabian Nights fantasy, with its vast sets and impressive trick effects.

WAXWORKS (Das Wachsfigurenkabinett). Germany. Director: Paul Leni. A tripartite whimsy evoking the exploits of Ivan the Terrible, Haroun al Raschid, and Jack the Ripper, chiefly known for its lighting devices and its distorted décors.

Short films and Documentaries

BALLET MÉCANIQUE. France. Director: Fernand Léger. More well known as a painter, Léger caused a stir with this avant-garde film in the cubist style.

ENTR'ACTE. France. Director: René Clair. A virtuoso and amusing short, prepared as an intermission *divertissement* for a ballet which was never, in fact, performed. Many celebrated figures of the time took part.

THE GIRL IN THE LIMOUSINE. United States. Larry Semon, who for some years had been among the highest paid comics in Hollywood, reaches new heights of energetic humor.

PICKING PEACHES. United States. Director: Erle C. Kenton. Harry Langdon's first appearance.

1924: Facts of Interest

M-G-M is founded by Sam Goldwyn, Louis B. Mayer, and Metro Pictures Corporation.
Columbia is also established as a major studio.
Death of Thomas Ince.

1925

BATTLESHIP POTEMKIN (Bronenosets "Potyomkin"). U.S.S.R. Script: Nina Agadzhanova-Shutko. Direction: Sergei M. Eisenstein. Photography: Edward Tissé. Art Direction: Vasili Rakhals. Assistants: Grigori Alexandrov, Alexander Antonov, Mikhail Gomarov, A. Levshin, Maxim Strauch. Players: Antonov, Alexandrov, Vladimir Barsky, Levshin, Gomarov, Strauch. Production: Goskino. (72 mins.)

In 1925 the 1905 Revolution was due to be celebrated in Russia. Eisenstein, at work on a study of the Cavalry Army in the Civil War, was assigned to film a scenario that covered the Revolution from the struggle with Japan to the domestic upheavals in Moscow. But Eisenstein concentrated all his attention on the mutiny aboard the *Potemkin* in June 1905, as it lay off Odessa in the Black Sea. The men are seen asleep in their hammocks, their bodies radiating strength and resilience despite their cramped and sordid surroundings. A carcass of rotten meat converts indignation into fury. The captain finds his men reluctant to shoot down their comrades; and so, in a terrible, dynamic struggle in the 'tween-decks and beside the huge guns, control passes to the "proletariat." In Odessa, the townsfolk take pity on the mutineers; they pay homage to the one dead member of the crew, a symbol of injustice. They take provisions to the *Potemkin* in their fishing boats. And then, down the broad marble staircase of Odessa marches a phalanx of Cossack soldiers. They shoot and trample on the men, women and children who resist. The *Potemkin* must now challenge the entire fleet if it is to survive. After an agonizing wait, the other ships in the squadron rally to their side. A famous victory has been won.

Eisenstein's achievement in this firm lies in the montage. Characterization is on a weak scale; the film is almost a documentary, and Eisenstein admitted that it "looks like a newsreel of an event, but it functions as a drama," divided into five distinct acts. But no image lasts more than a few seconds. As trouble foments aboard the battleship and along the quays of Odessa, one is caught up in an orchestration of movement that engenders its own suspense and that defies the limitations of the silent film. During the final lull, as the fleet creeps up on the *Potemkin* by night, the silence is turned to brilliant advantage by Eisenstein. As in *Strike* (see below), there is a fine admixture of close-ups and long shots, the scowling, frenzied faces of the officers thus dominating the crew on the deck, as they are photographed from above. *Battleship Potemkin* is surely not the best film the cinema has produced. In many ways, in its use of captions, in its propaganda, it seems crude when projected now. But its plastic symmetry, its humanity, and its throbbing power still command respect, and Eisenstein remains the world's finest film editor.

STRIKE (Stachka). U.S.S.R. Script: Proletkult collective (Valeri Pletnyov, Sergei M. Eisenstein, I. Kravchunovsky, Grigori Alexandrov). Direction: Eisenstein. Photography: Edward Tissé, Vasili Khvatov. Art Direction: Vasili Rakhals. Players: Alexandrov, Maxim Strauch, Mikhail Gomarov, Judith Glizer, Boris Yurtsev, Alexander Antonov. Production: Goskino and Proletkult. (6 reels.)

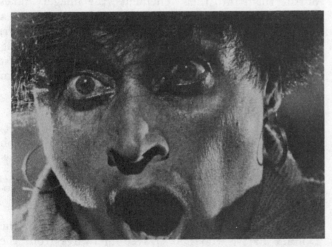

1925: From the Odessa Steps sequence in BATTLESHIP POTEMKIN.

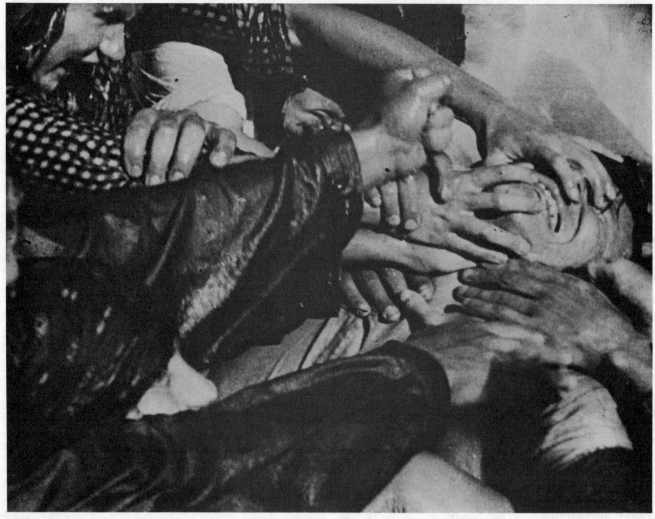

1925: "The hoses are turned on the crowds" in STRIKE.

Eisenstein's first film is almost more important than *Battleship Potemkin*. It is organized with the same dynamism and discipline, but it suffers increasingly with the years from its naïve view of class warfare and the power complex. *Strike* is split conveniently into six phases, each corresponding to the length of a reel (single-reel projection was prevalent in Russia at the time). Like *Battleship Potemkin,* the film deals with an incident prior to the 1917 Revolution. A workman in an industrial plant is accused of stealing a magnometer and hangs himself when the management threatens to withhold his pay. The other workers put down their tools in protest—the first great shot in Eisenstein's cinema is a lateral track along some overhead cables as the strikers stream from the factory, a concise image of the "collective action" that the early Soviet films determined to salute. As so often in his later work, Eisenstein uses an interlude—a space between urgent currents of action—to prepare his audiences for an intense emotional shock. Part 3 of *Strike* shows the workers happy and at leisure be-

fore the police intervene. They arrive on horseback; one striker is captured in the rain and brutally beaten. The hoses are turned on the crowds and, as the troops pursue them into their tenements, the imagery takes on a vicious quality. The final shots present a sea of dead men, piled like carcasses one upon the other, cunningly intercut with close-ups of a bull being slaughtered. Eisenstein was unquestionably the first director really to grasp the potentialities of the film as a medium of propaganda.

THE GOLD RUSH. United States. Script and Direction: Charles Chaplin. Photography: Rollie Totheroh and Jack Wilson. Editing: Harold McGahann. Players: Charles Chaplin, Mack Swain, Tom Murray, Georgia Hale, Henry Bergman, Malcolm Waite. Production: United Artists. (72 mins.)

Chaplin was partly inspired by an account of the Donner Party, who had strayed unawares from the trail to California and perished in the snow of the

70

Sierra Nevada. He even admits that the fact that some of these pioneers had resorted to eating their moccasins gave him the idea for the shoe-stewing scene in the film. He began shooting *The Gold Rush* without a script, but the finished film develops with sublime logic. It is situation comedy at its best, with Charlie first stumbling into view along a precipice, pursued by a disgruntled bear. As usual, in an effort to elude one crisis he plunges into another: the cabin that looks so comforting in the blizzard is inhabited by none other than the ferocious prospector, Big Jim. The core of the film is set within these wooden walls as the men resort to extremes (including the "shoe" meal), and the child-like romance that follows, with Georgia Hale, in the "Monte Carlo Dance Hall" seems to belong to another film, although in Chaplin's world pathos and comedy have always intermingled. Here Charlie the idealist is in full flow, concocting a dinner party for his beloved on New Year's Eve, and swearing to rescue her from her miserable life. In the concluding episode, as Charlie and Big Jim fight to escape from their cabin, which has been blown to the edge of an abyss, the familiar comic routine is brought to dazzling maturity. Suspense almost shores up one's laughter, until Charlie finally jumps to safety and the cabin disappears forever.

VARIÉTÉ. Germany. Script: Leo Birinski, from a novel by Felix Hollander. Direction: E. A. Dupont. Photography: Karl Freund. Art Direction: Oscar Werndorff. Players: Emil Jannings, Lya de Putti, Warwick Ward, Mady Delschaft, Georg John, Kurt Gerron. Production: UFA. (65 mins.)

In 1911 Ewald Dupont was one of the first film crit-

ics in Germany. Not until 1924, with *Baruch,* did he make his début as a director. Unlike other German productions of the period, his *Variété* does not rely for its impact on a ponderous accumulation of physical and psychological detail. The circus and music hall milieu gives plenty of opportunity for movement and dramatic highlights. "Boss" Huller (Emil Jannings) abandons his wife for a luscious young trapeze artiste (Lya de Putti). He even darns her stockings, and undresses her when she is exhausted after her act. But when in her turn she deceives him with Artinelli, a famous acrobat, the solicitous Huller is pushed to retaliate. As one sees him wash the dead man's blood from his hands afterwards, one realizes that the murder is to be recognized as nothing more or less than justified revenge. One crime has displaced another, and, after years of imprisonment, Huller tells the details of his story and is released to his wife. The vulgarity and anguish of the entertainer's life are given the same weight here as in Ingmar Bergman's *The Naked Night* (see *1953*). There is a similar sensation of spiritual guilt reflected in physical degradation. Karl Freund's camera follows the curling flight of the trapeze so as to make Lya de Putti a voluptuous and tantalizing creature in both men's eyes, and this contrasts chillingly with the shots of Huller in prison, viewed from above as he tramps in a circle with other criminals, or from behind as he shuffles towards the warden's room, the huge number 28 on his back implying at once anonymity and disgrace.

THE STREET OF SORROW (Die freudlose Gasse). Germany. Script: Willi Haas, from the novel by Hugo Bettauer. Direction: G. W. Pabst. Photogra-

1925: Emil Jannings as the murderer in VARIÉTÉ.

1925: *Greta Garbo in* THE STREET OF SORROW.

phy: Guido Seeber, Kurt Oertel. Art Direction: Söhnle, Erdmann. Players: Asta Neilsen, Valeska Gert, Greta Garbo, Agnes Esterhazy, Tamara Tolstoy, Werner Krauss. Production: Hirschal Sofar. (4200 ft.)

The opening scene of *The Street of Sorrow* shows a queue of women outside a butcher's shop. They are treated scornfully by the butcher who, it transpires, will only give his meat to girls of easy virtue. But these women do not belong to the working classes. They represent the unfortunate bourgeois families who have been caught in the somber aftermath of World War I in Vienna, where what money is left is grasped by racketeers and prostitutes. Greta Garbo plays the daughter of an ex-Councillor of the Imperial Austrian Court who has invested his pension in coal shares and lost it all. The daughter has to swallow her moral indignation and agrees to work in a night-club.

This third film of Pabst's confirmed his stature, especially in France, where it ran for two years and was regarded as a warning against the dangers of inflation. Censorship in one country after another has reduced the impact of the film over the years. The uncompromising view of squalor and privation, however, endures. "What need is there for romantic treatment?"

asked the director. "Real life is too romantic, too ghastly." *Street of Sorrow* ends with a spontaneous upheaval as the people tear at the doors of the Greifer brothel and crush the butcher beneath their feet. Even now Pabst's treatment of these scenes is conspicuously good. His editing creates the illusion of continuous movement from one frame to another, although he had not seen Eisenstein's work at the time. Some sequences suffer from overemphatic lighting and studio sets, just as others are enhanced by the beauty of Greta Garbo (in her first role outside Sweden) and of Asta Nielsen, the Danish actress who had lived in Germany since 1911.

Checklist of other important features

BEN HUR. United States. Director: Fred Niblo. M-G-M's costly spectacle—the budget soared to a reputed $4 million—with Ramon Novarro in the title role and Francis X. Bushman as Messala.

THE BIG PARADE. United States. Director: King Vidor. Assumed to be the most profitable silent film, *The Big Parade* is also among the most acute and best reconstructed of war films.

THE FRESHMAN. United States. Directors: Fred Newmayer and Sam Taylor. One of Harold Lloyd's most hilarious "character" comedies, with its climactic football game being an anthology piece of film humor.

LADY WINDERMERE'S FAN. United States. Ernst Lubitsch's sardonic visual wit replaces Wilde's repartee as far as the confines of the silent film permit. This film established the German director as a man able to hold his own in Hollywood.

THE LOST WORLD. United States. Director: Harry Hoyt. Outstanding for its special effects and "monsters" created by Willis O'Brien.

THE PHANTOM OF THE OPERA. United States. Director: Rupert Julian. Lon Chaney, with hideous swept-up nose and demoniac grin, bestrides one of the most flamboyant of early horror films, and after forty years the Phantom's fate still seems harsh and moving.

SALLY OF THE SAWDUST. United States. Director: D. W. Griffith. W. C. Fields established his film reputation with this comedy.

Short films and Documentaries

THE WIZARD OF OZ. United States. Larry Semon's Pierrot-like wit again in evidence. Semon's early death in 1928 was a great loss to the cinema.

1925: Facts of Interest

Death of Louis Feuillade and Max Linder, two bulwarks of the French cinema.

1926

MOTHER (Mat). U.S.S.R. Script: Nathan Zarkhi, from the novel by Maxim Gorky. Direction: Vsevolod Pudovkin. Photography: Anatoli Golovnya. Art Direction: Sergei Kozlovsky. Players: Vera Baranovskaia, A. P. Christiakov, Nikolai Batalov, Ivan Koval-Samborski, Anna Zemtzova. Production: Mezhrabpom-Russ. (106 mins.)

The individual, so often submerged in the mass Soviet cinema of the twenties, is crucially important in Pudovkin's films. "A mother is fearless," wrote Gorky, "when it comes to protecting a being she brought into existence," and the slow but definite change worked in the "mother" is a symbol of the overwhelming victory of the Revolution, a generation later in 1917. The film revolves on the ironic premise of a son's being responsible for the death of his father. At first his mother repudiates him and turns over to the soldiers the guns he has hidden for revolutionary action. But later she grows conscious of his grievances, and she asks his forgiveness in prison.

The ideological content of *Mother* is significant. The factory and the prison, two recurrent tokens of men-in-unison, are used organically in the narrative; authority, in the person of the police, the militia, or the court officials, is regarded with scorn and dislike. This appears forcefully in the many close-ups, where the tightly drawn, implacable features of a judge, for instance, contrast with the son's eager, candid response to the camera. Soldiers' faces are lit and observed from the side, so that they look like stone statues, incapable of sentiment. In the final sequence, the mounted troops cut down the demonstrators and become no more than black streaks hurtling across the screen, arousing the same palpable sense of outrage as the massacre on the Odessa Steps in *Battleship Potemkin* (see *1925*). Pudovkin's equation of the crowd's defiant progress with the surging tides of spring is not so effective as is often maintained, and his narrative style, so lucid when dealing with domestic situations, is fragmented and confusing in the strike and prison scenes. But *Mother* still foments acute emotional excitement, and it marks the arrival of Pudovkin as one of the silent cinema's greatest directors.

TRAMP, TRAMP, TRAMP. United States. Script: Frank Capra, Tim Whelan, Hal Conklin, J. Frank Holliday, Gerald Duffy, and Murry Roth. Direction: Harry Edwards. Photography: Elgin Lessley. Players: Harry Langdon, Joan Crawford, Tom Murray, Edward Davis, Alec B. Francis, Carlton Griffith. Production: Harry Langdon Corporation/First National. (62 mins.)

His distended white cheeks, his dreamy eyes, and his battered hat make Harry Langdon the gentlest and most vulnerable of the great silent comics. As Mack Sennett has said, "Langdon was as bland as milk, a forgiving small cuss, an obedient puppy, always in the way, exasperating, but offering his baby mannerisms with hopeful apology." *Tramp, Tramp, Tramp* was made during his vintage period at First National, and contains some of Langdon's finest gags, interspersed with leisurely romance and flights of fantasy as Harry joins a transcontinental walking race in order to help his ailing father. Burton's Shoes, "the sole of the nation," are offering a first prize of $25,000 and, with Joan Crawford as the coy young daughter of the firm eminently available too, the temptation proves too much for Harry. There are moments during the film that rival *The General* for sheer visual invention: when the electric fan shreds Harry's bed and drives feathers round the room; or when Langdon climbs a fence marked "Private" and finds that a precipice yawns on the other side . . . But the final scenes drift into fairy tale as Harry, with houses collapsing all around him, puts a cyclone to flight by hurling bricks at it, and then himself plays the baby in a cot, all curious and gawky in a frilly bonnet, as he is watched through the window by Miss Crawford and the real, proud Langdon.

METROPOLIS. Germany. Script: Fritz Lang and Thea von Harbou, from a story by the latter. Direc-

1926: The prison scene in MOTHER.

1926: Harry Langdon with Joan Crawford in TRAMP, TRAMP, TRAMP.

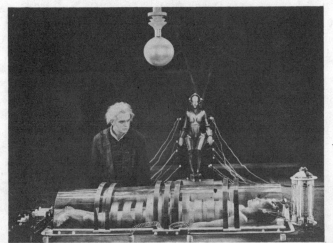

1926: The birth of the robot in METROPOLIS.

tion: Lang. Photography: Karl Freund, Günther Rittau. Music: Gottfried. Art Direction: Otto Hunte, Erich Kettelhut, Karl Vollbrecht. Players: Alfred Abel, Gustav Froehlich, Rudolf Klein-Rogge, Brigitte Helm, Heinrich George, Fritz Rasp, Theodore Loos. Production: UFA. (120 mins.)

The end of *Metropolis*, as the workers shake hands solemnly with the Master of the City, John Freder, is founded on the slogan, "There can be no understanding between the hands and the brain unless the heart acts as mediator." This, and much of the dialogue in the film, smacks of the false sentimentality and submission to power that were to engulf Germany ten years later. Lang was never a great director of actors, and the painful inadequacies of Gustav Froehlich as Freder's son now ruin the impact of *Metropolis*. But this city of the future, with its cubist architecture and its underground machinery, does provoke a certain wonder. The slow, lugubrious pace of the early sequences, as groups of workers relieve each other with the metronomic shuffle of robots, seems justified in view of the dynamic climax when the men run riot, destroying the machines and thus flooding their own homes. Karl Freund's photography of the crowds is brilliant, and the interaction of light and shadow, close-up and extreme long shot, has a more than melodramatic appeal. As Lotte H. Eisner has written, the human beings become part of the décor, gathered together in geometric and impersonal patterns. Lang transcends the limits of silent film technique through his choice of sights that imply noise—the jets of steam that *look* like sirens marking the end of a workers' shift, or the smooth, interlocking movements of each machine. It is a pity that the years have exposed the naïveté of the human relationships in *Metropolis*, for in terms of sheer realization Lang was ahead of other European directors at this time.

Checklist of other important features

THE BLACK PIRATE. United States. Director: Albert Parker. A glossy historical extravaganza starring Douglas Fairbanks, Sr. at his most agile and muscular.

DON Q, SON OF ZORRO. United States. Director: Donald Crisp. An extremely long but well controlled adventure film starring the irrepressible Fairbanks again.

FAUST. Germany. Director: F. W. Murnau. An imaginative and impressionistic version of the German legend, with Emil Jannings stout and leering as Mephisto.

NANA. France. A sardonic adaptation of Zola's great novel. Jean Renoir's second film, and his only major achievement during the silent period.

PAPER DOLL (Kami ningyo haru no sasayaki). Japan. The first distinguished film by Kenji Mizoguchi, later to become the most revered of Japanese directors.

THE SCARLET LETTER. United States. Director: Victor Seastrom. Hawthorne's novel about Puritanism at the time of the Pilgrims, with Lillian Gish as Hester and Lars Hanson as the minister. "I never worked with anyone I liked better than Seastrom," claimed Miss Gish.

SECRETS OF A SOUL (Geheimnisse einer Seele). Germany. Director: G. W. Pabst. An obsessive, nightmarish exercise in expressionism as a doctor goes steadily insane and pours out his dreams and hallucinations to a psychiatrist.

SON OF THE SHEIK. United States. Director: George Fitzmaurice. Filmed on location in Yuma, with Rudolph Valentino in probably his most shamelessly entertaining and swashbuckling role.

SO THIS IS PARIS. United States. Ernst Lubitsch took a decisive step forward in his Hollywood career with this magnetic and comic account of two young couples in Paris.

Short films and Documentaries

THE ADVENTURES OF PRINCE ACHMED. Germany. Lotte Reiniger, a German woman who later worked in Britain, created a niche of her own in the cinema by using silhouette figures to tell short stories, of which this is one of the most widely shown.

RIEN QUE LES HEURES. France. Director: Alberto Cavalcanti. The first documentary built around a time sequence and based on rhythmical editing.

1926: Facts of Interest

Walt Disney arrives in Hollywood and produces ten "Alice" shorts composed of animation and live action.
John Grierson uses the word "documentary" in a review of Flaherty's *Moana* in *The New York Sun*.
Death of Rudolph Valentino.
The world's first "art house," the Ursulines, is opened in Paris by Armand Tallier and Mlle Myrga.
The London Film Society is founded.

1927

THE JAZZ SINGER. United States. Script: Alfred A. Cohn, from the play by Samson Raphaelson. Direction: Alan Crosland. Photography: Hal Mohr. Editing: Harold McCord. Music: various, including "Blue Skies" by Irving Berlin. Players: Al Jolson, May McAvoy, Warner Oland, Eugenie Besserer, Cantor Josef Rosenblatt, Otto Lederer. Production: Warner Brothers. (90 mins.)

Sound comes to the cinema! There were many attempts to produce sound films before *The Jazz Singer* was shown in New York in October, 1927. The most convincing of these experiments were the De Forest Phonofilms which, though hampered by a static camera, managed to match an actor's lip movements with his voice on the soundtrack recording. *The Jazz Singer* was the first feature-length film to use sound, although it was essentially a silent film with a synchronized musical accompaniment. There are a few lines of dialogue, but these follow Jolson's songs, when he turns to talk to his accompanist or his old mother. Printed titles hurry the story along at a melodramatic pitch, and include gems like, "God Made her a Woman and Love Made her a Mother." The familiar plot tells of Jakie Rabinowitz, the son of a Jewish cantor, who turns to ragtime and then has to forego temporarily his big chance on Broadway because of his father's illness. Schmalz and sentimentality swamp the film except when Jolson is singing. At such moments, one tends to take for granted the excellent sound synchronization and to be fascinated by the charismatic persona that Jolson still projects. With his sad, sunken eyes, his beseeching glance, and his nasal voice, he establishes a pattern for what has become one of the most durable film genres—the musical, where naïve emotional appeal is counterbalanced by verve and good humor.

THE GENERAL. United States. Script: Al Boasberg, Charles Smith. Direction: Buster Keaton and Clyde Bruckman. Photography: Bert Haines and J. D. Jennings. Editing: Sherman Kell. Players: Marion Mack, Buster Keaton, Glen Cavender, Jim Farley, Frederick Vroom, Charles Smith, Frank Barnes. Production: United Artists. Eight reels. (Sound version: 75 mins.)

Buster Keaton's reputation has always sparkled among film critics; but his death in 1966 has encouraged claims that he was the greatest of all comedians. *The General* is probably his best, his most characteristic film. Keaton uses comparatively few gags, but he extends them and revives them so cleverly that they give his cinema a peculiar density. In *The General,* for instance, Keaton—a Southern engine driver—finds himself being chased in his turn along the railroad by the Yankees; and so it is only logical that he should resort to the same delaying tactics as he has overcome himself earlier in the film. Furthermore, his gags promote tremendous reverberations: the cannon ball that he fires (accidentally, of course) vertically into the air smashes a neighboring weir, thus inundating the Northern troops.

Keaton survives here, as elsewhere, because he can *adapt* himself to the most intimidating of situations. Keaton the director (with Clyde Bruckman) views Keaton the clown with a blank gravity that lends wit to a simple gesture—Buster offering his outstretched arm to Annabelle Lee as she climbs into the locomotive as if she were mounting a steed. For Keaton is always eager to please, where Chaplin is rapacious and opportunistic. His adherence to duty in *The General* is exemplary, epitomized in that superb shot, taken from a height, of his stumbling desperately down the track after the stolen train, while the troops just stand and stare. It is this measure of indomitable courage that attracts an audience's sympathies to Keaton. Life has taught him to present a mask of indifference to the world, but behind that impassive face lies the solution to every physical problem the world can pose.

LONG PANTS. United States. Script: Arthur Ripley. Direction: Frank Capra. Players: Harry Lang-

1927: Al Jolson in THE JAZZ SINGER.

don, Alan Roscoe, Gladys Brockwell, Priscilla Bonner, Alma Bennett, Betty Francisco. Production: Harry Langdon Corporation/First National. (87 mins.)

"Comedy is after all the most elemental form of tragedy," wrote Harry Langdon, and in his best films Harry's aspirations usually end in disaster. In *Long Pants* he is new to manhood and its desires, training himself with library books from the "Romance" section. But instead of marrying the girl next door, he pursues Bebe Blair, a beautiful lady gangster, as sloe-eyed and calculating as any of the predatory females in Langdon's world. One of the best protracted gags

in the film shows Harry circling Bebe's open car on his bicycle, while the chauffeur changes a wheel. By good fortune he runs into Bebe again when she escapes from San Francisco jail, and carries her round the city in a crate to avoid detection. Another example of Langdon's fertile invention comes when he tries to distract a dummy policeman which has been placed inadvertently on the crate. Finally, as Bebe gets involved in a fight with two accomplices, Harry decides to return to the family table, wearing that faintly guilty look of the schoolboy who has played truant. As he blinks at life in astonishment, Harry personi-

1927: *Langdon prepares to shoot his girl's lover in* LONG PANTS.

fies the shyness in all of us, and the floury, puffy face has the wistful quality of Pierrot.

Checklist of other important features

THE END OF ST. PETERSBURG (Konyets Sankt-Peterburga). U.S.S.R. Director: Vsevolod Pudovkin. An epic reconstruction of the events of 1917 and the history of Leningrad, commissioned for the tenth jubilee of the Russian Revolution.

FLESH AND THE DEVIL. United States. Director: Clarence Brown. The first film of a remarkable partnership—Greta Garbo and director Clarence Brown—noted for its love scenes and for the superb camera-work of William Daniels.

IT. United States. Director: Clarence Badger. Clara Bow's most famous film.

THE LOVE OF JEANNE NEY (Die Liebe der Jeanne Ney). Germany. Director: G. W. Pabst. A sensual and fluent glimpse of Russia at the time of the Revolution, with an emphasis on realistic detail rather than on the melodramatic story.

NAPOLÉON. France. Director: Abel Gance. A dynamic crescendo of epic cinema, with Gance stretching the screen wider still and wider, with parallel action in the same shot, superimpositions, and lyrical cutting. One of the longest films of the period.

SEVENTH HEAVEN. United States. Director: Frank Borzage. Janet Gaynor and Charles Farrell in the silent screen's most dearly loved romance.

SUNRISE. United States. Director: F. W. Murnau. Although a commercial disaster, this masterpiece has appealed strongly to a new generation of directors in Europe. Murnau's style is as lissome as ever, and the story (by Carl Mayer) has a passionate intensity. If, on the brink of the sound era, the cinema needed a film of great plastic beauty to emphasize its visual heritage, then *Sunrise* was that film.

THREE'S A CROWD. United States. Director: Harry Langdon. Langdon at his peak, using images of fairy-tale fragility that have been matched only by Chaplin and Clair, while Harry the clown acts the child and the tender lover.

UNDERWORLD. United States. Director: Josef von Sternberg. An early gangster film, distinguished by concise direction and a flair for lighting effects that reveal von Sternberg as a precocious master of the cinema.

Short films and Documentaries

BERLIN (Berlin, Die Symphonie einer Grosstadt). Germany. Director: Walther Ruttmann.

Ruttmann was primarily an aesthetic film-maker, and when Carl Mayer suggested to him the idea of a "symphonic" picture of Germany's capital, he seized on the idea not for moral reasons but because he wished to develop his undoubted talent for montage and the choice of shots, both aspects of cinema that *Battleship Potemkin* (see *1925*) had changed. Although critics at the time argued that Ruttmann had failed to produce a truly provocative social documentary on such an immense city, *Berlin* endures as the most fluid German film of the twenties. Especially competent are the swift montage sequences Ruttmann uses just before any important dividing point in the day (at 8 A.M., noon, and midnight, for example). These passages are so eloquent that sound—and certainly sub-titles—would have been almost superfluous. And Ruttmann does insert little dashes of comment that bring the people alive and touch on universal issues. He shows a suicide and the cold disdain mingled with curiosity in the faces of those watching the drowning girl from a bridge. This indifference is emphasized again and again with shots of tailor's dummies standing in shop windows. The inhabitants of Berlin are caught up in the rhythm of the city itself. They respond to its promptings just as automatically as do the machines when the levers are depressed. For all its mechanical structure, *Berlin* is a humane documentary, and its concept of the city as a daily symphony has been often resorted to in subsequent years.

FLYING ELEPHANTS. United States. Director: Frank Butler. Laurel and Hardy in the Stone Age,

1927: An ice-skating scene from the documentary BERLIN.

80

fighting for survival and for mates in the face of an edict commanding all men to marry within twenty-four hours.

PUTTING PANTS ON PHILIP. United States. Director: Clyde Bruckman. The first film featuring Laurel and Hardy as a team, though it was released after they had starred in several other comedies.

1927: Facts of Interest

The Academy Awards (later known colloquially as "Oscars") are instituted.
October 6: première of *The Jazz Singer* (see above).
Germany produces more films than the rest of Europe combined.

1928

LA PASSION DE JEANNE D'ARC. France. Script: Carl Th. Dreyer and Joseph Delteil. Direction: Dreyer. Photography: Rudolph Maté. Art Direction: Jean Hugo and Hermann Warm. Players: Falconetti, Silvain, Maurice Schutz, Antonin Artaud, Michel Simon. Production: Société Générale de Films, Paris. (114 mins.)

No silent film, apart from Eisenstein's masterpieces, grips one more consistently than *The Passion of Joan of Arc*. The Danish director Carl Dreyer was ideally fitted to make a study of the French martyr, for his early films revealed a vigorous obsession with the conflict between good and evil for mastery of the spirit. The fascination of the film stems from the extraordinary intimacy of its style (the action outruns the projection time by only a tiny amount). Dreyer examines his heroine from almost every angle and every distance; figuratively speaking, he lays bare her soul. Only when a soul is confronted by death, he seems to be saying, does its true richness and nobility appear. Everything in the film is subordinate to the ardent question of faith. Each gesture, each slow running tear, is minutely regarded. The camera sympathizes with Joan, and one feels that Falconetti sacrificed herself utterly to the part. The enormous close-ups assume a symbolism that could never be achieved in the theatre. Here, as in each of Dreyer's major works, there is a startling interest in the faces—alternately bloated and emaciated—of the inquisitors. And yet the final segment of the film, as Joan is burned at the stake, is more dynamic in movement than the earlier sequences, and shows that Dreyer could perform technical pyrotechnics when he wished.

THE WIND. United States. Script: Frances Marion, from the novel by Dorothy Scarborough. Direction: Victor Seastrom. Photography: Jack Arnold. Players: Lillian Gish, Lars Hanson, Montagu Love, Dorothy Cumming, Edward Earl, William Orlamond. Production: M-G-M. (71 mins.)

Victor Sjöström (or Seastrom, as he was known in America) brought to Hollywood his Scandinavian fatalism and interest in the powers of nature. This story of a girl, Letty (Lillian Gish), arriving in a desolate area of Texas and becoming a victim of the elements and of the primitive ritual of life, expresses that theme so familiar in Sjöström's work—that man drifts ultimately at the mercy of his environment. "Let me take you away where the wind can never follow you," says the smooth salesman who tries to seduce Letty. But the wind and sand are all-pervasive. Starvation is a constant threat. The harsh landscape and the people who live within it give off a menacing quality that unnerves the city girl. The climax, when she is driven to murder, is ferocious. The house, lashed by a gale, looks about to cave in on her as she begins to lose her reason. Slowly the shallow grave of sand in which her victim lies buried is swept away by the wind. Letty's fear is exorcized by her crime. She crosses the final barrier into hysteria, and is at one with the implacable elements: at the end she is a new personality, demoniac and yet infinitely pitiful. *The Wind* foreshadows the Westerns of John Huston (*Treasure of Sierra Madre, The Unforgiven*), and recalls *Greed* (see *1924*) with its uncompromising attention to human weakness, folly and sadism, as well as with the streak of ungratuitous humor that runs through several sequences. It is Sjöström's masterpiece, and it is blessed with one of the most truly "possessed" of all Lillian Gish's performances.

QUEEN KELLY. United States. Script and Direction: Erich von Stroheim. Photography: Ben Reynolds and Hal Mohr. Editing: Viola Lawrence. Art Direction: Richard Day and Stroheim. Players: Gloria Swanson, Walter Byron, Seena Owen, Sidney Bracey, William von Brincken. Production: Gloria Swanson/Joseph Kennedy. (105 mins.)

Stroheim's career in Hollywood was scarred with frustrations, but *Queen Kelly* is his authentic *film maudit*, a disjointed masterpiece that can probably

1928: "A startling interest in the faces . . . of the inquisitors"—from THE PASSION OF JOAN OF ARC.

never be seen in its entirety, although another twenty minutes of footage were found some years ago. Gloria Swanson as Kelly provokes havoc in the imaginary kingdom of Kronberg, buried somewhere in that "Mitteleuropa" that so fascinated Stroheim, the would-be aristocrat. Kelly is a girl in a convent near the Royal Palace, and she attracts Prince Wolfram while he is on a riding excursion. But the Queen, his cousin and fiancée, is a jealous vixen, and whips Kelly out of the Palace in a fit of rage as her impotent guards look on. The orphan is nearly drowned, but survives to experience further degradation in an African brothel.

In ten short years of activity, Stroheim established a new syntax of film expression that was to influence Buñuel, Welles, Renoir, and Ophüls. In an age of insouciant humour and frivolous comedies, he was not afraid to glance beneath the stones of human life and to fasten on depravity, passion, and perversion. His superb pastoral compositions at the beginning of Queen Kelly contrast tellingly with the images of viciousness, vulgarity, and tarnished opulence with-

1928: Lars Hanson and Lillian Gish in THE WIND.

1928: Gloria Swanson and her admirer in QUEEN KELLY.

in the Palace. The script is weighed down with the trappings of decadence but its characters remain nonetheless distinctly defined. The Queen (Seena Owen), resplendent in swirls of white fur, is voraciousness incarnate. Wolfram, fickle, and faintly effeminate, personifies an emasculated aristocracy, an outworn and corrupted generation. And Kelly, in the distraught, wild-eyed interpretation of Gloria Swanson, is the typical Viennese heroine, defiled by extravagance and the weakness of her admirer.

THE FALL OF THE HOUSE OF USHER (La Chute de la Maison Usher). France. Script and Direction: Jean Epstein, from two stories by Edgar Allan Poe, "The Fall of the House of Usher," and "The Oval Portrait." Photography: Georges and Jean Lucas. Art Direction: Pierre Kéfer. Players: Jean Debucourt, Marguerite Gance, Charles Lamy, Pierre Hot, Halma. Production: Jean Epstein Films. (55 mins.)

Jean Epstein is a director whose films are rarely seen today—except for *The Fall of the House of Usher*. Epstein was a theorist and a member of the avant-garde in the twenties (Buñuel was his assistant on this film). *Coeur Fidèle, Mauprat, Les Aventures de Robert Macaire,* and *Finis Terrae* (see *1929*), were among his most respected works. In *The Fall of the House of Usher* he commits himself to a visual style which is directly opposed to the bleak expressionism of contemporary German productions. "Death in his [Poe's] work has a kind of charm," said Epstein. "Life also has a charm. Life and death have the same substance, the same fragility." Nature itself—the sky, the parkland, the trees with their dead leaves—seems ghostly and mysterious. Slow motion, rickety travelling shots, and superimpositions are mingled to create a symphony of suspense, one which has been compared to Debussy's music and to Baudelaire's poetry. The locations, in the swamps of Sologne and on the coast

1928: THE FALL OF THE HOUSE OF USHER—"a symphony of suspense."

of Brittany, were chosen for their visual impact. But the sets, the costumes, and even the actors were also carefully selected for their response to the milky lighting which Epstein used to capture the weird atmosphere of Poe. Death, paradoxically, loses its terror in *The Fall of the House of Usher;* it beckons, like a dreamless sleep.

Checklist of other important features

THE CIRCUS. United States. Chaplin in melancholy mood in his now little-known but nimble comedy about the clown who tries to penetrate circus routine and loses his girl in the process.

CROSSROADS (Jujiro). Japan. Director: Teinosuke Kinugasa. One of the most momentous films in Japanese cinema: a melodrama compounded of hallucinatory flashbacks and close-ups that create an atmosphere of guilt and depression.

THE CROWD. United States. An urban masterpiece of the cinema, as Vidor dwells on one "average" man, his domestic tribulations, and his fruitless struggle against the masses of humanity—against "the crowd."

THE DOCKS OF NEW YORK. United States. Josef von Sternberg's glamorous vision of dockland, with a coal-stoker as its hero who marries a girl about to commit suicide and gets involved in her troubles.

A GIRL IN EVERY PORT. United States. Director: Howard Hawks. Early Hawks, with the now familiar emphasis on comradeship—"It's really a love story between two men," said Hawks. Starring Victor McLaglen, Louise Brooks, and Robert Armstrong.

AN ITALIAN STRAW HAT (Un Chapeau de Paille d'Italie). France. Director: René Clair. A delicate, impeccably timed comedy of manners tinged with the fantasy peculiar to Clair's Paris of the Belle Epoque (c.1895).

THE LITTLE MATCH GIRL (La Petite Marchande d'Allumettes). France. Jean Renoir's lively and experimental version of the Andersen fairy tale, superbly acted by Catherine Hessling.

85

OCTOBER. U.S.S.R. Director: Sergei M. Eisenstein. A vast fresco of the revolution in 1917. Eisenstein's theories of montage are taken to their logical extremes. One of the most exciting of all films from a visual standpoint.

PANDORA'S BOX (Die Büchse der Pandora). Germany. Director: G. W. Pabst. Louise Brooks's liquescent beauty haunts this ghastly story of a *femme fatale* who lures men to their death and is finally destroyed herself.

THE PATSY. United States. The first of two pictures starring Marion Davies, under the direction of King Vidor, in which she displayed a distinct talent for impersonation.

THE POWER OF THE PRESS. United States. Director: Frank Capra. One of the several comedy dramas (this time with a newspaper setting) that prompted Harry Alan Potamkin to label Capra as "the gem of Columbia's ocean."

STORM OVER ASIA (Potomok Chingis-Khan). U.S.S.R. Director: Vsevolod Pudovkin. The English army of occupation versus the partisans in Mongolia. The story is melodramatic, but the feel of life in this isolated country is captured in the bustling markets and religious ceremonies.

Short films and Documentaries

LEAVE 'EM LAUGHING. United States. Director: Clyde Bruckman. Laurel and Hardy reel into the rush hour traffic after an overdose of laughing gas at the dentist's. One of their most uproarious three-reelers.

MICKEY MOUSE Series. Although his first mouse character, Mortimer, was a failure, Walt Disney scored sensationally in 1928 with Mickey. The first short featuring MM was called *Plane Crazy*, and had to be given a soundtrack and be re-released after the enormous response to *Steamboat Willie* in 1928. Disney was put swiftly under contract by Columbia.

THE SEASHELL AND THE CLERGYMAN (La Coquille et Le Clergyman). France. Germaine Dulac's Freudian escapade, typical of the French avant-garde of the twenties: surreal, amusing, and probably meaningless.

1928: Facts of Interest

RKO (Radio Keith Orpheum Corporation) is established. Later liquidated in 1957.

1929

BLACKMAIL. Britain. Script: Alfred Hitchcock, Benn W. Levy, Charles Bennett, from a play by Bennett. Direction: Hitchcock. Photography: Jack Cox. Editing: Emile de Ruelle. Music: Hubert Bath, Henry Stafford. Art Direction: Wilfred Arnold. Players: Anny Ondra, John Longden, Sara Allgood, Charles Paton, Donald Calthrop, Cyril Ritchard. Production: British International (John Maxwell). (85 mins.)

The young Alfred Hitchcock had directed ten silent films prior to *Blackmail*, which began as yet another silent production. But owing to the competition from American sound pictures at the time, it was decided to re-shoot almost the entire film with synchronized sound. The opening sequence and other parts remained silent, but the significance of *Blackmail* rests in Hitchcock's experiments with the new process. The thud of a cell door, the incessant sound of taxi horns, and the sudden scream of a terrified woman overlaid from one scene to another, are accentuated deliberately so as to shock and to unnerve. One is little concerned with the story. The heroine (Anny Ondra, a Czech dubbed into genteel English by Joan Barry) strays one night from her steady boyfriend (John Longden), who is a policeman. She goes home with a flattering young artist (Cyril Ritchard), who tries to seduce her. In the struggle she stabs him fatally with a bread knife, and a blackmailer who finds one of her gloves on the scene attempts to compromise her with the police.

The film is flawed by an element of melodrama that seems an obvious legacy from the silent period, when Hitchcock was not the only director to underestimate the speed of his audience's reactions. But glimmers of his later mastery are visible. There is the ruthless portrayal of a woman under stress; the faintly sinister opening gambit by Cyril Ritchard, "Have you ever seen an artist's studio?"; and a tersely edited climax, with the villain plunging to his death through the glass dome of the British Museum.

APPLAUSE. United States. Script: Garrett Fort, from the novel by Beth Brown. Director: Rouben Mamoulian. Photography: George Folsey. Editing: John Bassler. Players: Helen Morgan, Joan Peers, Fuller Mellish Jr., Jack Cameron, Henry Wadsworth. Production: Paramount. (82 mins.)

Rouben Mamoulian's *Applause* is among the few really important sound movies of 1929. It is clear from the start that Mamoulian is a true *cinéaste,* as his inquisitive camera discovers the music hall *ménage* of Kitty Darling (Helen Morgan) and Hitch Nelson (Fuller Mellish Jr.). The flaxen-haired Kitty has her eyes on Broadway, but she is unmistakably condemned to second-rate burlesque. Hitch, vicious and irritable, is her lover, but soon switches his attention to her daughter April when the girl returns from a demure convent education. The film moves between extremes of sordidity and innocent pleasure. April Darling is shocked by the bustle and vulgarity of metropolitan life. The klaxons in the street, a dog's harsh yapping, even the voices of the stage hands, are used by Mamoulian to underline the discordance of this second-rate world. There is a raw, undisguised lustiness about the music hall show, as the fat-thighed chorus line parades along the stage and the audience gapes shamelessly. Kitty's shabby apartment, with its photos and its poison conveniently in the cupboard, is light years away from the skyscraper roof where the sailor proposes to April, or the café where the lovers talk so privately and intensely that it empties without their realizing the time. *Applause* is Mamoulian's most fluent film, marred by the occasional affectation of style but still unusually free from the artifices of period and inventive to the last shot.

THE DIARY OF A LOST GIRL (Das Tagebuch einer Verlorenen). Germany. Script: Rudolf Leon, from the novel by Margaret Boehme. Direction: G. W. Pabst. Photography: Sepp Allgeier. Art Direction: Ernö Metzner. Players: Louise Brooks, Joseph Roven-

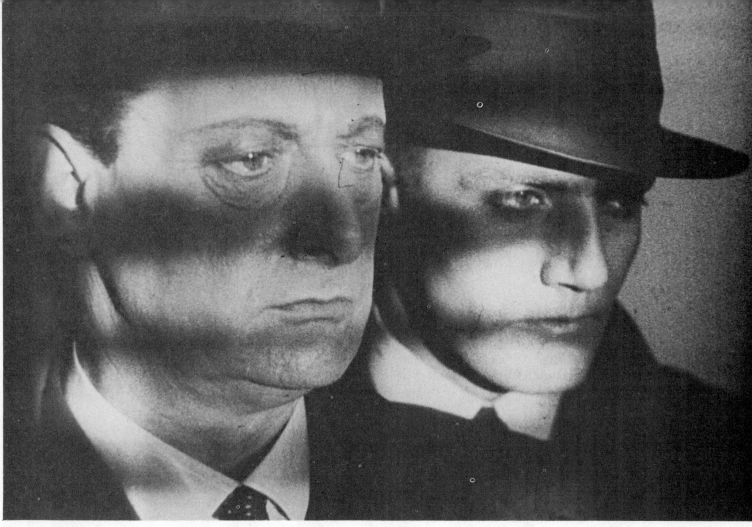

1929: A striking composition from BLACKMAIL.

1929: The chorus line in Rouben Mamoulian's APPLAUSE.

1929: Louise Brooks (right) in THE DIARY OF A LOST GIRL.

sky, Fritz Rasp, André Roanne, Edith Meinhard, Andrews Engelman, Valeska Gert, Vera Pawlova, Franciska Kinz, Siegfried Arno. Production: Hom-Film, Berlin. (3132 metres.)

The irridescent beauty of Louise Brooks had been exploited to dazzling effect by Pabst in *Pandora's Box* (see *1928*). In *The Diary of a Lost Girl,* her role is only slightly less sensual. She plays a chemist's daughter who is consigned to reform school when she gives birth to an illegitimate child. A major part of the film is devoted to the daily round at the formidable establishment. The matron in charge is clearly a sadist, and Tyvian is watched closely by a tall, bald-headed guardian, whose smiles are ingratiating and disturbing. Pabst's taste for close-ups lends an almost tangible evil to their features. When, eventually, there is a revolt at the school, Tyvian and her friend Erika escape, and are soon enrolled in a brothel. Here Pabst's style overflows with a mischievous *joie de vivre;* Tyvian quickly submits to the atmosphere of lechery and luxurious indulgence. Her dance with a client comprises one of the greatest erotic interludes on film. But the death of her father means that she is a wealthy young woman, and once more she returns to the drugstore where she grew up (although the original, censored version ended with her becoming "Madame" at the brothel). Even at the end, Pabst

includes an unforgettable sequence, as the funeral of a count who has committed suicide on Tyvian's account takes place in the local cemetery. All in all, the film affords a penetrating and often haunting picture of German bourgeois society in the late twenties, when authoritarianism and licence were alarmingly close neighbors.

NEW BABYLON (Novyi Vavilon). U.S.S.R. Script and Direction: Grigori Kozintsev and Leonid Trauberg. Photography: Andrei Moskvin, Yevgeni Mikhailov. Music: Dimitri Shostakovich. Art Direction: Yevgeni Enei. Players: D. Gutman, Sophie Magarill, A. Arnold, Sergei Gerasimov, Pyotr Sobolevsky, Yelena Kuzmina. Production: Leningrad Studio of Sovkino. (89 mins.)

The pent-up indignance of *New Babylon* gives it stature even among the great Soviet films of the twenties. Kozintsev and Trauberg broke away from the Revolution as a source of proletarian protest and turned instead to the fevered Paris of 1870–71. The brief flourish of the Commune, of the Parisians who refused to abandon the struggle against the Prussians, and who fought their own soldiers when it looked like they would demobilize, has an epic quality ideally suited to Soviet film techniques. *New Babylon* runs at a hectic pace, picking up its heroine, Louise, a midinette in a large department store, and dragging her into battle like a nineteenth-century Joan of Arc. The eye is assaulted with violent swirls of movement: cavalry gallop towards an already racing camera through the foggy streets; barricades are erected with an urgency and a desperation superbly communicated in Moskvin's photography. The destruction of the city becomes the passing of an order—the old man who plays the piano amid the carnage and the rubble is a grandiloquent symbol of decline more familiar in the cinema of the fifties. But despite the didactic

1929: Yelena Kuzmina in NEW BABYLON.

juxtaposition of shots—effete bourgeoisie gazing from the heights of Versailles as the army's cannon fire on the people—the directors are interested in individuals rather than masses. The faces flame out unforgettably from the chaos, faces soaked by the rain, faces swollen with arrogance, faces inhabited by courage. *New Babylon* stretches the propagandist potential of the cinema to the limit, and matches *Strike* or *Battleship Potemkin* (see *1925*) in its incandescent fervour.

90

a father is forced to kill his demented son in a lonely lighthouse.

THE GENERAL LINE or OLD AND NEW (Staroye i novoye). U.S.S.R. Eisenstein's view of the agricultural revolution under Lenin, filmed in the countryside with a sensuality and a voluptuous rhythm unparalleled in contemporary cinema. The most underrated of Eisenstein's works.

HALLELUJAH. United States. Director: King Vidor. The first feature film with an all-Negro cast, shot entirely on location in the southern states.

THE LOVE PARADE. United States. Director: Ernst Lubitsch. An early, dashing, and beguiling musical with Maurice Chevalier and Jeanette MacDonald.

SHOOTING STARS. Britain. Director: A. V. Bramble. Anthony Asquith began as an assistant director and editor on this gentle satire about film studios and the screen melodramatics that sometimes spill over into real life.

THE STRONGER (Den starkaste). Sweden. Director: Alf Sjöberg. The last Swedish film of consequence for many years. Shot in the Arctic Circle, where human rivalries aboard a whaling ship are played out in a flow of unpretentious action and personal crises.

A WOMAN OF AFFAIRS. United States. Director: Clarence Brown. Greta Garbo as the outrageous heroine of Michael Arlen's *The Green Hat*. With John Gilbert.

Short films and Documentaries

UN CHIEN ANDALOU. France. Directors: Luis Buñuel and Salvador Dali. The most famous achievement of Surrealism in the cinema, memorable for its stream of repulsive images (ants crawling out of a man's palm, a girl's eye being slit by a razor).

DRIFTERS. Britain. Director: John Grierson. The film that launched the documentary movement in Britain.

KARNIVAL KID. United States. One of the most brilliant of Walt Disney's cartoons, its effervescent style encompassing live hot dogs and several unusual sound effects.

THE MAN WITH A MOVIE CAMERA (Chelovek s kinoapparatom). U.S.S.R. Dziga Vertov is among the really influential directors of the twenties. In 1924 he had coined the term *cinéma vérité*. His outlook was strictly objective; he was not interested in the presence of people in his film at all. What fascinated him and his imitators were the possibilities inherent in a rhythmical treatment of city life and its patterns of behavior.

PEOPLE ON SUNDAY (Menschen am Sonntag). Germany. Director: Robert Siodmak. A documentary about four people spending Sunday at the Wandsee in Berlin, but scripted by Billy Wilder and Robert Siodmak, assisted by Fred Zinnemann and Edgar G. Ulmer. All four men were soon to leave for Hollywood as Hitler rose to power.

THE RACE SYMPHONY (Rennsymphonie). Germany. Director: Hans Richter. This remarkable documentary was produced for Maxim Emelka as a prelude to the play "Ariadne in Hoppegarten."

RAIN. Netherlands. Director: Joris Ivens. A superb photographic exercise by one of the cinema's greatest documentarists when the Dutch cinema was still in its infancy.

SKELETON DANCE. United States. Another Disney landmark, in which each movement is closely synchronized to the music. The first of the "Silly Symphonies."

1929: Facts of Interest

Films now projected at 24 frames per second to accommodate sound. (Silent pictures had been run at speeds varying from 16 to 22 f.p.s. and are usually distorted by modern apparatus.)

The Empire Marketing Board Film Unit is founded by John Grierson—a crucial step towards the establishment of an active British documentary school.

1930: A trench scene from ALL QUIET ON THE WESTERN FRONT.

1930

ALL QUIET ON THE WESTERN FRONT. United States. Script: Maxwell Anderson and George Abbott, from the novel by Erich Maria Remarque. Direction: Lewis Milestone. Photography: Arthur Edeson. Editing: Edgar Adams, Music: David Broekman. Players: Lew Ayres, Louis Wolheim, John Wray, Raymond Griffith, George "Slim" Summerville, Russell Gleason, William Bakewell. Production: Universal. (125 mins.)

Milestone's condemnation of World War I has stood the test of time rather better than Pabst's *Westfront 1918* (see *below*). Its dialogue is perhaps more obviously a blend of humor and sentimentality than it was in 1930, but it is as a spectacle, a comprehensive vision of war, that the film scores so persuasively. The group of German schoolboys who are urged by their teacher to enlist "for the Fatherland" are gradually swallowed up in battle. The comic stage of training under their local postman is meager preparation for the hideous phantasmagoria of the trenches, where food is in short supply and the continual bombardment is maddening. As one after another of Paul's comrades is killed, the primitive ardor of the film becomes overbearing, and it is only when Paul returns to his old school and expresses his disillusionment ("We sleep and eat with death") that Milestone again looks at the situation objectively. The final shots would fit into any anthology of the cinema. Paul is killed by a sniper as he reaches out tenderly for a butterfly and, like the ghosts in *J'Accuse* (see *1937*), the dead men march away into the distance, glancing back in disappointment at the audience. More than this personal tragedy, however, one remembers the minute organization of the crowd scenes in French villages, the wave after wave of attacks on the trenches, and the sophisticated use of sound at this period.

THE BLUE ANGEL (Der blaue Engel). Germany. Script: Josef von Sternberg, Carl Zuckmayer, Karl Vollmöller, Robert Liebmann, from the novel *Professor Unrat* by Heinrich Mann. Direction: von Stern-berg. Photography: Günther Rittau, Hans Schneeberger. Editing: Sam Winston. Music: Friedrich Holländer, with lyrics by Liebmann. Art Direction: Otto Hunte, Emil Hasler. Players: Emil Jannings, Marlene Dietrich, Hans Albers, Kurt Gerron, Rosa Valetti. Production: UFA-Paramount Publix (Erich Pommer). (90 mins.)

The Blue Angel revealed Marlene Dietrich as a star of distinctly durable proportions when it appeared in Germany. Josef von Sternberg, a Viennese, had made ten films in Hollywood before visiting Germany to adapt Heinrich Mann's novel about the humiliation of an elderly school teacher, Professor Rath (Emil Jannings), who is short sighted, punctilious, and pedantic. Sternberg shows Rath's position of awe in the classroom, so that he may be the more thoroughly degraded later in the film. He is an easy target for the bright eyed Lola (Marlene Dietrich) as she sings in "The Blue Angel" cabaret. He tries helplessly to preserve his dignity, but his weakness for alcohol and his banked-up desire for sex are his undoing. He loses his job, marries Lola, and joins the troupe of artistes in their picaresque progress from one nightclub to another. Five years later, he is forced to play the clown on the stage of "The Blue Angel." The part has so consumed him that he crows automatically, dreadfully, and in a frenzy he staggers through the gnarled streets to die in his old classroom.

A streak of cruelty lines much of von Sternberg's work, but *The Blue Angel* is his most relentless film. Rath symbolises Germany herself in the final days of the Weimar Republic, squatting in gloom and self-destructive lassitude. His sober boardinghouse room, cluttered with books, is in violent contrast to the cheap glitter and unfamiliar disrepute of "The Blue Angel." The tragedy of Professor Rath is that he struggles not so much against a flirtatious woman as against his own inferiority complex, and von Sternberg, with his skill in ordering sound and chiaroscuro, gives the film the contained power of a nightmare.

1930: *Emil Jannings and Marlene Dietrich in* THE BLUE ANGEL.

UNDER THE ROOFS OF PARIS (Sous les Toits de Paris). France. Script and Direction: René Clair. Photography: Georges Périnal. Music: Raoul Moretti and Armand Bernard. Players: Pola Ilery, Albert Préjean, Gaston Modot, Edmond T. Gréville. Production: Filmsonor-Tobis. (89 mins.)

René Clair and Marcel Carné are unfashionable directors now, because both men courted a kind of fabricated realism, where whole streets were constructed in or near the studios so as to flaunt a style that on location might be lacking. Clair's Paris, though, remains unique and charming. It is a city of cobblestoned streets where men in cloth caps contrive to be gallant despite their shabby surroundings;

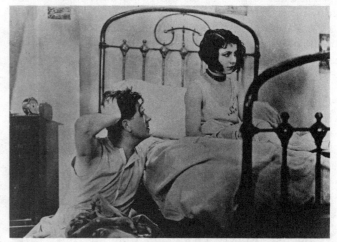

1930: *Unfamiliar awakening in* UNDER THE ROOFS OF PARIS.

94

where lovers are triumphantly self-sufficient, their lives bounded by tiny attic rooms and smoky bars; and where folk gather together at the squeal of an accordion to join in singing for its own sake. Evil does not exist. Instead, there are the sly, cowardly creatures who inhabit the margins of the crowd, and are regularly put to flight by the stout-hearted hero. The wisp of a story in *Under the Roofs of Paris* (the love of a street singer, Albert, for a lonely Rumanian girl named Pola) is perfectly aligned to the musical score. The title song passes from one person to another like a toast. It gives Albert courage in his melancholy moments, and when the camera curls up from the knot of people round him at the end, one knows that the loss of Pola will not affect this uncomplicated man. He will continue to sing, and Paris continue to live. Clair's gags still pace the film with brio, and in a mysterious, strongly appealing way, they gather momentum with the years.

THE GOLDEN AGE (L'Age d'Or). France. Script: Luis Buñuel and Salvador Dali. Direction: Buñuel. Photography. Albert Dubergen. Music: Georges Van

1930: Gaston Modot in full spate in L'AGE D'OR.

Parys, with extracts from Beethoven, Wagner, Mendelssohn, Mozart and Debussy. Art Direction: Schilzneck. Players: Gaston Modot, Lya Lys, Caridad de Laberdesque, Lionel Salem, Pierre Prévert, Max Ernst, Madame Noizet, Liorens Artryas, Duchange, Ibañez. Production: Viscount Charles de Noailles. (63 mins.)

"Art as an act of violence": so Susan Sontag has described the work of Luis Buñuel, the Spaniard whose monstrous shadow has loomed over the cinema for the past forty years, from *Un Chien Andalou* (see *1929*) to *Belle de Jour* (see *1967*). Buñuel had met Salvador Dali and Lorca at Madrid University, and between 1920 and 1923 he founded the first film society in Spain. In Paris in the late twenties he mixed eagerly with the Surrealists, and both *Un Chien Andalou* and *L'Age d'Or* are surrealist films. *L'Age d'Or*, still banned for public showing, is distinctly Freudian, suggesting Buñuel's violent reaction to the sexual perversions he had encountered at his Jesuit school. The swelling chords of Wagner's *Tristan und Isolde* on the soundtrack add to the erotic atmosphere; the lovers fight continually against everyone else in this symbolic world. Freedom, Buñuel appears to emphasize, exists only in sexual indulgence or,

95

1930: Edward G. Robinson (right) as LITTLE CAESAR.

more precisely, in complete unselfconsciousness. The film is rich in cinematic innovations—the interior monologue, the use of mirrors and so on—but it is still deliberately obscure in parts and this probably prevents it from achieving the magistral effect of *Nazarin* (see *1958*) or *Viridiana* (see *1961*). Throughout his career Buñuel's anti-clericalism has remained savage. "Surrealism taught me that life has a moral meaning that man cannot ignore," he has said. "Through Surrealism I discovered for the first time that man is not free."

LITTLE CAESAR. United States. Script: W. R. Burnett, Francis Faragoh. Direction: Mervyn LeRoy. Photography: Tony Gaudio. Players: Edward G. Robinson, Douglas Fairbanks Jr., Ralph Ince, Glenda Farrell, George Stone, Sidney Blackmer, Stanley Fields, William Collier Jr. Production: Warner Brothers (Darryl F. Zanuck and Hal Wallis). (80 mins.)

The American gangster film is founded on violence and brute ambition. "For all they that take the sword shall perish with the sword" is the Biblical text at the beginning of Mervyn LeRoy's *Little Caesar,* the first in the compulsive series of gangster portraits that Hollywood was to produce during the sound era. It is a chronicle of petty dictatorship on the part of little Rico (Edward G. Robinson), who is tempted by the power and the money involved in big-time gangsterism. He refuses to drink when all around him prohibition is flouted vehemently, and concentrates solely on bending people to his will. He leads a raid at a gala celebration in a prominent nightclub, and shoots a man dead without the slight-

est compunction. When the heat becomes intolerable, he turns viciously on his old friend, now happily married, and is eventually hunted down by the police. Robinson's characterization is almost brilliant. He struts and poses glibly for the press. He is disgruntled, and smolders in moments of crisis. Conceit ultimately fells him as swiftly as it has raised him. LeRoy's imaginative treatment of many scenes lingers in the memory: the robbery at the club is shown in a series of dissolves that imbues it with panic, and Tony's funeral in the streets, seen from aloft, gives almost a premonition of the death of Little Caesar himself.

Checklist of other important features

A COTTAGE ON DARTMOOR. Britain. The best of Anthony Asquith's early pictures; a melodramatic story enhanced by subtle pictorial rhythms and flashbacks.

EARTH (Zemlya). U.S.S.R. Alexander Dovzhenko's famous, languorous study of Ukrainian peasant life, in which death and beauty are intimately connected, but outmoded now in its plodding technique and lack of tension.

FEET FIRST. United States. Director: Clyde Bruckman. Harold Lloyd's succession of pure gags at its liveliest and most logical.

HELL'S ANGELS. United States. Director: Howard Hughes. An epic noted for its splendid aerial sequences, as early fighters engage each other in World War I. Stars Ben Lyon and Jean Harlow.

MOROCCO. United States. Director: Josef von Sternberg. Marlene Dietrich makes her début on the Hollywood screen, as a sultry café singer enamoured of Gary Cooper's laconic Legionnaire. Light and shadow predominate in this film, and evoke the desert atmosphere even though von Sternberg had never been to Morocco.

WESTFRONT 1918. Germany. Director: G. W. Pabst. Not quite on the same level as *All Quiet . . .,* but a stark and lucid indictment of war nonetheless, banned in Germany three years after it was made.

Short films and Documentaries

BRATS. United States. Director: James Parrott. Stan Laurel and Oliver Norvell Hardy came together under Hal Roach in 1926. Stan was a North Country Englishman who had shared rooms with Chaplin when both men were touring the U.S.A. with Fred Karno's music hall troupe. Ollie had opened a cinema in Georgia in 1910 and had worked in films since 1913, under Larry Semon and others. Their first comedy in tandem was *Putting Pants on Philip;* and *Flying Elephants, Battle of the Century,* and *Leave 'em Laughing* showed the potentialities of the partnership. *Brats* contained some of their finest gags and also shed light on their comic personalities. Stan, who supervised the editing, was never so rumbustious as Ollie, and relied on his outstanding gifts as a mimic for sparking the laughs. Ollie, the courtly, self-conscious partner, is also a mountain of compressed rage, "the dumb guy who thinks he's smart" (his own words). Both comedians are forever eager to help, and forever land in trouble. They bicker constantly, and yet they are fast friends again after even the loudest altercation. In *Brats* they play a pair of children dwarfed by gigantic sets, as well as the fathers supposed to be looking after the household for the evening. They play billiards (Stan proving lethal with a cue in his hands) while their "brats" run riot in the nursery overhead. Ollie is funny because of his clumsy, deliberate attacks; and Stan is funny because of his accidental, but effective retaliations, followed by a stare of mute apology. Both try hard to maintain what Stan later called their "phony dignity," and it is in describing the inexorable perversion of this dignity that *Brats* is so hilarious.

A PROPOS DE NICE. France. Directors: Jean Vigo and Boris Kaufman. An idiosyncratic gaze at the luxurious charade of the Riviera resort, imparting wit, irony, and a contagious feeling of revolt.

1930: Stan Laurel and Oliver Hardy.

THE LAUREL AND HARDY MURDER CASE. United States. Director: James Parrott. A superior three-reeler comedy with Stan and Ollie fleeing from each other as much as from the killer in an old house.

1930: Facts of Interest

The GPO Film Unit is founded in Britain.
The Barrandov Studios open in Czechoslovakia.

1931

M. Germany. Script: Thea von Harbou and Fritz Lang from an article by Egon Jacobson. Direction: Lang. Photography: Fritz Arno Wagner. Editing: Paul Fackenberg. Music: Edward Grieg: extract from "Peer Gynt." Art Direction: Emil Hasler and Karl Volbrecht. Players: Peter Lorre, Otto Wernicke, Gustav Gründgens, Ellen Widmann, Inge Landgut, Friedrich Gnas. Production: Nero Filmgesellschaft. (99 mins.)

Fritz Lang based *M* on the activities of Peter Kurten, the Düsseldorf child-murderer, but although the film appears on first acquaintance to be a suspense thriller, it is sown with disquieting symbols of the state of Germany on the eve of Nazi power. It was banned by Goebbels before the war, and its sympathy for the individual hounded for his crime by an angry populace is all too clearly a protest against the growth of Fascist methods. Peter Lorre plays Franz Becker, who has murdered eight children before the film even begins, and is a creature driven by an instinct he cannot understand. "I don't want to kill! I must kill!" he screams at the mock court of petty criminals that indicts him at the end. He hides from the public eye from shame, and with little subtlety: he whistles the same few bars from Grieg as he wanders furtively through the streets (sound is of the very essence of *M*) ; he buys balloons and toys for his victims; and at the moment of drawing his knife from his pocket a flicker of regret appears in the coarse, puffy face beneath the trilby. It is an indelible performance. Lorre *inhabits* the murderer.

Lang, faithful to the expressionist style that he had helped to pioneer in the twenties, invests the film with passages of great visual eloquence—the search for Becker in the office building, with its cluttered attic and hostile corridors, or the reflection of a girl in the window of a knife shop as the murderer spies on her. Lang does not exonerate Becker. He is more interested in the behavior of the crowds that hunt him. In one short scene, when an innocent elderly man is mistaken for the killer, and nearly lynched, the hideous events of the Nazi era are prefigured.

LE MILLION. France. Script and Direction: René Clair, from the comedy by Georges Berr and M. Guillemaud. Photography: Georges Périnal. Music: Georges Van Parys, Armand Bernard, and Philippe Pares. Art Direction: Lazare Meerson. Players: René Lefèvre, Annabella, Louis Allibert, Vanda Gréville, Paul Ollivier, Odette Talazac, Constantin Stroesco. Production: Films Sonores Tobis. (85 mins.)

Le Million is drawn from a musical comedy, like *An Italian Straw Hat* (see *1928*), but three years lie between the films, and *Le Million* gains considerably from the presence of sound. Clair proves that he is the heir to Marivaux, a master of that delightful wit that makes its point and then speeds ahead to ambush an audience again. Two down-at-heels artists, Michel and Prospère, are apparently redeemed when Michel hears that he has won a lottery worth a million francs. But the ticket has been mislaid, and as Michel and his friend pursue it from one person to another across Paris, so their creditors pursue them. The chase leads inevitably to a climax at the Opéra-Lyrique, where the ticket is in the possession of a monstrous tenor about to sail for America. Each sequence is in perfect visual and musical harmony with the next. The soundtrack is used with aplomb by Clair (note the thump of the rugby ball and the referee's whistle as everyone scrimmages together on stage). *Le Million* is on the verge of being a musical. But, except for the mock opera at the end, there are no set numbers. Clair's actors seem to express with their movements the same zest as a singer does in his songs. In the director's lesser films, this becomes an affectation: in *Le Million* it is the very heart of the entertainment, defying analysis as subtly as the lottery ticket eludes Michel.

VAMPYR, or The Strange Adventures of David Gray. France. Script: Carl Th. Dreyer and Christen Jul, from the novel *In a Glass Darkly* by Sheridan Le Fanu. Direction: Dreyer. Photographer: Rudolph Maté. Music: Wolfgang Zeller. Players: Julian West (Baron Nicolas de Gunzberg), Henriette Gerard, Jan

1931: The shadow of the murderer in Fritz Lang's M.

onimko, Maurice Schutz, Rena Mandel, Sybille
nitz. Production Dreyer Filmproduktion. (72
s.)

Although shot on location in France, *Vampyr* re-
ins the most expressionistic and Teutonic in tone
of Dreyer's films, reminiscent of *Nosferatu* (see *1922*)
or *Warning Shadows*. Some of the stylistic apparati
of the film have dated awkwardly—the sporadic use
of sound, for instance—and the Baron de Gunzberg's
acting seriously undermines one's willingness to believe in either David Gray or the bizarre events at
Courtempierre and in its adjacent parkland. But the
Baron was the chief financial sponsor of the film, and
must have had fairly clear ideas as to the dominance
of his role. Although palpably set in the present (the
flour mill in which the villainous doctor is suffocated
seems quite modern), *Vampyr* has an eerie, timeless
quality. David Gray strolls about in a misty, curiously
deserted limbo that coincides with a vision of the underworld in classical mythology—and the harvester

1931: René Lefèvre and Annabella in LE MILLION.

99

who tolls the bell for the ferry is certainly on the banks of Lethe. The film is a collector's piece from the photographic point of view. Rudolph Maté, later to become a Hollywood director, used illuminated black gauze in front of his camera to achieve the pale, supernatural imagery which suggests a loss of vitality in the inhabitants of Courtempierre.

THE THREEPENNY OPERA (Die Dreigroschen-oper). Germany. Script: Leo Lania, Ladislaus Vajda, Béla Balázs, from the play by Bertolt Brecht (derived from "The Beggars' Opera," by John Gay). Direction: G. W. Pabst. Photography: Fritz Arno Wagner. Music: Kurt Weill. Art Direction: André Andreiev. Players: Rudolf Forster, Carola Neher, Reinhold Schünzel, Fritz Rasp, Valeska Gert, Lotte Lenya, Hermann Thimig, Ernst Busch. Production: Deutsch-First National. (100 mins.)

Pabst's film of *The Threepenny Opera* caused an uproar in theatrical circles. Brecht and Kurt Weill (the composer) resorted to legal action, claiming that their songs had been emasculated and absorbed

The doctor is trapped in his own flour mill at the end of VAMPYR.

1931: From Pabst's THE THREEPENNY OPERA.

too irresponsibly into the narrative. The Brechtian satire so astringent on the stage is undoubtedly replaced here by an ambivalent blend of corruption (the brothel scenes) and social protest (the beggars' demonstration). But the *tone* of the score bathes the film in a current of decadence and eroticism. The wedding ceremony has an insidious, dishevelled splendor that is in keeping with the spirit of Gay's seventeenth-century operetta. It was not merely coincidental that Louise Brooks was at her most sensual in Pabst's films; Carola Neher as Polly in *The Threepenny Opera* also radiates a languorous, seductive charm that responds immaculately to Mackie's self-confident approaches in the café. The tale of Mackie Messer, head of the London apaches, also inspired *The Beggars' Opera* (directed in 1953 by Peter Brook). This coruscating dandy melts the resolution of every girl in Soho, and when he marries Polly Peachum he is harassed by the police. He leads them an elaborate chase through the district. Rudolf Forster is magnificent as Mackie, with his grey bowler, natty stick, and facility for scrambling over roofs when required. Pabst's technique is so assured that the complicated movements from scene to scene, from brothel to street, from street to roof, are dovetailed into one another, creating a mesmeric stream of incident. *The Threepenny Opera* is, with Mamoulian's *Applause* and *Love Me Tonight,* one of the key pioneer musicals, and it boasts a dimension of picaresque fantasy lacking in Hollywood films of the period.

Checklist of other important features

À NOUS LA LIBERTÉ. France. René Clair's fast-moving, balletic satire on factory life and social position in his own mythical France, tinged with anarchy as a tycoon and his ex-convict chum play games in a sumptuous drawing room.

LA CHIENNE. France. A brilliant example of Jean Renoir's early determination to catch in his cinema the sordid contentions of Paris life—with Michel Simon naïve and sensitive as the amateur painter driven to *le crime passionel.*

CITY LIGHTS. United States. The "little fellow" on a crusade for goodness's sake: he extracts from a millionaire money to restore a blind flower girl's sight. Silent, full of slapstick and pathos, and arguably Chaplin's best film.

DISHONORED. United States. Director: Josef von Sternberg. An extraordinary tale of espionage, set in Vienna, with Marlene Dietrich as X27, an enlisted prostitute determined to trap Russian spy Victor McLaglen.

DR. JEKYLL AND MR. HYDE. United States. Rouben Mamoulian's exciting and definitive version of the Stevenson story, with Fredric March earnest and pathetic as the Doctor.

FRANKENSTEIN. United States. Director: James Whale. Boris Karloff as the sympathetic monster in the forebear of a whole series of films based on Mary Shelley's novel. Uneven, but almost noble in its special effects and its respect for the unknown.

KAMERADSCHAFT. Germany. G. W. Pabst rubs a mixture of documentary power and human sympathy into his story of a coal mine disaster and the bravery that snatches so many of its victims from death.

MÄDCHEN IN UNIFORM. Germany. Director: Leontine Sagan. Romance and hysterics in a German girls' boarding school, realized with enthusiasm and candor by a woman director who had worked with Max Reinhardt.

MARIUS. France. Director: Alexander Korda. The first and least sentimental film of the Marcel Pagnol trilogy about life in Marseilles, with Raimu as the café proprietor giving one of the finest performances in the history of the cinema.

THE ROAD TO LIFE (Putyovka v zhizn). U.S.S.R. Director: Nikolai Ekk. One of the first successful Soviet sound films, taking as its subject the survival and haphazard education of children who had been left destitute after the Civil War.

TABU. United States. Directors: F. W. Murnau and Robert Flaherty. Two of the most successful filmmakers of the twenties combined here to produce an intense and exotic drama shot entirely in Tahiti and Bora-Bora, although the dominating hand is that of Murnau.

TELL ENGLAND. Britain. Director: Anthony Asquith. The massacre on the Gallipoli Beach in this film has taken its place among the most compelling war sequences ever made.

Short films and Documentaries

MOR-VRAN. France. Director: Jean Epstein. A grim and convincing picture of the Breton archipelago and its inhabitants.

1931: Facts of Interest

F. W. Murnau killed in an automobile accident after 18 months' work on *Tabu* (see *above*).
Ealing studios open in outer London.
D. W. Griffith closes his career as a director with *The Struggle.*

1932

BOUDU SAVED FROM DROWNING (Boudu sauvé des eaux). France. Script: Jean Renoir, from the play by René Fauchois. Direction: Renoir. Photography: Marcel Lucien, Asselin. Editing: Suzanne de Troyes. Music: Raphaël, and Johann Strauss's "The Blue Danube." Art Direction: Hugues Laurent, Jean Castanier. Players: Michel Simon, Charles Grandval, Marcelle Hainia, Séverine Lerczinska, Jean Dasté, Jacques Becker. Production: Michel Simon / Jean Gehret. (87 mins.)

Renoir's *Boudu* is sometimes referred to as a partial failure, an attempt by its maker to sweeten the French film industry after the antagonism shown towards *La Chienne*. But it has worn the years triumphantly and is a devastating indictment of crass, middle-class values and conformism. Boudu, the captious old tramp who, to his chagrin, is rescued from the Seine by a benevolent bookseller, Lestingois, be-

comes the scourge of the bourgeois household in which he is restored to normal health. Lestingois treats him like a new pet: he is fascinated by this monstrous, satyric creature whose beard scarcely disguises the lecherous glances he directs towards the maid and Madame. He wrecks a kitchen and a bedroom while cleaning his shoes. He spits in a first edition of Balzac's *Physiologie du Mariage,* and performs impromptu handstands in the hall. Then, to cap all his egregiousness, he seduces Lestingois's wife and, finding himself the winner of a lottery, marries the maid. But, suffering a last-minute prick of anti-bourgeois sentiment, he upsets the boat in which the bridal party is travelling, and drifts downstream to don a scarecrow's rags and to resume his former ways.

Boudu is a hymn to Pan, filled with the exuberance that Renoir and Truffaut alone in the French cinema seem capable of creating. Like Catherine in *Jules and Jim,* Boudu is "une force de la nature," cataclysmic in his effect on the merely bookish, on those ignorant of the vibrancy of life itself. Visually, the film reinforces this theme. The atmosphere of an idyllic summer is suggested sympathetically in the shots of Boudu's wandering in search of his dog in the Bois de Boulogne, and in the outing on the Marne with Boudu incongruous in morning suit and his far from virginal bride beside him. Boudu himself is given a sort of animal magnetism by the acting of Michel Simon, with tongue in dimpled cheek and eyes forever roving in search of fresh pastures to despoil: anarchy incarnate!

FREAKS. United States. Script: Willis Goldbeck, Leon Gordon, from Tod Robbins's novel *Spurs.* Direction: Tod Browning. Photography: Merrit B. Gerstad. Editing: Basil Wrangell. Art Direction: Cedric Gibbons. Players: Wallace Ford, Leila Hyams, Olga Baclanova, Roscoe Ates, Henry Victory, Harry Earles,

1932: Michel Simon casts his eyes to heaven in BOUDU SAVED FROM DROWNING.

Daisy Earles, Rose Dione. Production: M-G-M (Tod Browning). (61 mins.)

It is arguable that of all the celebrated horror films of the thirties, *Freaks* has survived the best. Tod Browning's *mise en scène* (especially during the wedding feast) has a weird brilliance, but it is his conception and treatment of the freaks themselves that command admiration. As the Prologue explains, in ancient times anything that deviated from the normal was considered as an evil omen. Freaks have always been the outcasts of society, and in order to protect and to justify themselves they adhere strictly to a code of behavior—"the hurt of one is the hurt of all." Robbins's slight little story of Cleopatra, the voluptuous trapeze artist, who patronizes the freaks in her circus and is repaid in ghastly fashion, is illuminated by an unexpected humanity and sympathy. The camera, perched at midget level, quickly ascertains where the evil and the sadism really lie—behind the magnificent physique of Cleopatra and her strong-arm lover. Beneath their makeup and their costumes they are ingenuous and egotistic (note the brief, sardonic shot of Hercules spraying himself with an unguent). By contrast, the freaks radiate a simply dignity and restraint that transcend their distorted appearance. During the terrible climax, as they are pursued implacably through a storm at night, it is as though

Cleopatra and Hercules were fleeing from the embodiment of their own base thoughts. Revenge has seldom seemed to be so hideous and yet so appropriate.

LOVE ME TONIGHT. United States. Script: Samuel Hoffenstein, Waldemar Young, George Marion Jr.

1378-72

1932: Maurice Chevalier and Jeanette MacDonald in LOVE ME TONIGHT.

Adaptation: Leopold Marchand, Paul Armont. Direction: Rouben Mamoulian. Photography: Victor Milner. Music and Lyrics: Richard Rodgers, Lorenz Hart. Art Direction: Hans Dreier. Players: Jeanette MacDonald, Maurice Chevalier, Charles Ruggles, Charles Butterworth, Myrna Loy, C. Aubrey Smith, Ethel Griffies. Production: Paramount (Rouben Mamoulian). (90 mins.)

Rouben Mamoulian, an Armenian who came to America in his twenties at the invitation of George Eastman, had already demonstrated his flair for cinema in *Applause* (see *1929*) and *Dr. Jekyll and Mr. Hyde* when he directed *Love Me Tonight*. The opening, as Paris shuffles rhythmically into wakefulness, is beautifully modulated and sophisticated in its use of sound effects. And Maurice Chevalier is immediately likeable as the cheerful tailor who is driven to masquerade as a baron in order to get his rightful money from the Vicomte de Varèze. In the ensuing gambols at a French château, one can detect the influence of many tastes, from Clair's (in the marriage of fragile sentiment and winning verve) to Lubitsch's (the crisp patter and wickedness of the dialogue). But even though his style is eclectic, and even though the Rodgers and Hart numbers are a massive asset to him, Mamoulian is constantly ready to stamp his own imaginative signature on the film. His experiments with overlapping sound are amusing in the context of the plot and also advanced for the period; his visual capers are never gratuitous (e.g. the speeded-up action as Chevalier gallops away on a rebellious horse is balanced neatly a few minutes later by the slow-motion as the hunt leaves the deer in peace and "tiptoes" home). *Love Me Tonight* has that infectious spontaneity that distinguishes the American musical at its best, and rarely makes the mistake of taking its romantic setting too seriously. "The son of a gun is nothing but a tailor" resounds through the château, and Jeanette MacDonald rides wildly, unforgettably, after her bourgeois hero.

SCARFACE. United States. Script: Ben Hecht, from a novel by Armitage Trail. Direction: Howard Hawks. Photography: Lee Garmes, L. William O'Connell. Editing: Edward Curtiss. Music: Adolph Tandler, Gus Arnheim. Players: Paul Muni, Ann Dvorak, Karen Morley, Osgood Perkins, George Raft, Boris Karloff, C. Henry Gordon. Production: Hughes Productions. (90 mins.)

This most cited of gangster films was based on the story of Al Capone. Howard Hawks wanted Tony Camonte (Paul Muni), Rinaldo and the rest to look "as if they were the Borgias set down in Chicago." *Scarface* was also made with the full approval of the City Police department, and this explains the didactic conversations among the detectives and newspapermen. Camonte's formula for survival in prohibition gangland is "Do it first, do it yourself, and keep on doing it." Ben Hecht's screenplay discreetly indicates the flaws in Camonte's character that contribute to his rise as well as his dramatic fall. There is the incestuous hold he wields over his sister, the unresisted temptation to sneer at his rivals, the unacknowledged dependence on henchmen like Rinaldo and even the pig-witted Angelo (who pulls a gun on

1932: Paul Muni and his sister in SCARFACE.

a telephone when the caller is insolent). These weaknesses only emerge fatally in the last scene, as Camonte realizes he is alone and that an essential part of him has died with Rinaldo and his sister. Hawks brings to the film his inimitable blend of irony and humor. There is something ghastly and at the same time farcical about the careering battles in the twilight streets, or the slaying of Gaffrey (Boris Karloff) in a North Side bowling alley. The only completely saturnine figure is George Raft's Rinaldo, tossing a half-dollar contemptuously with his hand while his snake-eyes fix on the nearest traitor or opponent in sight.

Checklist of other important features

BLOOD OF A POET (Le Sang d'un Poète). France. Jean Cocteau, who had earned a significant reputation in the twenties with his plays and novels, made his debut in the cinema with this extraordinarily "free" film, overflowing with visual symbolism and abstract effects.

I AM A FUGITIVE FROM A CHAIN GANG. United States. Director: Mervyn LeRoy. One of the toughest of all American sociological films, with Paul Muni as the convict. Sound is brilliantly used in this picture.

MOVIE CRAZY. United States. Director: Clyde Bruckman. Harold Lloyd inspired by his own experiences as a debutant in Hollywood; but by now he was one of the film colony's wealthiest stars.

L'OR DES MERS. France. Director: Jean Epstein. A convulsive and suspenseful drama played out by the fishermen of Brittainy, in which the wind and the sea have an important part.

POIL DE CAROTTE. France. Director: Julian Duvivier. An evocation of pastoral childhood based on Jules Renard's autobiographical novel, brilliantly acted by Robert Lynen and Harry Baur, both of whom were later killed in the war.

SHANGHAI EXPRESS. United States. Director: Josef von Sternberg. Marlene Dietrich enshrined in an Oriental extravaganza relieved only by the remarkable traceries of light and shade and a brilliant reconstruction of old Peiping.

TROUBLE IN PARADISE. United States. Director: Ernst Lubitsch. Herbert Marshall and Miriam Hopkins in Lubitsch's musically-timed comedy of two crooks who refuse to be reformed.

Short films and Documentaries

THE MUSIC BOX. United States. Direction: James Parrott. Photography: Walter Lundin. Editing: Richard Currier. Players: Stan Laurel, Oliver Hardy. Production: Hal Roach. (30 mins.)

The growing acceptance of Laurel and Hardy as comedians of the first rank was signalled by their winning an Academy Award for *The Music Box,* a three-reeler built on one brilliant visual gag. Stan and Ollie run a Transfer Company ("foundered," claims the sign on their vehicle, "in 1931"). They have to deliver a large pianola to a house which is approached by a large flight of steps. But it proves to be a task fit for Sisyphus. Stan and Ollie's stupidity escalates in inverse proportion to their progress towards the house. Each aggravates the other and thus their common position is weakened, while the protesting jangle of the pianola contributes to the confusion. There are some splendid sights—for instance, Ollie's being dragged down the steps by the pianola as it blunders towards the street like a sled on the Cresta Run. Stan is always on hand to dust him over and to add to his exasperation after such physical punishment. When eventually they do penetrate the house they inadvertently wreck everything in sight. Stout houses, indeed, were made to be destroyed by Laurel and Hardy.

THE BLUE LIGHT (Das blaue Licht). Germany. The first film directed by, and starring, Leni Riefenstahl, an overbearing, grotesquely-lit mountain fantasy.

L'AFFAIRE EST DANS LE SAC. France. Jacques Prévert was one of the key figures in the French cinema of the thirties. He wrote, and his brother Pierre directed, this pleasing trifle about a hatter bent on kidnapping the son of an American millionaire.

COUNTY HOSPITAL. United States. Director: James Parrott. Laurel and Hardy again, with Ollie in hospital with a broken leg and Stan bringing him hard-boiled eggs as a peace offering...

FLOWERS AND TREES. United States. Walt Disney won the first of his dozens of Academy Awards with this "Silly Symphony"—and also used the three-color Technicolor process ahead of anyone else.

LAND WITHOUT BREAD (Las Hurdes). Spain. Director: Luis Buñuel. A bleak study of the inhabitants of a poor region near Salamanca, filmed with ironic detachment.

OSCAR, CHAMPION DE TENNIS. France. Jacques

Tati's first film comedy, made on a shoestring from his own scenario and already affording a glimpse of the floundering hero later to become Monsieur Hulot.

1932: Facts of Interest

Technicolor introduces a three-color process.
Mary Pickford stars in her last film, *Secrets*.
The Venice Film Festival is inaugurated as a "Mostra" by Count Volpi.

1933

DUCK SOUP. United States. Script: Bert Kalmar and Harry Ruby, with additional dialogue by Arthur Sheekman and Nat Perrin. Direction: Leo McCarey. Photography: Henry Sharp. Editing: LeRoy Stone. Music: Bert Kalmar and Harry Ruby. Art Direction: Hans Dreier and Wiard B. Ihnen. Players: Groucho, Harpo, Chico, and Zeppo Marx, Margaret Dumont, Louis Calhern, Raquel Torres, Edgar Kennedy. Production: Paramount. (68 or 70 mins.)

Duck Soup is not only the best Marx Brothers film: it is also one of the funniest of all comedies. It lasts only just over an hour, but within that short span the team has demolished—physically and psychologically—every remnant of diplomacy, ceremony, and battlefield strategy in the mythical republic of Freedonia. Groucho is appointed leader of the country's affairs by wealthy widow Gloria Teasdale (Margaret Dumont). Chico and Harpo are ostensibly working for the administration, but are also spies by night for Sylvania, the neighboring state personified by the respectable

1933: *Groucho manhandles Margaret Dumont while Zeppo, as usual, takes a letter, in* DUCK SOUP.

figure of Trentino (Louis Calhern). But officialdom cannot cope with the Marxes, who thrive on insult: it gives them the excuse to revert to anarchy (*viz.* Harpo and Chico's interview with Trentino—they leave him shorn of his coat-tails and with his hand embedded in a mousetrap). But although the extended climax demonstrates without doubt that the Marxes dislike military pomp, other sequences suggest that this is far removed from class consciousness: for instance, Harpo's private war with the lemonade vendor. It is above all their talent for the unexpected improvisation that endows the exploits of the Marx Brothers with such fiendish power. Leo McCarey's direction gives *Duck Soup* an even flow that other Marx comedies lack, and for once, the lyrics, apparently a box-office necessity of the period, have a satirical edge.

THE PRIVATE LIFE OF HENRY VIII. Britain. Script: Lajos Biro and Arthur Wimperis. Direction: Alexander Korda. Photography: Georges Périnal. Editing: Stephen Harrison. Music: Kurt Schroeder. Art Direction: Vincent Korda. Players: Charles Laughton, Robert Donat, Merle Oberon, Binnie Barnes, Lady Tree, Elsa Lanchester, Franklin Dyall, Miles Mander. Production: London Film Productions. (95 mins.)

Alexander Korda, born in Hungary in 1893, had made films in Austria, the United States, and France before coming to England in 1931. For twenty years he nourished British films with his ideas; he gave young directors freedom to show their skill and his productions earned several million pounds for the British Treasury. As a director in his own right he achieved the height of panache with *The Private Life of Henry VIII.* The script dwells on characterization rather than plot, and the demise of one wife after another marks Henry's progress through life more

1933: Charles Laughton at one of his many banquets in THE PRIVATE LIFE OF HENRY VIII.

than any quarrel he might have had with Spain, or with Wolsey and More. The title role was a splendid challenge to Charles Laughton. He treats the king as a figure of fun—as Emil Jannings had done a few years before in *Ann Boleyn*. He swaggers, sneers, and bawls his way through banquets, love affairs, and meetings of the Privy Council, although his delight in music and his self-pity when he is without a wife afford moments of restraint. Many historians were enraged by the distortion of history, and Charles R. Beard spoke for many teachers when he complained that the film might be "good entertainment, but feeble history, bad psychology, and worse archaeology." *The Private Life of Henry VIII* brought fame to Korda in dozens of countries. It was the first British film of the brilliant French cameraman Georges

Périnal, who had made his reputation with René Clair, and most of the technicians involved with the production continued to work with Korda on such later successes as *Rembrandt* (see *1936*) and *Things to Come*.

KING KONG. United States. Script: Merian C. Cooper, James Creelman, and Ruth Rose, from the novel by Edgar Wallace. Direction: Merian C. Cooper and Ernest B. Schoedsack. Photography: Edward Linden. Editing: Ted Cheeseman. Music: Max Steiner. Art Direction: Willis O'Brien. Players: Fay Wray, Robert Armstrong, Bruce Cabot. Production: RKO (Merian C. Cooper and Ernest B. Schoedsack). (100 mins.)

1933: Special effects at their best in KING KONG.

King Kong, "the eighth wonder of the world," is the first of the great screen monsters not founded on a human image like the Golem or Frankenstein. But, as always, it is human curiosity and greed that stir him to fury. Carl Denham, a producer of travelogue films, sails to a remote island southwest of Sumatra. He takes with him the blonde Ann Darrow (Fay Wray), and when they arrive at their destination she is captured by the natives and presented as a sacrifice to Kong. This monstrous gorilla lives in a primeval forest, where he has to protect himself and his booty against pterodactyls, snakes, and dinosaurs. Somehow he cannot bring himself to destroy Ann. Her beauty fascinates him, and he is captured by the ship's crew with the help of gas bombs. But when, exhibited before the public in New York, he catches sight of the girl again, he breaks his steel chains and blunders through the streets, wreaking havoc as he goes. He treats skyscrapers like trees, and succumbs at last to machine-gun fire as he sits astride the Empire State Building.

The film is a landmark not so much by virtue of its message that beauty can charm the beast, but because it represents the first controlled and significant use of transparencies. The model monsters in the forest are very convincing. (Note how Kong always attacks that part of an opponent—head, beak, jaws—that is most dangerous.) Even the maneuvers of these gigantic creatures are reasonably smooth, and their size is always perfectly in proportion to their surroundings. This is the kind of deception that only the cinema can practice at all successfully. The music of Max Steiner contributes amply to the atmosphere of foreboding and violence.

QUEEN CHRISTINA. United States. Script: Salka Viertel and H. M. Harwood, from a story by Viertel and Margaret P. Levine, with dialogue by S. N. Behrman. Direction: Rouben Mamoulian. Photography: William Daniels. Editing: Blanche Sewell. Music: Herbert Stothart. Art Direction: Alexander Toluboff, Edwin B. Willis. Players: Greta Garbo, John Gilbert, Ian Keith, Lewis Stone, Elizabeth Young, C. Aubrey Smith, Reginald Owen. Production: M-G-M (Walter Wanger). (100 mins.)

Garbo had still not become a secure star when she left for Sweden in 1932 after her contract with M-G-M had expired. But when she returned to Hollywood in the following year to play Queen Christina, she was embarking on the great series of films that was to enshrine her name with the public at large as well as with discriminating filmgoers. By 1936 she was earning more than any female star in the world. Historically, *Queen Christina* is none too accurate: its center of focus is unashamedly on Garbo, and the production values are scaled appropriately. In the mid-seventeenth century, Christina's court was the flourishing cultural center of Sweden. She was excited by all things Southern, and reacted against the austere prudery of her Protestant ministers. In the film it is her passion for Antonio (John Gilbert), the suave Spanish diplomat, that forces her to abdicate and to

109

leave the country. (The last close-up, as she stands alone on the ship, sickened by the news of her lover's death in a duel, is rightly famous, for it signifies Garbo's unique combination of *hauteur*, tragic grace, and feminine emotion.) She looks every inch a Queen as she strides through the drafty palace in her black velvet costume, issuing orders, haranguing diplomats, occasionally and unexpectedly teasing with her throaty laughter. When she fingers each object in the room where she has spent a night of love with Antonio, her tenderness is extraordinarily touching. One suddenly realizes that this tall, proud woman is shackled by the powers she wields with such masculine verve, and that she is amused by the qualities of love, and by her own submission to their spell. Garbo's abiding presence as a star is due partly to her aloof control. Like Dietrich, she does not indulge her passions easily, and so her lonely face still mocks and tantalizes an audience.

Checklist of other important features

DESERTER (Dezerter). U.S.S.R. Director: Vsevolod Pudovkin. A militant attack on the rise of Nazism in Germany, with an experimental structure of sound and image (*Deserter* contains around 3,000 shots, according to Jay Leyda, where the average sound feature has between 800 and 1,000.)

1860. Italy. Director: Alessandro Blasetti. An episode in the campaign of Garibaldi that stands out from other Italian films of the time for its fine photography and marshalling of crowd scenes.

LE GRAND JEU. France. Director: Jacques Feyder. A remarkably atmospheric film about the French

1933: Greta Garbo with John Gilbert at the inn in QUEEN CHRISTINA.

Foreign Legion, with Françoise Rosay as the fortune-
teller in Morocco.

THE INVISIBLE MAN. United States. Director:
James Whale. Claude Rains made his debut as the
invisible man of H. G. Wells's imagination. Eerie and
humoro   in excellent proportions.

     WILL OF DR. MABUSE (Das Testa-
       r. Mabuse) . Germany. Mabuse is revived
       allegorical picture of Hitler's terrorism.
       ang's most exciting and inventive thrill-
       anti-Nazi tinge provoked his divorce
       or France.

       any. A romantic tragedy treated with
       bravura technique that it brought
       ls after he had begun his career
       atures.

       ted States. Director: George
       n, angular, athletic, and hot-
te   e four New England sisters
fr   vel.

ZER   éro de Conduite) . France.
A vi   hy that helped to make
Jean   tation in the cinema.
  (Rele

Short films and Documentaries

INDUSTRIAL BRITAIN. Britain. Assisted by Grierson, Wright, Elton and Anstey, Robert Flaherty makes
one of the truly significant "documentaries" of the
early thirties.

MOVIE STAR MICKEY. United States. Director:
Walt Disney. Fascinating caricatures of the great stars
of the period, as Mickey attends a film premiere in
Los Angeles.

A NIGHT ON THE BARE MOUNTAIN (Une
Nuit sur le Mont Chauve). France. Alexandre
Alexeieff launches his ghostly, unique animated style
—made up of light from a million pinheads, with a
dream-like film arranged to the frenzied gallop of
Moussorgsky's music.

1933: Facts of Interest

Constitution of the British Film Institute in London.

1934

L'ATALANTE. France. Script: Jean Vigo, Albert Riera, from an original scenario by Jean Guinée. Direction: Vigo. Photography: Boris Kaufman, Louis Berger. Editing: Louis Chavance. Music: Maurice Jaubert. Art Direction: Francis Jourdain. Players: Jean Dasté, Dita Parlo, Michel Simon, Gilles Margaritis, Louis Lefèbvre, Maurice Gilles, Raphael Diligent. Production: J. L. Nounez-Gaumont. (89 mins.)

Profuse claims have been made for the genius of Jean Vigo, the French director who died at twenty-nine with only two features and two shorts on film. The characters in *L'Atalante* act not according to orthodox dramatic rules but according to the whims of the moment, whether they be illogical, grotesque, or obscene. Jean, Juliette, and Père Jules are always truthful to themselves, and it is the beauty of their behavior that transcends the somber settings of this film, as the barge *L'Atalante* chugs along the canals towards Paris with its newlyweds on board, "always cooing or quarrelling," as Père Jules complains. Michel Simon plays Jules with a warmth and eccentricity that give him the stature of a Falstaff in Vigo's universe. His body a mass of tattoos, his cabin crammed with mementoes, his face wrinkled up in disgust at

1934: Michel Simon as Père Jules in L'ATALANTE.

life, he belongs among the great figures of the French cinema, a symbol of anarchy but also of generosity and understanding.

L'Atalante contains much conventional lyricism—the excursion to Paris, for instance—but in other strange, beguiling ways Vigo impresses his vision on the film: Juliette standing alone and disconsolate on the barge, her wedding dress barely visible in the dusk; the moment of violence when a thief is pursued by a crowd through the city streets; or the obsessive shots of Jean swimming underwater searching for the chimera of his bride. Vigo was buried a few hours before the première of *L'Atalante;* it is an imperishable tribute to his talent.

THE SCARLET EMPRESS. United States. Script: Manuel Komroff. Direction: Josef von Sternberg. Photography: Bert Glennon. Music: John M. Leopold and W. Frank Harling, based on themes by Tchaikovsky and Mendelssohn. Art Direction: Hans Dreier. Players: Marlene Dietrich, John Lodge, Sam Jaffe, Louise Dresser, Maria Sieber, C. Aubrey Smith, Ruthelma Stevens. Production: Paramount (Adolph Zukor). (97 mins.)

Much more vibrant and sardonic than Eisenstein's *Ivan the Terrible* (see *1944*), von Sternberg's *The Scarlet Empress* narrates the rise to power of that "Messalina of the North," Catherine the Great. Summoned to Russia in 1744 to marry the imbecilic Grand Duke Peter, she quickly learns that chastity and lack of guile are not the ideal weapons for a woman of the court. So Catherine turns into a relentlessly ambitious creature, gladly avenging herself on those who have taken advantage of her youth. Marlene Dietrich gives an immortal performance, progressing from a wondering Prussian girl to an Empress whose sophistication makes strong men like Count Alexei (John Lodge) quail before her.

The cinema is full of historical spectacles along these lines. But von Sternberg endows *The Scarlet Empress* with his unrivalled blend of visual bravura

and flippant disgust. The dialogue is at times oddly anachronistic; and the satirical stabs at decorum (the wedding ceremony and its aftermath) are hardly subtle. Yet von Sternberg spins with his camera a web of exotic intrigue that works on its own level, even to the hectic climax, with Dietrich and her Army supporters galloping up the great stairways of the palace until at last the throne is reached. The feeling of claustrophobic luxury and inert tradition is banished as Catherine smiles triumphantly into the camera. Corruption, as so often in von Sternberg's world, has been exploited, and the innocent defiled.

TRIUMPH OF THE WILL (Triumph des Willens). Germany. Direction: Leni Riefenstahl. Photography: Sepp Allgeier, Erna Peters, Guzzi and Otto Lantschner, Walter Prager. Editing: Riefenstahl. Music: Herbert Windt. Production: Walter Traut, Walter Groskopf. (120 mins.)

None of the numerous documentaries concerning the rise of the Third Reich in Germany have presented such a penetrating and horrifying vision of Hitler as *Triumph of the Will*. On September 20, 1934, the anniversary of the outbreak of World War I, the Nazis held a gigantic rally at Nuremberg. Leni

"A web of exotic intrigue"—THE SCARLET EMPRESS.

1934: From Leni Riefenstahl's TRIUMPH OF THE WILL.

Riefenstahl, an extrovert actress made famous by the Alpine films of Arnold Fanck, was instructed to record the occasion on film. Every facility was offered her; many of the Convention's maneuvers were planned to impress the cameras. The result was spectacular: a clever and ecstatic piece of propaganda. From the arrival of Hitler at the airport and his progress through the tumbled streets of the ancient town, to the nocturnal gatherings where thousands of torches pierce the darkness, the tone is Olympian. Riefenstahl's shots transmogrify the ordinary face into a symbol of Teutonic pride and physical perfection.

Myasnikova, L. Kmit, I. Pevtsov, S. Shkurst. Production: Lenfilm Studios. (99 mins.)

One still salutes a painstaking Soviet film of the thirties in which a heroic figure is depicted with affection, pride, and an honest awareness of human failings. Chapayev was a temperamental genius of a general, commanding his Red Division with a mischievous humor that those around him found unsettling but also inspiring. The brothers Vasiliev give a meaning to the strained hours of waiting for the next engagement, and if they give the battle scenes

1934: From CHAPAYEV.

The hundreds of tents call to mind the encampment of some medieval army. On the soundtrack, the Wagnerian music and the reverberating cheers of the crowd are compounded into a call to national solidarity that must, at the time, have been difficult to resist. *Triumph of the Will* was and remains a testimony to the noxious, animal magnetism of Hitler. In the light of subsequent events, the film is ghastly, even ludicrous. But the plastic brilliance and symmetry of Miss Riefenstahl's direction are undeniable.

CHAPAYEV. U.S.S.R. Script and Direction: Sergei and Georges Vasiliev, from the writings of D. A. and A. N. Furmanova. Photography: Alexander Sigayev, A. Ksenofontev. Music: G. Popov. Art Direction: I. Makhlis. Players: Boris Babochkin, B. Blinov, V.

a dimension of fantasy so that Chapayev's death in the broad river resembles that of the hero in a Western, then it is perhaps more attractive than the immaculate, "manipulated" heroism that had prevailed in the early Soviet cinema. With his ability to convert table-top strategy into success in the field, and his even more remarkable instinct for survival, as he crouches behind a machine gun holding off an entire company, Chapayev *demonstrates* his greatness by comparison with the patriarchal leaders of the Whites. Beside him for the first half of the film is Furmanov, his division commissar and the perfect foil for Chapayev's violent bluster. Their relationship is observed with splendid economy. Much of *Chapayev* has dated now—its sentimental romance in the margins of battle, its continual focus on comradeship—but the acting of Boris Babochkin as the general, naïve, quixotic, indefatigable, has the common touch that leaps over the years and the conventions.

Checklist of other important features

BOULE DE SUIF (Pyshka). U.S.S.R. Director: Mikhaïl Romm. A silent Soviet version of Guy de Maupassant's satirical short story which attacks the Church and all hypocrisy.

IT HAPPENED ONE NIGHT. United States. Director: Frank Capra. Clark Gable and Claudette Colbert were formidable players in several "screwball" comedies of the period. Smart dialogue and several witty incidents make the hackneyed story of *It Happened One Night* appear positively genial.

THE LOST PATROL. United States. Director: John Ford. Highly regarded, but often banal, study of a group of Legionnaires wasting away in a tiny oasis. With Victor McLaglen.

MADAME BOVARY. France. Director: Jean Renoir. Though depleted by over an hour, this dark, fanciful version of Flaubert's Norman tragedy exerts its spell and proves Renoir to be one of the cinema's master technicians.

THE MAN WHO KNEW TOO MUCH. Britain. Alfred Hitchcock's first and rather quaint version of the story of an innocent family involved in skulduggery beyond their ken. Peter Lorre excels as the smooth villain, matching the British for phlegm and efficiency.

Short films and Documentaries:

LA JOIE DE VIVRE. France. Directors: Anthony Gross and Hector Hoppin. One of the vintage pre-war cartoons that owes much of its charm to its balletic rhythm and the gaiety of its characters.

MAN OF ARAN. Britain. Director: Robert J. Flaherty. An inspiring account of life on the Arran Isles off Western Ireland, celebrating a specific kind of daily courage and stoicism in the face of a terrible climate.

LE MÉTRO. France. Directors: Henri Langlois and Georges Franju. A pioneer French documentary by two of the most well-known figures in the continental film world.

1934: Facts of Interest

Len Lye, the British animator, paints directly onto the frame in *Colour Box,* an important stage in the development of animation and cartoon technique.

1935

A NIGHT AT THE OPERA. United States. Script: George S. Kaufman and Morrie Ryskind. Direction: Sam Wood. Photography: Merritt B. Gerstad. Editing: William Le Vanway. Music: Herbert Stothart. Art Direction: Cedric Gibbons, Ben Carré and Edwin B. Willis. Players: Groucho, Harpo and Chico Marx, Margaret Dumont, Siegfried Rumann, Kitty Carlisle, Allan Jones, Walter King. For M-G-M (Irving Thalberg). (93 mins.)

The last vintage Marx Brothers film, produced by Irving Thalberg at M-G-M, enables the team to create havoc in fashionable opera circles. There are few of the unfunny interludes that mar the Brothers' films in later years, although the Kitty Carlisle–Allan Jones romance provides an obligatory streak of sentiment. The plot hardly concerns the Brothers, of course.

Groucho dominates the first half of the picture as, eyebrows undulating, he insults Margaret Dumont at front, rear, and everywhere, asking a waiter the while for a glass of milk from a milk-fed chicken. But Harpo, all faun-like leers and voracious appetite (for tie and cigar sandwiches, recalling the telephone receiver he devours in *The Cocoanuts*), swings into command at the climax in the New York Opera House. This unforgettable, beautifully paced scene, as the Brothers disrupt a gala performance of "Il Trovatore," includes some scalpel-sharp digs at American *moeurs*. As usual, the Marxes score through their incongruous behavior: Groucho sells peanuts to an affronted firstnight audience; Harpo and Chico toss a baseball to each other over the heads of the orchestra. Their cheekiness, their desire and ability to stultify bourgeois decorum, and the unparalleled combination of Groucho and Chico's linguistic wit with Harpo's demoniac miming, ensure victory for the Marxes as ever.

TOP HAT. United States. Script: Dwight Taylor, Allan Scott, from a story by Dwight Taylor. Direction: Mark Sandrich. Photography: David Abel. Editing: William Hamilton. Music: Irving Berlin. Art Direction: Van Nest Polglase, Carroll Clark. Dance Direction: Hermes Pan. Players: Fred Astaire, Ginger Rogers, Edward Everett Horton, Helen Broderick, Erik Rhodes, Eric Blore. Production: RKO-Radio. (105 mins.)

Fred Astaire has never been equalled as a dancer in musical comedy. His nine films with Ginger Rogers contain some of the most graceful numbers ever staged by Hollywood, and have a scintillating zest stemming from sheer expertise and love of dancing. In *Top Hat* the music and lyrics are by Irving Berlin, and are wedded deceptively to the narrative. Jerry Travers (Astaire) arrives in London to appear in a stage show and, while staying at his impresario's hotel, falls in love with a blonde called Dale Tremont (Gin-

1935: *The Marx Brothers in control in* A NIGHT AT THE OPERA.

116

ger Rogers) in the room below. Although there are some amusing incidents as Travers tries to woo Miss Tremont, the witticisms come thick and fast only when the impresario is accused of this flirtation, and has to confront his wife—and Miss Tremont's fiery Italian dressmaker—in the Venice Lido. Like Maurice

1935: Sheltering from the rain in TOP HAT.

Chevalier in *Love Me Tonight* (see *1932*), Astaire thrives on this case of mistaken identity. He breaks into song and dance at the slightest excuse, and always has a line of sophisticated repartee in reserve. The numbers have a professional gloss, and the obviously artificial replica of the Lido gives the film, if anything, a period charm, forcing one's attention onto the skirmishing couples and Astaire's whirling feet. In the Piccolino number at the end, Mark Sandrich directs with unorthodox skill, creating a sense of space and ensemble rhythm. *Top Hat* has retained its enervating, mischievous gaiety over the years, and must be accounted the classic musical of the thirties.

THE YOUTH OF MAXIM (Yunost Maksima). U.S.S.R. Script and Direction: Grigori Kozintsev and Leonid Trauberg. Photography: Andrei Moskvin. Music: Dimitri Shostakovitch. Art Direction: Yevgeni Enei. Players: Boris Chirkov, Stepan Kayukov, Valentina Kibardina, Mikhail Tarkhanov. Production: Lenfilm Studios. (2678 metres.)

This is the first part of what is known as "The Maxim Trilogy," showing the imaginary adventures

1935: From THE YOUTH OF MAXIM.

of a young man growing up with the 1917 upheaval in Russia. It has an enthusiasm and a charm in sharp contrast to the "realism" of other Soviet films. (Kozintsev and Trauberg had already founded "FEX," the Factory of the Eccentric Actor, in 1921, whereby film performances stemmed from a music-hall or circus tradition.) The opening scenes, on New Year's Eve 1909, show a delight in the use of sound (then new to Soviet studios) as sleigh-bells fill the air and partygoers sing wildly in the snow. This exuberance sets the tone for the trilogy. Maxim, though he sees his compatriots fretting in the last years before the Revolution, never abandons his *joie de vivre*. He is involved in a factory protest after two workers have died at their posts. He goes to prison, and later he is ambushed in a wood with other revolutionaries. His old mentor, Polivanov, is wounded, and Maxim realizes that the torch has been passed to his generation. The social criticism implicit in the film is best at its satirical moments. Maxim stumbles on a picnic in the woods where a fat employer is lying in a hammock while his primitive phonograph blares out insanely and his beribboned family sprawl around in the grass. The police chiefs behave with a blend of harshness and pomposity that seems far nearer the truth than the inhuman monsters of Eisenstein and Pudovkin's world. *The Return of Maxim* (1937) and *The Vyborg Side* (1939) extend Maxim's story to the capture of the Winter Palace and beyond.

Checklist of other important features

CARNIVAL IN FLANDERS (La Kermesse Héroïque). France. Jacques Feyder's near masterly recreation of life in Flanders, every composition echoing the Dutch painters and every exchange of sentiments reflecting the fastidiousness that made Feyder so influential in the French cinema of the thirties.

THE DEVIL IS A WOMAN. United States. Marlene Dietrich's last film with her champion, Josef von Sternberg. A series of exotic set-pieces, a "Caprice Espagnol" to be noted more for its imagery than for its plausibility.

THE INFORMER. United States. John Ford's celebrated film about the Irish troubles. Sadly dated now, though Victor McLaglen's monumental performance as the intoxicated Gypo still gives reason to the sentimentality.

MUTINY ON THE BOUNTY. United States. Director: Frank Lloyd. One of the earliest and most enduring of sea films, with Charles Laughton as Captain Bligh and Clark Gable as Fletcher Christian locked in a merciless quarrel.

THE REVOLT OF THE FISHERMEN OF SANTA BARBARA (Vostaniye Rybakov). U.S.S.R. Direction: Erwin Piscator. An eclectic but often dazzling exercise in film style, built round a fisherman's strike and its violent aftermath, directed by the well-known theatre producer, Piscator.

RUGGLES OF RED GAP. United States. Direction: Leo McCarey. Charles Laughton again, as the squeamish English butler who is taken into service by an American millionaire and quickly assimilates his new surroundings without losing any of his bland comportment.

TONI. France. Jean Renoir revolted successfully against the vogue for studio sets and heavy makeup in the French cinema. *Toni*, an ironic tale of frustrated love set in the south of France, is among his most beautiful films and one which recalls his father's search for realism in painting.

THE WHOLE TOWN'S TALKING. United States. Director: John Ford. A consistently hilarious satire on gangsterism, with Edward G. Robinson as the meek little clerk who is an unfortunate double for "Killer" Mannion.

Short films and Documentaries

EASTER ISLAND (L'Ile de Pâques). France. A stirring and mature study of the tribe and its legendary statues, edited by Henri Storck, scored by Maurice Jaubert and directed astonishingly, by a man of only 20, John Ferno.

L'HIPPOCAMPE. France. Director: Jean Painlevé. An underwater description of the habits of the sea horse that verges on the abstract.

SONG OF CEYLON. Britain. Director: Basil Wright. A queen among documentaries, evoking the spirit of Ceylon through its religious traditions and its developing industry.

1935: Facts of Interest

Rouben Mamoulian's *Becky Sharp* is the first feature filmed in three-color Technicolor (although Disney had used the process sporadically since 1932).
Museum of Modern Art Film Library is established.
The firm of J. Arthur Rank, subsequently to dominate film distribution in Britain, is launched.

1936

LE CRIME DE MONSIEUR LANGE. France. Script: Jacques Prévert, from an idea by Jean Renoir and Jean Castanier. Direction: Renoir. Photography: Jean Bachelet. Editing: Marguerite Renoir. Music: Jean Wiener, with song by Joseph Kosma. Art Direction: Jean Castanier, Robert Gys. Players: René Lefèvre, Jules Berry, Marcel Levesque, Henri Guisol, Florelle, Nadia Sibirskaïa, Sylvia Bataille. Production: Les Films Minerva (Oberon). (84 mins.)

Renoir again! Hindsight has revealed him as the master director of the thirties. Lange works in a publishing house and devotes his spare time to the writing of lurid Westerns. Batala, the publisher and a swindler whose creditors are rapidly foreclosing, learns of Lange's talent and tricks him into giving him the copywright of his "Arizona Jim" adventures. But the business collapses before the popularity of Lange's work can save it, and Batala flees from Paris. When his train is derailed, he cunningly exchanges clothes with a dead priest, and eventually returns to his old haunt. Lange, driven almost berserk by the blackmailing tactics of a man he believes to have been killed, shoots Batala. Then, with Valentine, a laundress and former mistress of Batala, he makes for the frontier.

1936: The death of Batala in LE CRIME DE MONSIEUR LANGE.

Le Crime de Monsieur Lange is more than a murder story. It is an attack on the church (people accept Batala in the guise of a priest and are purblind to his shark-like smile), on patronage, on class prejudice, and even on the cantankerous type of military hero—the concièrge, forever boasting about his exploits in Tonkin—that Franju was to expose later in *Hôtel des Invalides* (see *1952*). Prévert's influence on the script can be discerned in the idea of the "cooperative" that runs the publishing house with spectacular success after Batala's disappearance, and in the poetic justice of the murder itself. Prévert's hero is shown to be an innocent man at heart, who is drawn into a vortex of disaster in spite of himself. The final shot of Lange and Valentine's escape across the sands is charged with significance. The future seems grey and bare; the lovers are lost and it is as though Batala were still leering over their shoulders, obscuring the sun from their lives. Lange has now changed places with his evil genius: like Batala, he will spend the years ahead afraid of detection and scandal. Jules Berry's handling of Batala is quite magnificent—one of the greatest performances in the cinema. So rounded is the character, so human his devilish contortions, that one even admits to a twinge of sympathy for him as he coughs out his life beside a dry fountain.

A DAY IN THE COUNTRY (Une Partie de Campagne). France. Script: Jean Renoir, from the story by Guy de Maupassant. Direction: Renoir. Photography: Claude Renoir. Editing: Marguerite Renoir, Marinette Cadix. Music: Joseph Kosma. Players: Sylvia Bataille, Georges Darnoux, Jane Marken, Gabriello, Jacques Borel (J-B. Brunius), Paul Temps. Production Panthéon (Pierre Braunberger). (36 mins.) (Released in 1946.)

A Day in the Country, shot in 1936 and left incomplete because of *force majeure*, shows the artistic relationship between Jean Renoir and his father, Auguste Renoir, at its closest. The film has a visual felicity which, to an almost intoxicating degree, decants the flavor of the French countryside. Monsieur Dufour, an ironmonger from Paris, takes his wife and daughter for a Sunday excursion in 1860. Two men meet them at a restaurant beside the river, and in the drowsy heat of the afternoon they squire the mother and daughter upstream. For a brief moment, Henri, dark and thoughtful, kisses Henriette in a glade on the bank. But the magic passes; the weather deteriorates; and years later, when the two meet again, they can scarcely speak for their emotion. The interlude is treated like a melody, while the sunshine and the meadows recall the canvases of Renoir *père*. The river, the symbol of life's changing moods in so many Renoir films, witnesses the shy attachment between Henri and Henriette in all its stages, teasing the eye with its reflections, and then cheerless beneath the

1936: "Pictorial beauty and . . . precipitate romance" in Renoir's A DAY IN THE COUNTRY.

unexpected rain. Yet for all its pictorial beauty and its precipitate romance, *A Day in the Country* is the least self-conscious of films, made with simplicity and love by a director in full command of his medium.

FURY. United States. Script: Fritz Lang and Bartlett Cormack, from a story by Norman Krasna. Direction: Lang. Photography: Joseph Ruttenberg. Editing: Frank Sullivan. Music: Franz Waxman. Art Direction: Cedric Gibbons, William Horning, Edwin B. Willis. Players: Spencer Tracy, Sylvia Sidney, Walter Abel, Bruce Cabot, Edward Ellis, Walter Brennan. Production: M-G-M (Joseph L. Mankiewicz). (92 mins.)

Fritz Lang came to Hollywood in 1934 at the instigation of M-G-M. *Fury* was thus his first English-language film, and has been described as an abstract study of mob hysteria. While travelling to join his fiancée, Joe Wilson (Spencer Tracy) is arrested on suspicion of kidnapping a young girl. Circumstantial evidence accumulates against him. A frenzied crowd surrounds the prison where he is being held and eventually sets fire to the building. There is a trial, and the mob leaders are about to go free when Joe, having escaped surreptitiously from the blaze, arrives to provide evidence against them. He has become tainted with the same desperate desire for revenge as his assailants. The innocent victim has been changed by his experience into a vindictive enemy of society, and this development stands in ironic contrast to the behavior of the sheriff, who defends his prison so loyally and then fails to speak against the "respectable" citizens in court. *Fury* was made at a time when there was an average of one lynching every three days in the United States, and Lang's skeptical vision lays emphasis squarely on the mechanics and consequences of such violence. Melodrama and romantic incidents are given short shrift, and even the early part of the film has an ominous atmosphere. *Fury* can be seen today as one of the most outspoken and disturbing productions of the thirties.

1936: The crowd outside the prison in FURY.

121

Checklist of other important features

THE CHEAT (Le Roman d'un Tricheur). France. Written, directed, and generally dominated by that paragon of French entertainment in the thirties, Sacha Guitry, *The Cheat* is a stimulating *conte* about an irredeemable trickster whose style prefigures the Ealing comedies.

MR. DEEDS GOES TO TOWN. United States. Director: Frank Capra. The Oscar-winning comedy with Gary Cooper and Jean Arthur that suggested a solution to the aftermath of the Depression—that property should belong to the people.

MODERN TIMES. United States. Chaplin's virtually silent satire on the mechanical age and the individual's plight therein. Charlie is the tramp for the last time in this rather disunified picture.

THE PETRIFIED FOREST. United States. Director: Archie Mayo. A strange gathering in the desert, filled with intellectual dialogue ("The Petrified Forest" corresponds to the world of outmoded ideas), offset by a laconic performance from Humphrey Bogart as the gangster. With Bette Davis and Leslie Howard.

REMBRANDT. Britain. Director: Alexander Korda. An underestimated biography of the Dutch painter, with Charles Laughton reciting long, virtuoso passages and conveying Rembrandt's increasing disillusion, with splendid pathos.

Short films and Documentaries

NIGHT MAIL. Britain. Directors: Basil Wright and Harry Watt. A documentary on British postal communications equipped with a lyrical rhythm by W. H. Auden's commentary and the music of Benjamin Britten.

THE PLOW THAT BROKE THE PLAINS. United States. Director: Pare Lorentz. A challenging film about the perils of drought, made for the New Deal administration.

RAINBOW DANCE. Britain. Director: Len Lye. An advertising film (for the Post Office Savings Bank) becomes a lively and inventive abstract cartoon, many years ahead of its time.

1936: Facts of Interest

Foundation of La Cinémathèque Française, probably the most significant of the national archives for preserving films.

1937

LA GRANDE ILLUSION. France. Script: Charles Spaak and Jean Renoir. Direction: Renoir. Photography: Christian Matras. Editing: Marguerite. Renoir. Music: Joseph Kosma. Art Direction: Lourié. Players: Jean Gabin, Pierre Fresnay, Erich von Stroheim, Dalio, Julien Carette, Gaston Modot, Jean Dasté, Sylvain Itkine, Jacques Becker. Production: R.A.C. (Frank Rollmer, Albert Pinkovitch, Alexandre). (117 mins.)

For Renoir at the age of forty two, the horror of World War I had already been replaced by a recollection of chivalrous behavior. *La Grande Illusion* is concerned with the people involved in the upheaval rather than with the mechanics of warfare. Two French officers are shot down over Germany and become prisoners of war. They are the aristocrat Boildieu (Pierre Fresnay), and the bourgeois Maréchal (Jean Gabin). Rauffenstein (Erich von Stroheim) accords them the privileges of their rank be-

fore he returns to the fray as a flier. The Frenchmen drift from one camp to another, always eager to join an escape attempt, until they arrive at a redoubtable fortress commanded by none other than Rauffenstein, who has been terribly wounded in the intervening months. Here the core of the film is to be found, as the two aristocrats discuss their impending redundance and reflect on the fortunes of war. Maréchal, thanks to a diversion provoked by Boildieu, escapes at last and enjoys a short interval of contemplation and romance in the Bavarian mountains before crossing the Swiss border with his friend Rosenthal.

That the war will end is the illusion that disturbs Renoir, the pacifist. His remedy is a companionship and mutual respect that traverse national and racial barriers. Rauffenstein, with his patrician conduct and his reluctance adherence to duty, personifies this spirit of maganimity so close to Renoir's heart. With the passing years, *La Grande Illusion* has acquired a certain quaintness, a stylized nostalgia that enhances the warmth of its sentiments, the courage of its faith in human friendship.

DROLE DE DRAME. France. Script: Jacques Prévert, from the novel *His First Offense* by J. Storer Clouston. Direction: Marcel Carné. Photography: Eugène Schuftan. Editing: Marcel Carné. Music: Maurice Jaubert. Art Direction: Alexandre Trauner. Players: Louis Jouvet, Michel Simon, Françoise Rosay, Jean-Louis Barrault, Jean-Pierre Aumont, Nadine Vogel, Alcover. Production: Corniglion-Molinier. (95 mins.)

Drôle de Drame is a comic fantasy that emphasized a new talent in Marcel Carné, whose first feature was *Jenny* in 1936. It suggests in retrospect that Jacques Prévert was as adept at writing farcical dialogue as he was the doom-laden lines of *Quai des Brumes* (see *1938*) or *Le Jour se Lève* (see *1939*); and it represents a courageous attempt by the French cinema to match

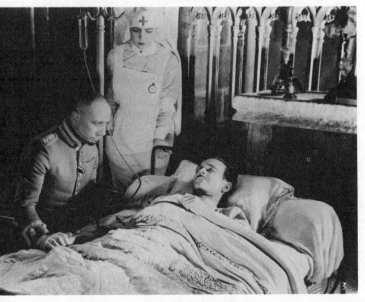

1937: Erich von Stroheim at Pierre Fresnay's bedside in LA GRANDE ILLUSION.

the flow of sophisticated Hollywood comedies of the period. The film takes place in London, where Louis Jouvet holds court unctuously as an Anglican bishop with a brood of young children, and decides that his wife has been murdered by Michel Simon (his cousin, masquerading as a botanist when he is really a thriller writer). The humor is compounded of twirling music, baroque décor, and suppliant lovers (Jean-Pierre Aumont and Nadine Vogel). *Drôle de Drame* celebrates great players, and Simon, whether drunk or sober, is a worthy foil for Jouvet, who dresses severely as a Scottish laird (with dark glasses). Its picture of Edwardian London is uproariously off-balance, with the milkman, the police inspector, and the nether reaches of Limehouse all being treated with more than a tinge of burlesque; and in the antics of Jean-Louis Barrault, as "the slaughter-house terror" who despatches butchers with relish, there is clearly the same anarchic glee as in *Zero for Conduct* and *Boudu saved from drowning*.

1937: Michel Simon and a suspicious Louis Jouvet in DROLE DE DRAME.

Checklist of other important features

J'ACCUSE. France. Abel Gance's sound version of his 1918 film of the same name, in which the dead of Verdun rise to haunt a country shortly to be engulfed again in war. Essentially a passionate fantasy, it still impresses with its wild-eyed performances and its brooding photography.

UN CARNET DE BAL. France. The peak of Julien Duvivier's career: an assortment of splendid players emerges as Marie Bell decides to trace her suitors at a ball twenty years before, and meets them again in episode after episode of wit and poignance. With Raimu, Jouvet, Françoise Rosay.

THE EDGE OF THE WORLD. Britain. Given complete freedom for the first time in his career, Michael Powell made a remarkable quasi-documentary on the eroding community life of a lonely Scottish isle.

GRIBOUILLE. France. Director: Marc Allégret. Raimu was primarily a stage actor; but in *Gribouille* he again proves his subtlety in screen acting as a French shop-keeper on the jury in a murder case. Michèle Morgan made her name in this film.

LA MARSEILLAISE. France. Jean Renoir's documentary (or almost) reconstruction of episodes from the French Revolution, invested with the director's lissome style and unfailing faith in human sincerity.

OH, MR. PORTER! Britain. Director: Marcel Varnel. Will Hay's peculiarly British kind of farce is close to perfection in this film, while Moore Marriott and Graham Moffat provide hilarious support at the expense of the British railways.

PÉPÉ LE MOKO. France. Director: Julien Duvivier. Jean Gabin again as the solitary gangster, trapped in Algiers; the film is characteristic of its period, as fatalistic as *Quai des Brumes* and *Le Jour se Lève*.

LES PERLES DE LA COURONNE. France. An uneven period extravaganza in which Sacha Guitry, at the height of his theatrical fame, takes four roles and impresses as always with his Gallic zest for comedy.

YOU ONLY LIVE ONCE. United States. Another trenchant essay by Fritz Lang on the meaning and infectiousness of guilt in American society, as an ex-convict (Henry Fonda) is "framed" and finds himself displacing the real murderer.

Short films and Documentaries

THE SPANISH EARTH. United States. Full of images of conflict and destruction, Joris Ivens's famous documentary is ennobled by Hemingway's commentary and by the fearlessness of its photography (by Ivens and John Ferno).

1937: Facts of Interest

Jean Harlow dies.
Opening of Cinecittà in Rome, probably the largest studio in Europe at the time.

1938

ALEXANDER NEVSKY. U.S.S.R. Script: Peter A. Pavlenko and Sergei M. Eisenstein. Direction: Eisenstein and D. I. Vasiliev. Photography: Edward Tissé. Editing: Eisenstein. Music: Sergei Prokofiev. Art Direction: I. Shpinel. Players: Nikolai Cherkassov, Nikolai Oklopkov, A. L. Abrikosov, Dimitri Orlov, Vassili Novikov, Nikolai Arski, Vera Ivasceva, Anna Danilova. Production: Mosfilm Studios. (108 mins.)

In certain respects *Alexander Nevsky* is Eisenstein's masterpiece. Organized with the polyphonic complexity of grand opera, it has the advantage of sound over *Strike* and *Battleship Potemkin* (see *1925*), and is more vibrant and less academic than the *Ivan the Terrible* films (see *1944*). Its construction is faultless, with its centerpiece the battle on Lake Peipus between the Russians and the Teutonic Knights in 1242. Before this, Eisenstein shows the towns of Novgorod and Pskov reduced to terror and panic by the enemy, and afterwards these same places filled with celebrations of victory.

Eisenstein fixes on a spirit that has never died in the Russian people, a spirit that makes the film's events, so remote in history, seem relevant and alive on the screen. As always, Eisenstein's visuals are closely linked to the theme of the film. Flaming torches in the streets of Novgorod express the roused ardor of the peasants; the intimidating helmets of the Teutonic Knights bear down *en masse* on the camera; they are the quintessence of tyranny and implacability. Eisenstein and Vassiliev watch the action now like a hawk from above, now with a violently shifting camera in the thick of the hand-to-hand fighting, where sheer strength of arm and axe expose the unwieldy strategy of the Knights. Then the aftermath, as the aggressors are sucked under the crumbling ice and only a terrible silence remains. But even in the condensed frenzy of battle, Eisenstein's puckish sense of humor emerges through the characters of Vassili and the Master Armorer. Thus *Alexander Nevsky* is not completely the stark and chilling film that its setting might suggest. It is illuminated by a profound patriotism, and exhorted by the music of Prokofiev.

QUAI DES BRUMES. France. Script: Jacques Prévert from the novel by Pierre Mac Orlan. Direction: Marcel Carné. Photography: Eugène Schuftan. Music: Maurice Jaubert. Art Direction: Alexandre Trauner. Players: Jean Gabin, Michèle Morgan, Michel Simon, Pierre Brasseur, Robert Le Vigan, Aimos, Delmont, Pérès, René Génin. Production: Grégor Rabinovitch. (89 mins.)

Because in the thirties he was younger than most of his peers in the French cinema, Carné was fascinated with the problems deriving from youth and inexperience. For these men and women, the tragedy of life is far more shattering than it ever was for the mature heroes of Renoir; they recall instead the hapless figures in Louis Delluc's films (made in 1921–1922). *Quai des Brumes* is a tale of impossible love. Jean is an army deserter who arrives in a foggy Le Havre and falls in love with Nellie (Michèle Morgan). But he also stumbles into gangsters' territory and is shot in the stomach as he is about to leave on a ship for Venezuela—the promised land that beckons so many of Carné's heroes. The mood of the film is thus a bewitching mixture of dejection and idealism, right to the final scenes when the despairing screams of Nellie as she kneels over Jean's corpse mingle with the wailing of the ship's siren as it prepares to sail.

Carné once commented, "One must compose images as the old masters did their canvases, with the same preoccupation with effect and expression," and in *Quai des Brumes* he concentrates on *visual* narrative more than on anything else. Nevertheless the lyrical compositions and the carefully planned patterns of movement rarely distort the social scene that is being described. Realism is an interior element of Carné and Prévert's films (as it was in Clair's and is in Truffaut's); characters behave rigidly according to the "Good-Evil" and "Light-Dark" codes laid down by Prévert in his scripts. Predestination is all.

PYGMALION. Britain. Script: W. P. Lipscomb, Cecil Lewis, and Anthony Asquith, from the play by George Bernard Shaw. Direction: Asquith. Photography: Har-

1938: Nikolai Cherkassov in the title role in ALEXANDER NEVSKY.

1938: Michel Simon and Jean Gabin in PORT OF SHADOWS.

1938: Wendy Hiller as Eliza Dolittle in PYGMALION.

ry Stradling. Editing: David Lean. Music: Arthur Honegger. Art Direction: Laurence Irving. Players: Wendy Hiller, Leslie Howard, Wilfrid Lawson, Marie Lohr, Scott Sunderland, Jean Cadell, Everley Gregg, David Tree. Production: Gabriel Pascal Productions. (96 mins.)

Alfred Hitchcock and Anthony Asquith were the only two English directors of distinction in the thirties. Parts of *A Cottage on Dartmoor* (see *1930*), *Tell England* (see *1931*), and *Dance Pretty Lady* (1932) are worthy of any anthology of the prewar cinema. There had been two previous film versions of *Pygmalion,* made in Holland and Germany, but Asquith's was the one to which Shaw himself paid most attention. Asquith suggested the sequence at the Ambassador's Ball. "For some reason or other," he recalls with characteristic modesty, "Shaw liked my phrase, 'She came up the stairs with the frozen calm of a sleepwalker,' and he wrote the scene for us." As well as providing touches like the superb removal of his hat by Higgins in the final shot, Asquith succeeds in tempering the Shavian wit with a warmth, and an understanding that is ironic without ever being malicious. Both Wendy Hiller (as Eliza) and Leslie Howard (as Higgins) act at the height of their powers. The film was reissued four times after the war, a tribute to its zest, its satire, and its timeless theme. It still moves faster and more intelligently than *My Fair Lady* (1965).

OLYMPIA (Olympische Spiele 1936). Germany. Direction and Editing: Leni Riefenstahl. Assistant: Walther Ruttmann. Photography: Hans Ertl, Walter Frentz, Guzzi Lantschner, Kurt Neubert, Hans Scheib, Willy Zielke and others. Music: Herbert Windt. Production: Leni Riefenstahl/Tobis-Filmkunst. (220 mins.)

Leni Riefenstahl's film can be seen as a propagandist banner which conveniently transfers the prestige of the Olympic movement and its lofty ideals as laid down by the Baron de Coubertin to the Nazi movement. In 1933, Miss Riefenstahl had been accorded the title "Film Expert to the National Socialist Party." In 1936 she was commissioned—by the International Olympic Committee—to film the Berlin Olympiad, and was given reasonable artistic and financial latitude (although it now appears that she was balked on several issues by Goebbels). The two-part documentary cost about 2.2 million marks, and only six cameramen were allowed inside the stadium. But apart from the athletic events, there was coverage of much else. More than 3,000 runners apparently carried stainless steel Krupp torches from Olympia in Greece to the Berlin stadium for the opening sequence. More than money and equipment, however, was needed to produce such a startlingly beautiful film. Leni Riefenstahl's talent lay not merely in her conception of sequences—the ebb and flow of movement that could later be captured aesthetically in the editing room—but in her awareness that even top-class athletes were prey to human considerations, and her close-ups of runners tensed before the gun, or of swimmers straining towards the finish, radiate the same humility and anguish as they do in Kon Ichikawa's equally impassioned film of the 1964 Tokyo Olympiad (see *1965*).

1938: The sacred flame is lit in Leni Riefenstahl's OLYMPIA.

Checklist of other important features

LA BETE HUMAINE. France. Director: Jean Renoir. A naturalistic adaptation of Zola's novel about the train-driver who feels impelled to kill all that he loves most.

BLOCKHEADS. United States. Director: John Blystone. Laurel and Hardy meet again for "the first time" since the Flanders trenches, and Ollie's wife doesn't take kindly to Stan's arrival in their fifteenth-floor apartment. Some excellent belly-laughs, but the pace is slowing already, unfortunately.

THE CHILDHOOD OF MAXIM GORKY (Detstvo Gorkovo). U.S.S.R. Director: Mark Donskoi. The first film in a famous trilogy about the youth of the Russian author, overflowing with song and dance, incident and enthusiasm. A unique portrayal of life in the Russian provinces.

ENTRÉE DES ARTISTES. France. Director: Marc Allégret. A distinguished cast again saves another French melodrama of the thirties from extinction. Jouvet, Carette, Dalio... The film takes place in the Paris Conservatoire (school of acting), with the ambivalent atmosphere born of the clash between fantasy and real experience.

THE BAKER'S WIFE (La Femme du Boulanger). France. Marcel Pagnol was a better writer for the screen than a director, but in this Provençal comedy —from a novel by Jean Giono—his hand is sure and clever, with Raimu as the baker who stops baking the moment his wife has fled with the local shepherd.

HOTEL DU NORD. France. Director: Marcel Carné. Much admired in its time, this semiclassic now looks too precious, its artificial landscape in painful contrast to the wholehearted, delightfully laconic playing of Arletty as the prostitute and Jouvet as her ponce.

THE LADY VANISHES. Britain. Director: Alfred Hitchcock. The high point of Hitchcock's British career: a very English type of thriller set in central Europe, with Naunton Wayne and Basil Radford more concerned about the cricket Test Match at home than about the skulduggery aboard their train.

SNOW WHITE AND THE SEVEN DWARFS. United States. Walt Disney's first essay in full-length animation. It cost some $700,000 and was drawn by 570 artists. A tremendous commercial success, it opened the way for other fairy tale cartoons such as *Pinocchio, Bambi,* and *Cinderella.*

1938: Facts of Interest

George Méliès dies in France.
The International Federation of Film Archives is set up.

128

1939

THE RULES OF THE GAME (La Règle du Jeu). France. Script: Jean Renoir and Carl Koch. Direction: Renoir. Photography: Jean Bachelet. Editing: Marguerite Renoir, Madame Huguet. Music: Mozart, Chopin, Monsigny, Saint-Saëns, Johann Strauss. Art Direction: Eugène Lourié, Max Douy. Players: Marcel Dalio, Nora Grégor, Jean Renoir, Roland Toutain, Mila Parély, Paulette Dubost, Julien Carette, Gaston Modot. Production: La Nouvelle Edition Française (Claude Renoir). (110 mins.)

Renoir described this brilliant tragicomedy as "a sort of reconstructed documentary on the condition of a society at a given moment"—the moment being 1939, with a disastrous phase of French history in the offing. *The Rules of the Game* is a satirical study of a way of life that stifles all opportunity for love and friendship. A November house party at the château of Marquis Robert de La Chesnaye (Marcel Dalio) provides the ideal setting. All spirit and enterprise have departed from the gentry at the gathering. They are as petrified as the Chinese statues that line the vast rooms, as mechanical in their decorum as the musical boxes the baron loves so dearly. André, the intrepid pilot, is the acknowledged outsider. He does not behave like the hero society expects him to be; he disregards the rules of the game, and his dispute with the Marquis for the love of Christine becomes a clumsy fracas, a significant substitute for the duel of prouder times. The distressing finale of the film is also ironic because Octave (Jean Renoir) finds that his honorable sacrifice rebounds on him with a vengeance.

While he remains an individualist, Renoir always returns to the essential need for companionship among men. His heroes and heroines, from the enraged gamekeeper to the sophisticated Geneviève, harbor the same emotions at heart. Renoir demonstrates their sad predicament in one of the best sequences in French cinema. The game-shoot is filmed on a perfect spring day, with low luminous clouds

Nora Grégor and Jean Renoir in THE RULES OF THE GAME.

prevailing as the beaters march through a young wood on their time-honored mission. The camera zips along behind each luckless hare and then hovers dispassionately while the animal squirms and suddenly dies, just as André falls at the end of the film, a victim of society rather than of circumstance. Humanity, warmth, generosity: these are the qualities that infuse *The Rules of the Game* and that confound one's intellectual disapproval of Renoir's occasional flippancy and lack of discipline. Is he not indeed the father of the *Nouvelle Vague*?

STAGECOACH. United States. Script: Dudley Nichols, from the story "Stage to Lordsburg" by Ernest Haycox. Direction: John Ford. Photography: Bert Glennon. Editing: Dorothy Spencer, Walter Reynolds. Music: Richard Hageman, Frank Harling, John Leipold, Leo Shuken. Art Direction: Alexander Toluboff. Players: John Wayne, Claire Trevor, John Carradine, Thomas Mitchell, Andy Devine, Donald Meek, Louise Platt, Tim Holt, George Bancroft, Ber-

Ultimately, it is the visual communication of speed and danger that distinguishes *Stagecoach:* the high shots of the stage moving away unprotected across the vast salt flats; the stirring race against the Indians; the arrival of the cavalry.

LE JOUR SE LÈVE. France. Script: Jacques Prévert, from an original scenario by Jacques Viot. Direction: Marcel Carné. Photography: Curt Courant. Editing: René Le Hénaff. Music: Maurice Jaubert. Art Direction: Alexandre Trauner. Players: Jean Gabin, Jacqueline Laurent, Jules Berry, Arletty, Mady Berry, René Genin, Bernard Blier, Marcel Pérès. Production: Sigma (J-P. Madeux). (85 mins.)

With Renoir, Carné is the most impressive French director of the thirties; but only when his talent is harnessed to that of Jacques Prévert, whose script for *Le Jour se Lève* breathes the same melancholy aroma of Destiny as do *Quai des Brumes, Les Visiteurs du Soir,* and *Les Enfants du Paradis.* The partnership is remarkable because while Carné concentrates on establishing a hard, prehensile sense of locality and character, Prévert's dialogue and situations are on a more romantic, and often poetic level. Jean Gabin as François, the factory worker who shoots his evil genius (Jules Berry) and then himself, is the embodiment of spiritual defeat. Trapped of his own volition in the tall, gaunt, suburban block, he meditates on the derisory sequence of events that has driven him to murder. The heroes of Carné and Prévert have an innate awareness of Fate; only thus can they view their past and accept their future with lucidity and equanimity. Each of the three flashbacks illuminates the grey futility of François's life—the love affairs first with the shy young girl, then with the mature Arletty, and always the voracious rivalry of Jules Berry. Each of Trauner's sets seems fabricated to reflect a state of mind: the hothouse where Gabin and Jacqueline Laurent talk of solitude and travel; the music hall where Berry and Arletty try to delude themselves as well as their audience; and the drab attic room where, as the dawn seeps in and an alarm clock rings from habit, Gabin lies sprawled in death.

ONLY ANGELS HAVE WINGS. United States. Script: Jules Furthman from a story by Howard Hawks. Direction: Hawks. Photography: Elmer Dyer, Joseph Walker. Editing: Viola Lawrence. Music: Dimitri Tiomkin, Morris W. Stoloff. Art Direction: Lionel Banks. Players: Cary Grant, Jean Arthur, Richard Barthelmess, Rita Hayworth, Thomas Mitchell, Sig Rumann, Victor Kilian, John Carrol, Noah Beery Jr. Production: Columbia (Howard Hawks). (121 mins.)

ton Churchill. Production: Walter Wanger, released by United Artists. (96 mins.)

Stagecoach is probably the most famous of all Westerns, although many Ford enthusiasts might prefer *My Darling Clementine* (see *1946*) or *Wagonmaster* (see *1950*). It marks the arrival of John Wayne among the leading stars of the genre, and is graced by one of Dudley Nichols's more perceptive scripts. The journey across Monument Valley, from "Tonto" to "Lordsburg," establishes a framework in which the characters can act on one another. The film thus achieves a psychological depth hitherto unattempted in the Western. There are five passengers—Hatfield, the gambler; Dallas, a girl of distinctly dubious virtue; Boone, a bibulous doctor; Lucy Mallory, travelling to her husband at an Army post; and Peacock, a tweed-capped liquor salesman. When Ringo Kid (John Wayne) joins the stage, he soon strikes up an *entente cordiale* with Dallas, and their romance lasts throughout the journey, despite a violent Indian attack. Eventually the coach reaches Lordsburg, escorted by a troop of cavalry, and Ringo has to settle a feud with the Plummer brothers. It is perhaps a weakness of construction that the fight comes as an anti-climax after the tension of the running battle with the Apaches.

Ford proves that he is unsurpassed at evoking the "wide open spaces" of America's Southwest. His characters respond to this environment, drawing from it a kind of nobility that—in a crisis—enables them to act beyond their reputations (Doc Boone's sobering up and delivering Mrs. Mallory's baby, for instance).

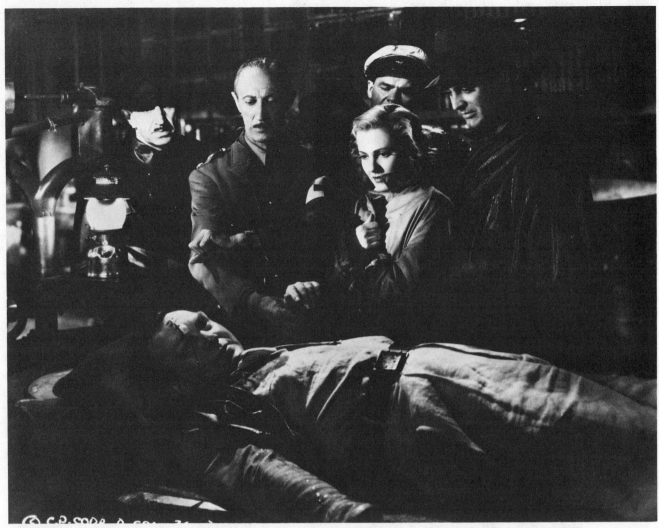

1939: ONLY ANGELS HAVE WINGS: Jean Arthur, Cary Grant, and (on the bunk) Thomas Mitchell.

Those who regard Howard Hawks as a director of more than artisan ability find their admiration justified in *Only Angels have Wings*. Here is the familiar Hawksian assortment of men in a lonely stretch of the world; here is the newcomer (Richard Barthelmess), who acts as a catalyst for the events that drive the film on. Geoff Carter (Cary Grant) runs an airline in Barranca, "port of call for the South American banana boats." His pilots have assimilated some, but not all, of his bitterness. Trust breeds unwillingly in such a mirthless and precarious occupation. Death is a daily fact, a force not fit to be challenged, merely to be resorted to as an incitement to professional cynicism. Geoff is quick to brush aside any emotional commitment, but Jean Arthur gradually masters him, as Angie Dickinson masters John Wayne in *Rio Bravo* (1959). Hawks's rigorous, purposeful direction allows the characters no spare time for sentimentality, and the screenplay deploys its arbitrary crises to perfection. There are many spectacular and intrepid flying sequences, but none are assembled so adroitly as

the first, horribly conclusive crash among the palm trees, with the searchlights failing to peer through the glutinous fog, and the pilot's queries bouncing hopelessly out of the field-set.

Checklist of other important features

DRUMS ALONG THE MOHAWK. United States. Director: John Ford. Frontier days, with war again destroying the parochial atmosphere, and Henry Fonda involved in a memorable chase with the Indians at the climax.

ESPOIR—Sierra de Teruel. France. André Malraux, now Minister of Culture in the French government, made this film while in Spain with the Republicans, and its accumulation of incident gives it a kind of stark, exalted bravery. Known in the U.S.A. as *Man's Hope*. Hidden from the Nazis until the Liberation.

GONE WITH THE WIND. United States. Director:

Victor Fleming. Until a year or two ago, this Civil War epic was the biggest-grossing film in cinema history, and sealed David O. Selznick's reputation as a producer of spectacular pictures. Vivien Leigh as Scarlett O'Hara gives her most axiomatic performance.

JUAREZ. United States. Director: William Dieterle. Arguably the best of the Warner "bio-pics" of the thirties. An attack on totalitarianism, with Paul Muni playing the Indian-born democrat whom the Mexican people oppose to Maximilian (Brian Aherne), the Emperor sent from Paris. With Bette Davis.

NINOTCHKA. United States. Director: Ernst Lubitsch. A sophisticated comedy set in Paris, with Greta Garbo as a female commissar involved with Melvyn Douglas. The script by Billy Wilder, Charles Brackett, and Walter Reisch, still tingles with witticisms.

SHCHORS. U.S.S.R. Another unforgettable picture of the Ukraine by Alexander Dovzhenko, but this time the country is ravaged by war as Shchors, the nationalist, fights for a new society. Jay Leyda has called Dovzhenko "the foremost Communist in Soviet films."

THE STARS LOOK DOWN. Britain. Director: Carol Reed. This film established Reed as the most resourceful English director of his generation. Michael Redgrave is outstanding as the miner in the Northeast who seeks to educate himself and to fight for the men's rights, though the characterisation of the pit-owner (Emlyn Williams) is too banal by far.

Short films and Documentaries

VIOLONS D'INGRES. France. Jacques Brunius's study of painters and amateur scientists that was made for the French Pavilion at the New York World's Fair of 1939.

1939: Facts of Interest

The National Film Board of Canada is established. A now famous film school, Centro Sperimentale, is founded in Rome.

1940: The family group in THE GRAPES OF WRATH.

1940

THE GRAPES OF WRATH. United States. Script: Nunnally Johnson, from the novel by John Steinbeck. Direction: John Ford. Photography: Gregg Toland. Editing: Robert Simpson. Music: Alfred Newman. Art Direction: Richard Day, Mark Lee Kirk. Players: Henry Fonda, Jane Darwell, John Carradine, Charley Grapewin, Doris Bowden, Russell Simpson, John Qualen, Eddie Quillan, Zeffie Tilbury. Production: Twentieth Century Fox (Darryl F. Zanuck). (129 mins.)

This sober, bleak adaptation of John Steinbeck's novel presents as sorry a chronology of squalor and bitterness as any in the American cinema. The Joad family are driven from their homestead in the Oklahoma Dust Bowl and journey Westward to California. But prosperity retreats before them like a mirage. Ma Joad's ample resolution sustains the others—young Tom (Henry Fonda), home on parole from the penitentiary, Uncle John, the grandparents, the pregnant daughter, even the ex-preacher, Casy (John Carradine). But the incessant misery outwears even family ties, and as one after another dies—Casy is struck down beneath a bridge by racketeers at night—so hope fails too.

The landscape lies behind all the Joads' distress, and Ford imbues the dusty roads and illimitable skylines with such intensity that the loaded truck appears like an ark, bearing one or two from each generation away from a wind-swept desert. The darkness brings fear and uncertainty, the sunlight encourages and stirs the family. Through Nunnally Johnson's articulate script, Ford is pleading, pleading, pleading, and in the film's last quarter he offers perhaps too optimistic a salve, in the form of the government camp, with its hearty, patronizing welcome, and its luxurious facilities. Jane Darwell as Ma gives a wholly committed performance, but it is Fonda, with his cat-like walk and his deep-etched gaze, who takes on the features of an Everyman, suffering with grace and every so often lashing out against exploitation. Few

Hollywood films have taken so stern a stand against the realities of social injustice.

THE WESTERNER. United States. Script: Jo Swerling and Niven Busch, from a story by Stuart N. Lake. Direction: William Wyler. Photography: Gregg Toland, Archie Stout. Editing: Daniel Mandell. Music: Dimitri Tiomkin. Players: Gary Cooper, Walter Brennan, Fred Stone, Doris Davenport, Forrest Tucker, Lilian Bond, Chill Wills, Dana Andrews. Production: Samuel Goldwyn. (100 mins.)

William Wyler and Gary Cooper worked together on only two films, *The Westerner* and *Friendly Persuasion,* both of which contain some of the most congenial scenes in the Western genre. In *The Westerner,*

1940: Gary Cooper and Walter Brennan in THE WESTERNER.

135

Cooper succeeds in curbing his cavalier spirit as well as making full use of the physical peculiarities that, though they undoubtedly contributed to his popularity, caused him also much annoyance (he suffered a fractured hip early in life, and his arms were singularly long and ungainly). Like all the finest Western heroes, he plays in this film the lonely man, heading westwards, who pauses on his journey to right some wrongs and in so doing loses his heart to a local girl. The story is set in the eighties, and concentrates on the struggle between the rapacious cattlemen and the stubborn homesteaders who refuse to budge from their land until their crops are fired. Cooper's performance is outstanding because the dialogue is written perfectly for him, and his dry comments, his mischievous eyes, his gawky walk, and his swiftness on the draw all combine to create a figure of humor and depth. There is a nonchalance and an irony about the film that are missing from all too many Westerns of the thirties.

1940: "One of the brightest, and most sophisticated comedies ever made in Hollywood"—THE PHILADELPHIA STORY.

But this most resilient of screen actresses was not to be ousted; she scored an incredible triumph on Broadway in *The Philadelphia Story* and consequently played in George Cukor's film adaptation. Tracy Lord, with her shrewish, tomboyish attitude towards the male sex, was an ideal character for Hepburn. The film dwells on the dangerous hours before a marriage (Tracy's second) is celebrated. Enough happens in this short span to shock even James Stewart, as the yellow journalist conniving rather facetiously with Miss Lord's first husband (Cary Grant). The opening scene is typical of the whole film, as Grant comes flying out of the Lord mansion pursued by an infuriated Hepburn. She throws down his golf clubs and snaps one of them over her knee. "You can go right back where you came from!" she tells him tartly. Tracy Lord is scornful, rapacious, witty, and entrancing by turns; Hepburn manages all such moods with ease, as ferocious in riding-breeches as she is attractive in her flowing white dress during a sequence by the swimming pool. Stewart too, who won an Oscar for his performance, has some nice moments, muttering with disgust at the society capers around him. Cukor's direction is competent, but it is the dialogue of Philip Barry and Donald Ogden Stewart that makes *The Philadelphia Story* one of the brightest, and most sophisticated comedies ever made in Hollywood. It was re-made in 1956 as a musical, *High Society,* losing much of its venom and sparkle in the process.

Checklist of other important features

FANTASIA. United States. Walt Disney's ambitious attempt to interpret classical music through animation—only partially successful, but the prehistoric beasts illustrating Stravinsky's "Rite of Spring" are really impressive.

THE GREAT DICTATOR. United States. Chaplin's burlesque on Hitler—and his first talkie. Some excellent pantomime, but the final speech sounds pompous today.

THE PHILADELPHIA STORY. United States. Script: Donald Ogden Stewart, from the play by Philip Barry. Direction: George Cukor. Photography: Joseph Ruttenberg. Editing: Frank Sullivan. Music: Franz Waxman. Art Direction: Cedric Gibbons and Wade B. Rubottom. Players: Katherine Hepburn, Cary Grant, James Stewart, Ruth Hussey, John Howard, Roland Young, John Halliday, Mary Nash. Production: M-G-M (Joseph L. Mankiewicz). (112 mins.)

In 1938 a group of American cinema owners declared Katharine Hepburn to be "box-office poison."

THE LONG VOYAGE HOME. United States. John Ford's community of Irishmen at sea, bound for Ireland. John Wayne as the drunken Swede; magnificent photography by Gregg Toland.

NORTHWEST PASSAGE. United States. Director: King Vidor. The high point of a line of M-G-M films concerned with pioneer days, with Spencer Tracy as Major Rogers at war with the Indians, his men gradually collapsing under the strain of the expedition. Gory, realistic, and on occasion rather *too* colorful.

REBECCA. United States. Alfred Hitchcock's first Hollywood film after he had emigrated from London, and a signpost to the psychological and moral complexities of his later period. Laurence Olivier and Joan Fontaine as husband and second wife in a gloomy mansion, filled with suspense and mementoes.

THE MARK OF ZORRO. United States. Director: Rouben Mamoulian. A re-make of the swashbuckling Fairbanks vehicle, with Tyrone Power as the masked swordsman who infuriates and finally defeats Basil Rathbone's Esteban Pasquale.

THEY STAKED THEIR LIVES (Med livet som insats). Sweden. Director: Alf Sjöberg. Human relationships begin to count again in the Swedish cinema after ten barren years. This film deals with a group of underground agents in a Baltic country on the eve of World War II.

1941

CITIZEN KANE. United States. Script: Herman J. Mankiewicz and Orson Welles. Direction: Welles. Photography: Gregg Toland. Editing: Robert Wise, Mark Robson. Music: Bernard Herrmann. Art Direction: Van Nest Polglase, Perry Ferguson. Players: Orson Welles, Joseph Cotten, Dorothy Comingore, Everett Sloane, Ruth Warrick, Agnes Moorehead, Ray Collins, Production: Mercury (Orson Welles), released by RKO. (119 mins.)

With Eisenstein's *Strike* (see *1925*), *Citizen Kane* marks the most impressive début in the cinema. Orson Welles, only twenty-five, with a reputation in radio and stage circles and notorious for his "War of the Worlds" broadcast in 1938, took nine months to edit the film, which can still stagger an audience by its director's ability to synthesize and harmonize all possible stylistic methods into a coherent instrument for telling his story. But, in his search for this technical cohesion, Welles does not forget his characters. Kane, newspaper tycoon extraordinary—clearly, but never openly, modelled on William Randolph Hearst—looms grotesquely large in Welles's own magnetic performance. His rise and decline are charted through a series of flashbacks, while the newsreel at the start of the film presents Kane's public image. ("Few private lives were more public," booms the commentary.) Each flashback, narrated by an intimate of the dead man, impinges on another, so that prejudices and discrepancies add to the enigmatic quality of Kane.

In his misuse of power, Kane is the father to all the heroes of Welles's cinema. Power is established only to be destroyed; the more gigantic the power, the more reverberating its fall. Kane subordinates everyone—wife, mistress, business associates—to his vaulting ambition. And yet, uncannily, he somehow retains one's sympathy; for he stumbles on that terrible, arid loneliness that haunts the selfish Midas. On his deathbed, a cherished memory from childhood surges to his lips —"Rosebud"—but it is an indication

1941: Kane's wife learns of his infidelity. From Orson Welles's CITIZEN KANE.

of the film's quality that the solution to the mystery of Rosebud never seems so important as the investigation it provokes. As Thompson the reporter says, "I guess 'Rosebud' is just a piece in the jigsaw puzzle." *Citizen Kane* has the dimensions of a tragedy, but the tragedy is expressed in a dazzling cluster of cinematic metaphors and devices. Quite suddenly, in 1941, the cinema comes of age, with a film that—triumphantly, vividly—proclaims its independence and its mesmeric fascination.

Checklist of other important features

THE FLAME OF NEW ORLEANS. United States. Director: René Clair. Marlene Dietrich's crisp, ironic performance as the adventuress who fascinates the cosmopolitan society of New Orleans in 1841 is in tune with Clair's own style of satire here.

49th PARALLEL. Britain. Director: Michael Powell. Primarily a propagandist film, set in Canada, where a German U-boat is sunk with only six survivors, *49th Parallel* opposes two ways of life—the Nazi and the individualist—with surprising perception. Laurence Olivier, Leslie Howard, Anton Walbrook, and Eric Portman head the cast.

HELLZAPOPPIN. United States. Director: H. C. Potter. This crazy farce ran for several years on the New York stage before being filmed, and the screen version, for all its surrealism and half-digested gags, is remarkably meaningful now, when so many advanced films are resorting to "alienation" tactics, reminding their audience that they are watching a film, and a fragile potpourri of emotions at that.

THE LADY EVE. United States. Henry Fonda and Barbara Stanwyck in one of Preston Sturges's most literate and ferociously ribald comedies about wealthy society.

THE LITTLE FOXES. United States. Director: William Wyler. Bette Davis at her astringent best as the harridan of a family in the deep South at the turn of the century.

REMORQUES. France. Director: Jean Grémillon. Jean Gabin as the tugboat captain who falls in love with Michèle Morgan. Notable for its description of life at sea.

SERGEANT YORK. United States. Director: Howard Hawks. Gary Cooper as the reluctant Tennessee hero of World War I, whose homespun marksmanship earns him decorations in Flanders. A film of humor and sincerity.

WESTERN UNION. United States. The second of three Westerns by Fritz Lang, *Western Union* dwells on the pioneer progress of telegraphic communications across Indian country from Omaha to Salt Lake City, and has a sense of color remarkable for 1941.

Short films and Documentaries

LA NAVE BIANCA. Italy. Director: Roberto Rossellini. The first full-length Italian documentary (about a hospital ship during the war); also the forerunner of neo-realism.

LISTEN TO BRITAIN. Britain. Director: Humphrey Jennings. An original and stirring picture of British life in war, immortalizing sights and sounds that seemed threatened and vulnerable in the darkest period of the struggle with Hitler.

1942

OBSESSION (Ossessione). Italy. Script: Mario Alicata, Antonio Pietrangeli, Gianni Puccini, Giuseppe De Santis, and Luchino Visconti, from the novel *The Postman Always Rings Twice* by James M. Cain. Direction: Visconti. Photography: Aldo Tonti and Domenico Scala. Editing: Mario Serandrei. Music: Giuseppe Rosati. Players: Massimo Girotti, Clara Calamai, Juan De Landa, Elia Marcuzzo, Vittorio Duse, Dhia Cristiani. Production: I.C.I. (Libero Solaroli). (135 mins.)

Throughout the thirties the Italian—like the Swedish—cinema had been stultified by a series of comedies and artless "white telephone" films that had no connection with the daily life of the working population. Visconti's début with *Ossessione* is doubly significant: as a determinist tragedy it excels through the force of its narrative, and at the same time it takes a searching look at the dinginess and the frustrations of the lower classes. The film is based on James M. Cain's novel *The Postman Always Rings Twice*. Gino (Massimo Girotti), a truck driver, falls in love with the dissatisfied proprietress of a roadside inn, and together they murder her husband. The inevitable conclusion has since been echoed in films like *Death of a Cyclist* (see *1955*) and *Thérèse Raquin*. Visconti observes the couple's schemes with a detached rigor that was to become the hallmark of neo-realism, just as the atmosphere of guilt was to recur in the director's subsequent work. He stresses the poverty that goads the ill-matched lovers into action: the squealing cats, the tattered clothes, the litter after a party. These were rare ingredients in the cinema of 1942. Huge close-ups alternate unnervingly with high crane shots so that moments of shock for Gino and his mistress carry a physical weight for the audience too. The characters are rooted in their surroundings; *Ossessione* is as much the tale of a geographical predicament as it is of an emotional one. But there is also much effective understatement: the murder of the husband and the first seduction scene between Gino and Giovanna are both omitted. The film's earthy realism, coupled with its tacit championship of the proletariat, enraged the Fascist authorities, and they cut it unmercifully.

THE MAGNIFICENT AMBERSONS. United States. Script: Orson Welles, from the novel by Booth Tarkington. Direction: Welles. Photography: Stanley Cortez. Editing: Robert Wise. Music: Bernard Herrmann. Art Direction: Mark Lee Kirk. Players: Tim Holt, Joseph Cotten, Dolores Costello, Anne Baxter, Agnes Moorehead, Ray Collins, Erskine Sanford, Richard Bennett, Don Dillaway. Production: Mercury (Orson Welles) released by RKO. (88 mins.)

According to Welles, about forty-five minutes were cut out of *The Magnificent Ambersons*—"the whole heart of the picture really," and the closing sequence in the hospital was not written and directed by him. But the film still has a fine Proustian flavor. Rarely has Welles been so gentle and affectionate in his approach, while at the same time expressing a conflict as important and as bitter as that in Indianapolis between a landed aristocracy fast drifting into decadence and an industrial bourgeoisie anxious to gain control of society. Georgie Minafer (Tim Holt) is the last bastion of this aristocracy, and Eugene Morgan (Joseph Cotten) is the representative of the industrial pioneers. Georgie is egotism incarnate; he belongs to the scorpions of Welles's world: like Kane, or like Quinlan in *Touch of Evil* (see *1958*), he frustrates and blights the lives of those around him almost in spite of himself. Acting as an intermediary between the rivals is Fanny Minafer, whose secret love for Eugene builds up inside her to a pitch of self-pity. Thanks mainly to Agnes Moorehead's superlative acting, Fanny is as enduring a character as anyone in the film, a creature ruled by her instincts, revelling in the Indian summer of a respected family.

Welles the creative technician is in evidence as usual. For example, by merging several soundtracks he achieves the babble of voices that lends such conviction to the leavetaking at the Amberson ball and

1942: Massimo Girotti in OBSESSION.

1942: Dolores Costello with Tim Holt in THE MAGNIFICENT AMBERSONS.

to the excursion in the snow. But, perhaps untypically, Welles observes rather than manipulates his characters, and this discreet style imparts an enormous emotional charge to such scenes as the death of old Wilbur Minafer, and the conversation between Lucy and Eugene in the garden, where an Indian folk tale is told so subtly that only later does one realize that it parallels the Amberson saga itself.

THE ROAD TO HEAVEN (Himlaspelet). Sweden. Script: Alf Sjöberg and Rune Lindström, from a play by the latter. Direction: Sjöberg. Photography: Gösta Roosling. Editing: Oscar Rosander. Music: Lillebror Söderlundh. Art Direction: Arne Akermark. Players: Rune Lindström, Eivor Landström, Gudrun Brost, Anders Henrikson, Arnold Sjöstrand, Holger Löwenadler, Emil Fjellström, Anita Bjork. Production: Wivefilm. (106 mins.)

The peasant painters of medieval Sweden interpreted the Bible in the light of their own conditions and surroundings. *The Road to Heaven*, written by Rune Lindström while he was preparing for the priesthood, is inspired by the church murals in Dalarna.

141

1942: THE ROAD TO HEAVEN, "inspired by the church murals in Dalarna."

It is part allegory, part fantasy. Mats Ersson (Rune Lindström) is a Candide, the very spirit of optimism. When his fiancée is burned unjustly at the stake for being a witch, he strides off on "the road to heaven" to seek recompense. The film shows how he is encouraged and tempted along his route. He falls under the Devil's influence and he discovers a gold mine in the fields. The lofty aims of his youth seem remote and ridiculous, and so he marries and grows rich and bloated, old and cruel. Only on his deathbed does he repent in the presence of the Good Father (Anders Henrikson), and finds himself reunited with his long-lost fiancée in paradise.

The period costumes, the use of genuine locations, and the astonishing conviction of Lindström's performance give stature to *The Road to Heaven*. It is probably the most nationalistic of all Swedish films, and yet it bears a universal message, in the manner of *The Pilgrim's Progress*. The roistering tones of the drinking song, and the headlong dash in a chariot across the plain to the City of Desire, contrast with the pastoral contentment and quietness of other scenes —the final encounter of Mats and the wife he married

on his travels, for instance. Alf Sjöberg, the director, repeatedly overcomes sentimentality with sincerity, and if at the time of its release *The Road to Heaven* was considered as a flight from the realities of war, it has nonetheless survived on account of its pictorial values and its spiritual strength.

LES VISITEURS DU SOIR. France. Script: Jacques Prévert and Pierre Laroche. Direction: Marcel Carné. Photography: Roger Hubert. Editing: Henri Rust. Music: Maurice Thiriet, with Joseph Kosma. Art Direction: Georges Wakhévitch. Players: Alain Cuny, Arletty, Marie Déa, Jules Berry, Fernand Ledoux, Marcel Herrand. Production: André Paulvé. (120 mins.)

Based on a fifteenth-century legend, Marcel Carné's *Les Visiteurs du Soir* marks the French cinema's resolve to evade the sour pessimism of the Nazi occupation. Censorship forbade directors to be the "witnesses of their time." Propaganda was the only theme permitted. So the Middle Ages attracted Carné and Prévert as an epoch in which hope and beauty could be stylized.

iting: Thomas Richards. Music: Adolph Deutsch. Art Direction: Robert Haas. Players: Humphrey Bogart, Mary Astor, Gladys George, Peter Lorre, Barton Mac-Lane, Lee Patrick, Sydney Greenstreet, Ward Bond, Elisha Cook Jr. Production: Warner Brothers (Hal Wallis). (100 mins.)

John Huston, son of the distinguished actor Walter Huston, made his début as a director with *The Maltese Falcon*, the third Hollywood adaptation of the thriller Dashiell Hammett wrote in 1930. The narrative combines suspense and wit. It moves forward swiftly, but never at the expense of the characterization and never obscuring the seemingly endless convolutions of the plot. Sam Spade (Humphrey Bogart) is a private eye whose partner is killed when the pair start to investigate the suspicions of a girl named Miss Wonderly (Mary Astor). It soon becomes clear that she is involved in a search for a priceless statuette, known as "The Maltese Falcon," as are two other mysterious people, Joel Cairo (Peter Lorre), craven beneath his bluster, and Kaspar Gutman (Sydney Greenstreet). The meetings between Gutman, obese and inperturbable, and Spade, laconic to the end,

1942: Humphrey Bogart in THE MALTESE FALCON.

The Devil sends two of his creatures to earth so that they may frustrate humanity. Thus Gilles (Alain Cuny) and Dominique (Arletty) arrive at a baron's castle and sing before the high table. They throw a spell over the court (a wonderful *frisson* when Arletty slows the formal dancers into immobility with the sound of her mandolin), and steal the passion of, respectively, Anne, the baron's daughter, and Renaud, the knight who has been her admirer. The Devil (played with suave, sly brio by Jules Berry) intervenes when his emissaries become too involved in earthly love. He turns them into stone, but he cannot still the beating of their hearts. . .

Prévert's scenario is as rhetorical as the tale will allow, and the dialogue lacks that impassioned sensibility which lifts *Les Enfants du Paradis* (see *1945*) out of time altogether. But Carné's picture of a medieval court matches it with an unexpected harmony. The pace is slow and measured; the characters wear their values—Goodness, Truth, Evil—quite unselfconsciously, and the exquisite compositions in garden and castle still remind one of the charm and mystery of *Childe Roland*.

THE MALTESE FALCON. United States. Script: John Huston, from the novel by Dashiell Hammett. Direction: Huston. Photography: Arthur Edeson. Ed-

provide the richest moments of the film, and Huston directs with the waggish humor that has been associated with his best work since. The Huston hero is usually engaged in a search for paradise, which itself is lent concrete and also symbolic value—the statuette here, the gold in *Treasure of Sierra Madre* (see *1948*), the money in *The Asphalt Jungle* (see *1950*). But almost invariably he finds, as Spade does in *The Maltese Falcon,* that his victory turns to ashes. The bird is a fake, and Gutman's rumbustious laughter epitomizes the derision inherent in Huston's outlook. He, and Huston, know just how dangerous it can be to take oneself seriously.

CAT PEOPLE. United States. Script: DeWitt Bodeen. Direction: Jacques Tourneur. Photography: Nicolas Musuraca. Editing: Mark Robson. Music: Roy Webb. Art Direction: Albert S. D'Agostino, Walter E. Keller. Players: Simone Simon, Kent Smith, Tom Conway, Jane Randolph, Jack Holt, Alan Napier, Elizabeth Russell. Production: RKO Radio (Val Lewton). (73 mins.)

A producer of shrewd imagination, Val Lewton died in 1951, but in the early forties he instigated a series of psychological horror films of which *Cat People* was the first. Irena Dubrovna (Simone Simon) is a dress designer fighting a legacy of evil from her childhood in Serbia. Her village had reeked of witchery; and now, in New York, she feels pursued by some malignant force that can change her temporarily into the form of a panther, rather as Jekyll must change into Hyde. She charms an engineer called Oliver Reed (Kent Smith) and they marry. But the relationship crumbles, and Irena, remote and averse to psychiatric aid, grows mortally jealous of Oliver's friend at the office.

The horror in *Cat People* is not explicit. It lurks in the dialogue, in the cavernous shadows, in Irena's apartment, and in the deserted transverse on Central Park where footsteps suddenly cease to echo . . . Even the most amazing scene of all—where a girl in a swimming pool treads water frenziedly while the light ripples in rhyme with the darkness and the constricted space is filled with the coughing sound of a panther —even here the cause of the panic is only suggested. Simone Simon gives off a helpless sincerity that still accommodates the more dated of DeWitt Bodeen's lines, and Tom Conway's bland portrayal of the psychiatrist contributes a dash of wry wit to the film's macabre constitution.

Checklist of other important features

CASABLANCA. United States. Director: Michael Curtiz. An ornate cast—Bogart, Bergman, Rains, Greenstreet, Lorre *et al.*—assembled as refugees and scoundrels in Casablanca in the last war. Melodrama at its best, and one of the biggest box-office triumphs of the forties.

IN WHICH WE SERVE. Britain. Directors: David Lean and Noël Coward. "The story of a ship" in World War II: designed as a call to patriotism, this film has a deadpan efficiency, personified in Coward's own performance as the captain. It also suggests well the unspoken rivalry that exists between home and sea in wartime—or even in peace.

THIS GUN FOR HIRE. United States. Director: Frank Tuttle. The arrival of Alan Ladd as a star, playing Graham Greene's slouch-hatted killer with a fondness for cats and for Veronica Lake.

TO BE OR NOT TO BE. United States. Director: Ernst Lubitsch. A mixture of comedy and suspense that still appears full of barbed innuendoes, and which at the time told more truths about Nazism than its audiences probably realized. With Jack Benny and Carole Lombard.

1942: Simone Simon in CAT PEOPLE.

Short films and Documentaries

THE LAND. United States. Director: Robert J. Flaherty. This harshly moving picture of a poverty stricken American countryside was banned when it first appeared, but it remains sociologically significant and accurate.

1942: Facts of Interest

Carole Lombard is killed in an air disaster. The term "neo-realism" is coined in Italy.

1943

DAY OF WRATH. (Dies Irae or Vredens Dag). Denmark. Script: Carl Th. Dreyer, Mogens Skot-Hansen, and Poul Knudsen, from "Anne Pedersdotter," a play by Wiers Jensen. Direction: Dreyer. Photography: Carl Andersson. Editing: Edith Schlüssel and Anne Marie Peterson. Music: Poul Schierbeck. Art Direction: Eric Aes and Lis Fribert. Players: Thorkild Roose, Preben Lerdoff, Sigrid Neeiendam, Lisbeth Movin, Anna Svierkier. Production: Palladium Film. (100 mins.)

The world of Carl Th. Dreyer, like that of Kierkegaard and even Hans Andersen, is haunted by a belief in the supernatural and charged too with the Nordic artist's hatred of intolerance. *Day of Wrath* shows that, as in *The Passion of Joan of Arc* (see *1928*), Dreyer's brilliant visual sense is firmly allied to his interest in the human spirit. A young girl is the victim of the film. She falls in love with her stepson and her husband's mother deliberately accuses her of being a witch. Eventually, with even her lover against her, she resigns herself to the stake by refusing to deny the charges. One of the film's several merits is its strict adherence to reason: Dreyer never overtly condemns the girl as a witch and yet his description of her mind and the grudge that she harbors against her stern husband do suggest strange, perversive powers. Like *The Passion of Joan of Arc, Day of Wrath* is a protest against the bigotry which spread like a shadow across the lives of ordinary people in the middle ages. The film is, appropriately, a formal masterpiece. Practically every composition has the clean, measured proportions of a Flemish painting. The white ruffs contrast sharply with the dark robes of the characters and some of the faces could have been chosen by Rembrandt. The scenes in the presbytery are claustrophobic. Every movement is furtive, and the soundtrack is so discreetly composed that when someone does cry out in terror or anguish, the sound strikes like a dagger. The ponderous narrative is faithful to a state of mind and a way of life at a certain point in history. In *Day of Wrath* slowness becomes a terrible inevitability.

THE CROW (Le Corbeau). France. Script: Henri-Georges Clouzot and Louis Chavance. Direction: Clouzot. Photography: Nicolas Hayer. Editing: Marguerite Beaugé. Music: Tony Aubin. Art Direction: André Andreiev, Hermann Warm. Players: Pierre Fresny, Pierre Larquey, Ginette Leclerc, Héléna Manson, Micheline Francey, Noël Roquevert, Bernard Lancret, Sylvie, Brochard. Production: Continental. (100 mins.)

Clouzot is, with Hitchcock, the cinema's leading specialist in suspense. Films like *The Wages of Fear* (see *1953*), and *Diabolique* have brought him an international reputation, but *The Crow*, exploited as anti-French propaganda by its German sponsors in 1943 and banned for two years after the Liberation, is his most incisive, least meretricious work. A tiny French town is suddenly unsettled by a series of poison-pen letters, signed by "The Crow." The revelation of a murderess at the end does not yield a simple answer to the source of the letters. All the characters are guilty, all interlock and nudge one another into temptation. The letters are merely a catalyst in the terrible proceedings, a dramatic device used by Clouzot with sly and increasingly perceptive skill. The Doctor (Pierre Fresnay), around whom life in the town revolves, is the principal victim of "The Crow," but even he admits to a dubious past. Clouzot's achievement is in showing how the letters, couched in a tone of coarse sarcasm, gradually assume a pregnancy and an influence almost irrespective of their content. Dark shadows (the figure of the Sister or the mother in mourning) steadily predominate over the sunlit streets. Visual and aural shocks abound: the sudden arrival of the Sister in the church while Fresnay is *tête-à-tête* with Héléna Manson, and the baying of an unseen crowd as the Sister herself dashes in alarm through the town after the appearance of yet another letter.

146

DAY OF WRATH (1943): "The clean, measured proportions of a Flemish painting."

1943: The Sister arrives home in THE CROW.

147

Suspense is not exploited for its own sake in *The Crow*, but rather as a means of sociological analysis, and nearly a quarter of a century later the film still seems psychologically valid and disconcerting.

came together as an efficient team when things really mattered—one remembers the moment when Barrett, hitherto depicted as rather snobbish and aloof, sits at the piano and plays "One man went to mow" with

1943: FIRES WERE STARTED—"a supreme effort of will and patriotism."

FIRES WERE STARTED (I was a Fireman). Britain. Script and Direction: Humphrey Jennings. Photography: C. Pennington-Richards. Editing: Stewart McAllister. Music: William Alwyn. Art Direction: Edward Carrick. Players: George Gravett, Philip W. Dickson, Fred Griffiths, Loris Rey, Johnny Houghton, T. P. Smith. Production: Crown Film Unit (Ian Dalrymple). (63 mins.)

Apart from the Ealing comedies (see *1949*), one or two films by David Lean or Carol Reed, and the Shakespeare films by Laurence Olivier, the British cinema's finest work has been in the field of documentary—at least until the sixties. Humphrey Jennings is regarded by many as the most gifted of all English directors. After an outstanding career at Cambridge, Jennings joined the GPO Film Unit and, in a series of films between 1940 and 1945, captured the spirit of a nation at war. *Fires were Started* is the record of a typical night's work by the Auxiliary Fire Service in London during the blitz of 1940, but Jennings's discerning treatment of events marvellously conjures up the rough and ready comradeship demanded by a crisis. Men of different backgrounds

thundering fluency. The grey metropolitan landscape takes on a lyrical quality as the night begins and the brigade is called out on duty. Jennings handles the pace of his film with self-effacing skill, so that in retrospect, the actual fire-fighting is like a supreme effort of will and patriotism for which the preceding days have been merely a meditation.

Checklist of other important features

LES ANGES DU PÉCHÉ. France. This extraordinary debut by Robert Bresson is concentrated on life in a Dominican convent, where women criminals are rehabilitated as novices. It is the intensity and plastic force of Bresson's imagery that endure even more than Jean Giraudoux's dialogue.

THE DEMI-PARADISE. Britain. Director: Anthony Asquith. Laurence Olivier enjoying himself hugely as a Russian inventor who is first puzzled and then captivated by the peculiarities of English life and manners.

THE CHILDREN ARE WATCHING US (I Bambini ci Guardano). Italy. A story of a broken marriage, viewed through a child's eyes. The first major film by Vittorio De Sica.

JANE EYRE. United States. Director: Robert Stevenson. Orson Welles plays Rochester, "proud, satanic, harsh" and inspires the production generally, with Bernard Herrmann's music recalling the brooding chords of *Citizen Kane*.

LUMIERE D'ÉTÉ. France. Director: Jean Grémillon. Made after censorship troubles with the Vichy government, this film is concerned with the triumph of simple love amid corruption and decadence in southern France. The script by Prévert lifts the affair to a tragic, majestic, if sometimes theatrical level.

THE OX-BOW INCIDENT. United States. Director: William A. Wellman. A bitter denunciation of the lynch mob, starring Henry Fonda and Anthony Quinn.

ROMANZE IN MOLL. Germany. Director: Helmut Käutner. A period romance, made in Nazi Germany but refreshingly free of political propaganda.

SHADOW OF A DOUBT. United States. Joseph Cotten as the bland-faced criminal who hides with his unsuspecting sister and is little by little unmasked by his niece. Hitchcock at his most hermetic, using suspense to penetrate his characters.

Short films and Documentaries

THE SCARECROW (L'Épouvantail). France. Director: Paul Grimault. An excellent cartoon, more complex than its American model, but just as amusing.

A SUMMER TALE (En sommarsaga). Sweden. One of Arne Sucksdorff's finest nature films, with its preoccupations with the passage of the seasons and the struggle for survival among the animals.

1943: Facts of Interest

Death of Leslie Howard.
Eisenstein, the Soviet director, publishes *The Film Sense*, a key book of film theory.

1944

1944: *Nikolai Cherkassov as IVAN THE TERRIBLE.*

IVAN THE TERRIBLE Part One (Ivan Grozny). U.S.S.R. Script: and Direction: Sergei M. Eisenstein. Photography: Andrei Moskvin (interiors), Edward Tissé (exteriors). Music: Sergei Prokofiev. Art Direction: Yosip Spinel. Players: Nikolai Cherkassov, Ludmila Tselikovskaya, Serafima Birman, Pavel Kadochnikow, Mikhail Nazvanov, Andrei Abrikosov. Production: Alma-Ata Film Studios. (105 mins.)

At first sight Eisenstein's interest in and sympathy for Ivan the Terrible seem odd. This sixteenth-century autocrat emasculated the power of the Boyars and welded together the Russian principalities into one Tsardom. His methods were harsh and sometimes treacherous. But with his Marxist outlook Eisenstein sees Ivan as the product of his times and society, as a man of vision, leading his country unsteadily but heroically towards the nationalist state of the twentieth century. Any other interpretation, one suspects, would have caused the film to be banned by Stalin. In Part One, there is the Tsar's coronation, his victory over the mongols at Kazan, the murder of his wife Anastasia, and his lonely vigil at Alexander Liberty. The film is in acute contrast to Eisenstein's dynamic work of the twenties. The camera rarely shifts. Ivan's deliberate, often sanctimonious gaze has the same naïveté as an ikon's. The low-slung corridors of the Kremlin provide an apt setting for the intrigues of Ivan's aunt and her Boyar friends. The brutal execution of the hostages at Kazan recalls Eisenstein's Mexican venture. But the bathos of the dialogue and the groupings spoils the film now, and the savage pomp of the Russian court had been captured just as effectively a decade earlier by von Sternberg (*see The Scarlet Empress, 1934*). The impressive aspect of *Ivan the Terrible,* as of all Eisenstein's films, lies in its sense of massive, latent force, in the military parade before the fight with the Tartars, or in the marvellous final sequence when the people of Moscow wind over the snow to beg for Ivan's return to power.

1944: Alf Kjellin in TORMENT.

TORMENT (Hets). Sweden. Script: Ingmar Berg-man. Direction: Alf Sjöberg. Photography: Martin Bodin. Editing: Oscar Rosander. Music: Hilding Rosenberg. Art Direction: Arne Akermark. Players: Alf Kjellin, Mai Zetterling, Stig Järrel, Olof Winner-strand, Gösta Cederlund, Stig Olin, Jan Molander, Gunnar Björnstrand. Production: Svensk Filmin-dustri. (101 mins.)

Certain films loom large in the history of the cin-ema because they reflect a moment in time or because they signal a new spurt forward in a country's film-making progress. *Torment* was made in the spring of 1944 by Alf Sjöberg, who had already proved that he was a director of high calibre with *The Strongest*

(see *1929*) and *The Road to Heaven* (see *1942*). More significantly, the film was scripted by Ingmar Berg-man, who had joined Svensk Filmindustri a year or two earlier, after a stormy youth in the Stockholm theatre world. Its story of a young man in revolt against the pompous characteristics of an older gen-eration was allied to Sjöberg's own interest in the class strife that existed in Sweden even after the ar-rival of the welfare state. Jan-Erik is a butt for the sadistic taunts of his schoolmaster, nicknamed "Ca-ligula," and when he discovers that his girlfriend has been driven to her death by this creature, he protests. He steps beyond the bounds of convention. Jan-Erik is disqualified from sitting for his finals. He becomes the prefiguration of Bergman's desolate anti-heroes in such films as *A Ship Bound for India* and *Prison* (see *1949*). Descendants of the predatory and craven Caligula too are often to be found in Bergman's later work. *Torment* is thus a seminal film, full of the complexes and preoccupations that one associates with the postwar Swedish cinema.

Checklist of other important features

ARSENIC AND OLD LACE. United States. Director: Frank Capra. The insane habits (sly poisoning, sadism, megalomania) of the Brewster family made a brilliant stage play. The film, starring Cary Grant, Peter Lorre, and Raymond Massey, is only a degree less subtle and cynical.

LE CIEL EST A VOUS. France. Another curious and little known film about French provincial life by Jean Grémillon, based on the true story of Madame Dupeyron, a garage owner's wife who broke a solo flying record in 1937.

CURSE OF THE CAT PEOPLE. United States. A skilful blend of melodrama and psychological thriller, directed by Robert Wise and produced by Val Lewton.

DOUBLE INDEMNITY. United States. Director: Billy Wilder. A typically black thriller about an insurance swindle that is redeemed by some really crackling dialogue from Messrs. Wilder and Chandler, interpreted with bravura wit by Edward G. Robinson and Fred MacMurray. With Barbara Stanwyck.

GOING MY WAY. United States. Director: Leo McCarey. Bing Crosby at the peak of his screen career in a sentimental comedy about the zealous young priest who has to take over an older man's parish in Manhattan, and finds Barry Fitzgerald as the incumbent quite a querulous colleague and opponent.

HAIL THE CONQUERING HERO. United States. Small-town antics maliciously exposed by Preston Sturges when a sick marine is elevated to the status of a hero and swept into the mayoral election.

LAURA. United States. After directing five mediocre films, Otto Preminger, a former theatre producer in Vienna, found his form with a thriller both efficiently told and sharply acted (by Clifton Webb and Dana Andrews).

THE MASK OF DIMITRIOS. United States. Director: Jean Negulesco. Based on a devious thriller by Eric Ambler, *The Mask of Dimitrios* stars two of the most memorable "heavies" of the forties, Peter Lorre and Sydney Greenstreet, both contriving to be sinister and pathetic by turns.

1944: Facts of Interest

Death of Harry Langdon.

1945

CHILDREN OF PARADISE (Les Enfants du Paradis). France. Script: Jacques Prévert. Direction: Marcel Carné. Photography: Roger Hubert. Editing: Henri Rust, Madeleine Bonin. Music: Maurice Thiriet. Art Direction: Alexandre Trauner. Players: Arletty, Jean-Louis Barrault, Pierre Brasseur, Marcel Herrand, Maria Casarès, Pierre Renoir, Etienne Decroux. Production: S.N. Pathé Cinéma. (195 mins.)

The partnership of Carné and Prévert reached its apogee in *Les Enfants du Paradis,* a long, tragicomic recreation of the Paris of 1840 with its characters based on celebrated figures of the period—Debureau, the mime, Lacenaire, the suave villain who profited from many an aristocratic indiscretion, and Lemaître, the actor whose vanity takes him to the height of his profession.

In the film, all three men are linked through their adoration for Garance (Arletty), elegant, enigmatic; one who prizes her liberty intensely. In their passion for this peerless woman, Debureau, Lemaître and Lacenaire uncover their souls and their aspirations. The mime (Jean-Louis Barrault) is afraid at first to sacrifice his romantic vision to the reality of lovemaking, and Garance slips from his grasp into the arms of Lemaître: "Paris is small for lovers like us," he says gaily, and when they meet again near the end of the film this sentence, first spoken in irony by Garance, has a wrenching melancholy. Lacenaire, meanwhile, is watching; and when Garance becomes the mistress of a wealthy count, he cannot stomach the blow to his pride—and kills, but, uncharacteristically, for love and not for money.

If Prévert's achievement resides in the study of these folk and their ambiguous identities, Carné's is undoubtedly in the supremely confident evocation of the past. From the opening shots of the Boulevard du Temple, with its teeming crowds and sideshows stretching into the distance, to the murder of the count in the Turkish baths, the period detail is precise. The film is also a tribute to the mystique of the stage: Lemaître and Debureau play out their emotions in the theatre. They share them with the packed, vociferous audience for, as Debureau says of the "gods," "Their lives are small but their dreams are big." The costumes by Mayo, the sets by Trauner, and the photography by Hubert all contribute to the spell that *Les Enfants du Paradis* perennially exerts. It hovers outside time, somehow the apotheosis of romance in the cinema.

ROME OPEN CITY (Roma Città Aperta). Italy. Script: Amidei, Federico Fellini, Roberto Rossellini, from a story by Sergio Amidei in collaboration with Alberto Consiglio. Direction: Rossellini. Photography: Ubaldo Arata. Editing: Eraldo Da Roma. Music: Renzo Rossellini. Art Direction: R. Megna. Players: Anna Magnani, Aldo Fabrizi, Marcello Pagliero, Harry Feist, Maria Michi, Francesco Grandjaquet, Giovanna Galletti. Production: Excelsa Film. (100 mins.)

Rossellini's *Open City,* made as it was before the Nazi surrender, still has the look of a newsreel. The film is composed of rough-hewn slabs of action; the dialogue has an earthy wit that stems from the unrhetorical delivery of nearly everyone (except the *Sturmbandführer*). And at the eye of this patriotic storm is the forthright Anna Magnani, shot down screaming in the hot streets as her fiancé is driven away by the Gestapo. The film is, then, a study of a city thrown off balance by war, divided into fourteen zones by the Nazis, and struggling surreptitiously for its freedom through a National Liberation Committee to which even the priest Don Pietro offers his life. Rossellini seizes the drab, miserable quality of life during this period. He expresses the disillusionment of many Romans through Marina, the girl who betrays her friends in order to obtain drugs that, in turn, alleviate her discomfort. He expresses the pure strength of will of others through Manfredi, who refuses to yield to the tortures of the Gestapo. But although the film is a roar of defiance, like *Paisa* the following year, it is given greater stature by a medi-

1945: Arletty with her lover Count in CHILDREN OF PARADISE.

1945: Marcello Pagliero after torture in ROME OPEN CITY.

tative quality (when the prisoners are alone before their interrogation, for example), and by its conviction that the children who walk back to the city in despair after the priest's execution, will inherit a cleaner world.

BRIEF ENCOUNTER. Britain. Script: Noël Coward, David Lean, and Anthony Havelock-Allan. Direction: Lean. Photography: Robert Krasker. Editing: Jack Harris. Music: Rachmaninov's Second Piano Concerto, played by Eileen Joyce. Art Direction: L. P. Williams. Players: Celia Johnson, Trevor Howard, Stanley Holloway, Joyce Carey, Cyril Raymond, Everley Gregg, Margaret Barton. Production: Cineguild. (86 mins.)

"If my content is a bit trivial perhaps I am a bit trivial, and I like trivialities," David Lean has said. His key film is *Brief Encounter*, redolent of the English suburbs and capturing a postwar monotony marked by ration cards and prim, provincial tea rooms. It is a story of an affair—aching and furtive—between two respectable married people: Laura Jesson (Celia Johnson), whose husband is well meaning but insensitive; and Alec Harvey (Trevor Howard), the doctor. The inspired choice of Rachmaninov's Second Piano Concerto raises moments of quite familiar emotion to unbearable heights. Laura's agony is kept within private bounds: there is no melodramatic rupture with her family. David leaves for Africa, and her life continues as before, with only memories to console and frustrate her. Lean is one of the most highly skilled technicians the British film industry has produced. Although his use of close-ups and angled shots recalls the work of the great expressionist directors, he assimilates them successfully into his basic narrative form. Noël Coward's dialogue is tart and rather quaint, although some of the satire still stabs playfully—the announcements of "forthcoming attractions" in the local cinema, the gossip in

1945: "Moments of quite familiar emotion" in BRIEF ENCOUNTER.

the station bar . . . It is a tribute to Celia Johnson's acting that, while *Brief Encounter* gathers charm like ivy with the years, her domestic upheaval continues to appal.

1945: Ray Milland imagines the room full of bats in **THE LOST WEEKEND.**

THE LOST WEEKEND. United States. Script: Charles Brackett and Billy Wilder, from the novel by Charles Jackson. Direction: Billy Wilder. Photography: John F. Seitz. Editing: Doane Harrison. Art Direction: Hans Dreier, Earl Hedrick. Music: Miklos Rozsa. Players: Ray Milland, Jane Wyman, Philip Terry, Howard Da Silva, Doris Dowling. Production: Paramount (Charles Brackett). (101 mins.)

Behind the snappy dialogue and the seemingly flippant expertise of Wilder's films, a moralist is striving to make himself heard. *The Lost Weekend* is a call to sobriety directed at all alcoholics. Don (Ray Milland) is an intellectual in his early thirties, a writer who lacks the fibre to finish his stories. At the start of the film, he is allegedly ten days dry and about to leave for a long weekend with his brother. But he is already hiding liquor in the flat, and a ten dollar bill left for the cleaning woman tempts him to buy a couple of bottles of rye and visit the local bar. So the time drifts by in maudlin conversations and memories of his meeting with Helen (Jane Wyman), now his fiancée. Desire grows into desperation: he steals a girl's handbag in order to pay for more whisky—and is caught. He cannot pawn his typewriter because the pawnbrokers are closed. Soon he is taken to the alcoholics' ward of a hospital, where a sadistic male nurse treats him like a criminal. Only when

suicide is imminent does his fiancée manage to shift his allegiance from the bottle. So persuasive is Ray Milland's playing that his appeals and recollections speak from *within* Don's character. He suggests perfectly the bitter attitude and the ingenuousness of the alcoholic. He cannot believe that one tiny drink will harm him. "It's like falling off a roof and expecting to fall just one floor," remarks his brother. *The Lost Weekend* never submits to sentimentality; Wilder's dark, expressionistic style sees to that as always.

Checklist of other important features

DEAD OF NIGHT. Britain. Directors: Alberto Cavalcanti, Basil Dearden, Robert Hamer, Charles Crichton. A genuinely unsettling group of supernatural stories, made by a team from Sir Michael Balcon's Ealing Studios.

THE LADIES OF THE BOIS DE BOULOGNE (Les Dames du Bois de Boulogne). France. Director: Robert Bresson. A grave, sombre tale of revenge in Paris, with Maria Casarès dispensing feline sarcasm that calls to mind Racine as she lures her ex-lover into marrying a whore. Bresson's style is already elliptical and dispassionate.

MEET ME IN ST. LOUIS. United States. Director: Vincente Minnelli. Regarded by musical fans as the greatest masterpiece in the genre, with Judy Garland as Esther Smith singing "The Trolley Song" and other numbers.

THE SPIRAL STAIRCASE. United States. Director: Robert Siodmak. One of the vintage RKO thrillers, with a reliable cast directed with stealth and an intermittent sense of domestic humour.

THE WAY TO THE STARS. Britain. Director: Anthony Asquith. The British and the Americans together in war at an airbase in the heart of England. Understated and convincingly acted by such players as Michael Redgrave, John Mills, Renee Asherson and Trevor Howard.

YOLANDA AND THE THIEF. United States. Vincente Minnelli and Fred Astaire combine their talents in a lively musical fantasy tinged with South American color and rhythm.

Short films and Documentaries

A DIARY FOR TIMOTHY. Britain. The last important film by Humphrey Jennings. Timothy is a newborn baby, who symbolizes a postwar future for the British people. A sensitive mosaic of impressions from a country still at war and not yet accustomed to the idea of peace.

1945: Facts of Interest

UPA, America's most egghead cartoon group, is founded by Stephen Bosustow.

The cinema is nationalized in Czechoslovakia, Poland, and Yugoslavia.

1946

MY DARLING CLEMENTINE. United States. Script: Samuel G. Engel, W. Miller, Sam Hellman, from a treatment by Stuart N. Lake. Direction: John Ford. Photography: Joe MacDonald. Editing: Dorothy Spencer. Music: Alfred Newman. Art Direction: James Basevi and Lyle Wheeler. Players: Henry Fonda, Linda Darnell, Victor Mature, Grant Withers, Walter Brennan, Tim Holt, Alan Mowbray. Production: Fox (Samuel G. Engel). (95 mins.)

Ford based this film on the "Battle of the O.K. Corral," which took place in 1880 in Tombstone, Arizona, between the Clanton gang of rustlers and the local Marshal, Wyatt Earp. But there is infinitely more to *My Darling Clementine* than the gun-fighting, good though this is. Henry Fonda as Wyatt Earp is the epitome of restraint; he has a laconic, beaten look; his eyes hold a hundred sorrows; he is a kind of deliverer, a chivalrous figure on horseback. The dusty little town yields characters and incidents typical of Ford's world, such as the band of wandering players led by Alan Mowbray as Hamlet, and the open air dance that has such lyricism that it provides one with a shared experience, an unrivalled simplicity of emotion. Between old Pa Clanton, cracking his whip with fury, and Earp, unruffled, cat-like in his walk, there stands Doc Holliday (Victor Mature), a figure neither black nor white—jealous, drunk, and ailing, but siding with the forces of good in the final battle. The excellent characterization of *My Darling Clementine* raises it to the level of the finest Westerns, and with this performance Fonda joins the screen's immortals.

SHOESHINE (Sciuscia). Italy. Script: Cesare Zavattini. Direction: Vittorio De Sica. Photography: Anchise Brizzi. Music: Alessandro Cicognini. Art Direction: Ivo Batteli, G. Lombardozzi. Players: Rinaldo Smordoni, Franco Interlenghi, Aniello Mele, Bruno Ortensi, Claudio Ermelli, Emilio Cigoli, Maria Campi. Production: Alfa Cinematografica (W. Tamburella). (90 mins.)

Very few directors—Donskoi, Vigo, Clément, Truffaut, Satyajit Ray perhaps—have contemplated the world of childhood quite so movingly as De Sica. In *The Children are Watching Us* (see *1943*), he and his scriptwriter treated the failure of a boy's parents to measure up to his illusions. In *Shoeshine*, the guilt lies with society as a whole. Pasquale and Giuseppe ape the very adults who have so clearly failed to communicate or sympathize with them. These puny adolescents are already as cynical and as sophisticated as the aftermath of war can make them. They are driven

1946: Henry Fonda as Wyatt Earp in MY DARLING CLEMENTINE.

1946: The delinquents in De Sica's SHOESHINE.

to petty crime and to black-market dealings, and thence into the hands of the authorities, who quarter them in a crowded prison, where competition for survival is even more intense. Pasquale and Giuseppe are separated; each betrays the other until in the end Giuseppe is killed. Yet as in all De Sica's films, some inner goodness emerges from the characters to transmute the images of squalor; a goodness warped by misunderstanding and desperation. For if *Shoeshine* may be interpreted as a documentary on poverty and juvenile delinquency, it is equally valid as a study of the human failings that lead to catastrophe—the means by which Giuseppe and Pasquale are turned against each other. The last shot shows the horse they have bought galloping away like their innocence, while Pasquale yields to the police and Giuseppe's body is recovered. It is symbolic, too, of the "poetic neo-realism" that divides De Sica from Rossellini and Visconti in the Italian cinema of the forties.

PAISA. Italy. Script: Sergio Amidei and Roberto Rossellini, from ideas by Klauss Mann, Alfred Hayes, Federico Fellini, Marcello Pagliero, and Roberto Rossellini. Direction: Rossellini. Photography: Otello

1946: PAISA: "in war, expectancy is always diminished and depressed by experience."

Martelli. Editing: Eraldo Da Roma. Music: Renzo Rossellini. Players: Carmela Sazio, Robert Vanloon, Dots M. Johnson, Alfonsini, Maria Michi, Gar Moore, Harriet White, Renzo Avanzo, Bill Tubbs, Dale Edmunds, Cogolani. Production: O.F.I. and F.E.P. (115 mins.)

This is the second of Rossellini's two great films about World War II and its impact on Italian life. It is compounded of documentary footage and fictional interludes. These two extremes of realism sustain the film and have their psychological parallel in each of the six stories told by Rossellini. The Americans liberate Sicily and then gradually move north through the mainland of Italy. The six stories represent stages in this organized chaos. The fleeting encounters stress the failure, or rather the inability, of so many people to adapt to new conditions and codes of conduct. The endless clash of languages sets up a barrier between the U.S. troops and the Italians they meet. G.I. Joe from Jersey is shot by the Germans in an old Sicilian castle as he tries to convince a local girl that he is her friend. A Negro M.P. runs berserk in a puppet theatre in Naples and is helped by a destitute child. In Rome, there is the tired, drunken G.I. who fails to recognize—even in bed—the girl who had charmed him on his arrival in the city a few months before. Harriet, an American nurse, searches frantically for her Italian lover among the partisans of Florence. Three smug U.S. chaplains are accommodated at a monastery and are puzzled by the serene and frugal behavior of the Franciscan monks. Finally, in the marshes of the Po, some partisans fighting alongside the OSS are captured by the Nazis and drowned at dawn. Out of these chastening episodes comes a protest against war, not merely against the physical destruction but also against the spirit-

ual anguish it causes. It is a protest made more harrowing and truthful by Rossellini's refusal to glamorize the campaign and by his continually emphasizing that, in war, expectancy is always diminished and depressed by experience.

THE BIG SLEEP. United States. Script: William Faulkner, Leigh Brackett, Jules Furthman, from the novel by Raymond Chandler. Direction: Howard Hawks. Photography: Sidney Hickox. Editing: Christian Nyby. Music: Max Steiner. Art Direction: Carl Jules Weyl. Players: Humphrey Bogart, Lauren Bacall, John Ridgely, Martha Vickers, Dorothy Malone, Peggy Knudsen, Elisha Cook Jr. Production: Warner Brothers (Howard Hawks). (114 mins.)

If one had to select a representative of the dozens of thrillers produced by Hollywood during the forties, one would turn instinctively to *The Big Sleep,* just as one would probably choose Raymond Chandler, its author, as the most characteristic crime writer of his generation. "All we were trying to do was to make every scene entertain," recalls Howard Hawks, and one has to admit that *The Big Sleep* is one of the most intricate fantasies Chandler ever wrote, with a mysterious summons to Sternwood House embroiling private eye Philip Marlowe (Humphrey Bogart) in one murder after another. The film is content to ripple along from climax to climax, letting Bogart and Lauren Bacall exchange their disenchanted repartee while the villains are gradually killed off. Despite its attenuated plot and its heavy bouts of dialogue, the film still gives an impression of tight, economical story-telling. All the familiar forties trademarks are there: a Max Steiner score that drowns even a thunderstorm as Marlowe tracks his man to a dingy house by night; the wide-shouldered girls (Dorothy Malone and Martha Vickers); and the sudden, chilling murders that catch almost everyone by surprise. *The Big Sleep* is professional movie-making at its best and at its most entertaining.

THE DIARY OF A CHAMBERMAID. United States. Script: Jean Renoir and Burgess Meredith, from the novel by Octave Mirbeau, and the play by André Heuse, André de Lorde, Thielly Nores. Direction: Renoir. Photography: Lucien Andriot. Editing: James Smith. Music: Michel Michelet. Art Direction: Eugene Lourié. Players: Paulette Goddard, Burgess Meredith, Hurd Hatfield, Reginald Owen, Francis Lederer, Judith Anderson, Florence Bates, Irène Ryan. Production: Camden Productions for United Artists. (86 mins.)

Renoir's talent prospered better in Hollywood than almost any European *émigré's* during the forties. *This Land is Mine* and *The Southerner* (1943 and 1945 respectively) have many admirers, and *The Diary of*

1946: Humphrey Bogart as Philip Marlowe in THE BIG SLEEP.

1946: From Renoir's most successful Hollywood film, THE DIARY OF A CHAMBERMAID.

a *Chambermaid,* though dismissed at the time, gathers strength and vitality over the years. It is based, like Buñuel's film of the same name (see *1964*), on a turn of the century novel by Octave Mirbeau, about a French provincial family and the arrival in its midst of a new housemaid, Célestine (Paulette Goddard), whose innocence is assailed by the corruption above and below stairs. The texture of the film is an unnerving blend of flippancy and menace. There is Burgess Meredith as the preposterous captain next door who eats flowers and lusts merrily after Célestine. And there is Francis Lederer as Joseph the coachman-cum-butler who kills a goose sadistically with a steel needle and tries to escape the crowd at a carnival by slashing right and left with his whip. Meanwhile, Hurd Hatfield as the consumptive son of the house broods in his room and conceives a gentle love for Célestine. The acting and the costumes embrace many styles and pitches of intensity, but somehow one grants them licence in the weird ménage,

which never for a moment pretends to be realistic. (This is the only film Renoir has shot entirely in a studio).

Checklist of other important features

BATAILLE DU RAIL. France. A famous reconstruction, as coarse and as truthful as a newsreel, of the French underground resistance on the railways during World War II.

BEAUTY AND THE BEAST (La Belle et la Bête). France. Jean Cocteau's enchanting symbolist tale, with Josette Day as the princess and Jean Marais as the Bête playing with dignity and simple, infectious faith in the fairy story.

THE BEST YEARS OF OUR LIVES. United States. Director: William Wyler. Hollywood's long, hard, but occasionally poignant picture of postwar ills, as three soldiers return home and find themselves ill at ease in civilian life. With Myrna Loy, Fredric March, Dana Andrews etc.

IVAN THE TERRIBLE—The Boyars' Plot (Ivan Grozny). U.S.S.R. Director: Sergei M. Eisenstein. The sequel to part one, even slower and more sumptuous, with a finale in color that does justice to Eisenstein's theories on panchromatic cinema and contains some of Prokofiev's most enervating music. (Not released until September 1958.)

THE KILLERS. United States. Director: Robert Siodmak. The shadowy tension of the opening minutes, with two killers putting paid to Swede Lunn, derives from Hemingway's short story, and this raw-nerved quality is lost in the profusion of flashbacks that follow the murder. Stars Burt Lancaster.

MARIA CANDELARIA. Mexico. Director: Emilio Fernandez. Dolores del Rio and Pedro Armendariz as Indian lovers in a doom-laden village; one of the rare Mexican films of note.

THE MURDERERS ARE AMONG US (Die Mörder sind unter uns). East Germany. Director: Wolf-gang Staudte. The first postwar film from Germany, which placed its sympathies squarely behind the miserable Berlin doctor who, out of a mixture of hatred and guilt, tries to kill his former Nazi C.O.

NOTORIOUS. United States. Director: Alfred Hitchcock. Cary Grant and Ingrid Bergman tracking down Nazi criminals in Brazil. Implausible, infuriating, but gripping and seductive in Hitchcock's inimitable manner.

Short films and Documentaries

NAISSANCE DU CINÉMA. France. Director: Roger Leenhardt. An intelligent and affectionate documentary on the pre-history and "archaeology" of the cinema.

1946: Facts of Interest

Death of W. C. Fields, and William S. Hart.
The first film festival is held at Cannes, in France.

1947

ODD MAN OUT. Britain. Script: F. L. Green and R. C. Sherriff, from Green's novel. Direction: Carol Reed. Photography: Robert Krasker. Editing: Fergus McDonell. Music: William Alwyn. Art Direction: Ralph Brinton. Players: James Mason, Kathleen Ryan, Robert Beatty, Robert Newton, W. G. Fay, Fay Compton, F. J. McCormick. Production: Two Cities. (115 mins.)

The combination of James Mason's acting and Carol Reed's inspired technique makes *Odd Man Out* one of the very few masterpieces of the English cinema. It unfolds its story with the sharp, angry pace of a.thriller, but still allows time for reflections on life and art. Johnny McQueen (James Mason) is a political leader who has escaped from prison in Belfast and resolves to rob a mill to muster some funds for his organization. But at the crucial moment of the raid he suffers an attack of dizziness and—badly wounded—has to stagger away on his own, the "odd man out." This doomed flight, as Johnny is sought by his friends and hunted by the police as well as by his enemies, is analyzed in detail by Reed. Shell, an informer, follows Johnny like a conscience until his death at last in the snow, with the ship that he hoped to board sailing away beyond the railings of the harbor. *Odd Man Out* has almost an embarrassment of fine sequences—Fay Compton as the London woman befriending Johnny and slowly discovering his predicament, or the scene in the bar where Lukey (Robert Newton) recognizes Shell, his *bête noire,* just as Johnny's cry of anguish from an inner room transfixes the gathering. If film directing can best be described as a craft, then Carol Reed is unquestionably a master craftsman.

DUEL IN THE SUN. United States. Script: David O. Selznick, suggested by a novel by Niven Busch. Direction: King Vidor. Photography: Lee Garmes, Hal Rosson, Ray Rennahan (Technicolor). Editing: William Ziegler, John D. Faure. Music: Dimitri Tiomkin. Art Direction: James Basevi. Players: Joseph Cotten, Gregory Peck, Jennifer Jones, Lionel Barrymore, Herbert Marshall, Lillian Gish, Walter Huston, Charles Bickford, Harry Carey. Production: David O. Selznick. (135 mins.)

Although King Vidor is credited with the direction of *Duel in the Sun,* the monster Western of the forties, there is no doubt that William Dieterle and Josef von Sternberg were also engaged on the film, and David O. Selznick is even thought to have managed certain sequences himself. *Duel in the Sun,* which cost approximately $7 million, is the apogee of Hollywood melodrama, attended by the most lavish production values. At times it is so portentous as to verge on a parody of the traditional Western; at other moments it scales intoxicating heights of emotion, carefully constructed to attract a vast audience. Visually magnificent, morally disreputable, it tells the story of half-breed Pearl Chavez—"a wildflower, sprung from the hard clay, quick to blossom and early to die." She has been brought up on the McCanles ranch with two brothers, Lewt and Jessie, who soon quarrel for her affections. The struggle between the brothers is only the prelude to the film's greatest climax: the

1947: *James Mason as the hunted leader in* ODD MAN OUT.

DUEL IN THE SUN. Gregory Peck and Jennifer Jones.

LE DIABLE AU CORPS. France. Director: Claude Autant-Lara. One of the few completely successful films by a director whose career began in the early twenties. Gérard Philipe is the young student who falls ardently in love with a soldier's wife (Micheline Presle) in the France of 1917.

MACBETH. United States. Director: Orson Welles. A cheaply-made, sometimes hollow version of Shakespeare's tragedy, but rewarding for Welles's habitual use of trick perspectives, hideous caverns, and abstract forms to create impact (the castle, for instance).

MONSIEUR VERDOUX. United States. Chaplin's bittersweet satire on the Bluebeard theme, with Charlie reduced to a murderer in order to maintain his family and his status in an inimical society.

PURSUED. United States. Director: Raoul Walsh. A story of revenge and rivalry between two families that is dominated by a young Robert Mitchum and by Walsh's command of violence in a pastoral landscape. An unusual, intelligent Western.

QUAI DES ORFEVRES. France. Director: Henri-Georges Clouzot. A detective thriller lifted out of the rut by its director's uncanny feeling for the atmosphere of the Parisian music-hall and by Louis Jouvet's first-class performance.

Short films and Documentaries

L'ÉCOLE DES FACTEURS. France. A brief and effective comedy by Jacques Tati, a kind of preliminary sketch for *Jour de Fête* (see *1949*).

FIDDLE-DE-DEE. Canada. Director: Norman McLaren. Violin music on the soundtrack is followed by a flow of colors on the screen. McLaren paints whole sections of film, several feet at a time.

RHYTHM OF A CITY. Sweden. Director: Arne Sucksdorff. A distinguished dawn-to-dusk portrait of Stockholm and its inhabitants.

1947: Facts of Interest

Death of Ernst Lubitsch, the comedy director.
The Actors' Studio is formed in New York. This has influenced a generation of Hollywood stars, among them Marlon. Brando, Joanne Woodward, Paul Newman, and James Dean.

agonizing, attenuated encounter on Squaw's Head Rock, when Pearl shoots Lewt and dies herself in his arms. Closely entwined with the love-hate relationship is the extension of the railroad across the Texas of the eighties, resisted by old McCanles at the point of a gun. But *Duel in the Sun* is too grotesque to be analyzed seriously. It is a stranded whale of a film, strangely unmoving and unfunny, signifying the end of Hollywood's great era and the start of a period when tastelessness excelled wit and economical direction was to be regarded as a sin.

Checklist of other important features

BRUTE FORCE. United States. Director: Jules Dassin. This vivid indictment of American prison life shows how a sadistic guard (Hume Cronyn) rouses the men (Burt Lancaster and others) against the warden. Within its self-imposed limits the characterization is unusually acute.

CROSSFIRE. United States. Director: Edward Dmytryk. A brutal and timely attack on anti-Semitism and, perhaps even more strongly, on wartime conditions, as a group of G.I.s (with Robert Ryan as the sergeant) needle an inoffensive civilian to death.

1948

THE BICYCLE THIEF (Ladri di Biciclette). Italy. Script: Cesare Zavattini, from a story by Luigi Batolini. Direction: Vittorio De Sica. Photography: Carlo Montuori. Music: Alessandro Cicognini. Players: Lamberto Maggiorani, Enzo Staiola, Lianella Carell, Gino Saltamerenda, Vittorio Antonucci. Production: PDS (ENIC) Umberto Scarpelli. (90 mins.)

De Sica's film has figured prominently in every critics' pool for "The Best Film of all Time," and it won an Oscar in 1949. Certainly it is regarded as the supreme achievement of neo-realism in the Italian cinema. Its story is simple, almost banal. Antonio is hopelessly poor. One morning the labor bureau offers him a job as a bill-sticker—if he has a bike. His wife pawns their sheets to retrieve Antonio's machine, and he starts his rounds. But no sooner has he paused to fix his first poster than a thief rides away with his bicycle. So Antonio spends all Sunday searching for his vital tool, his means of survival in an unscrupulous city. He tramps through the markets, the churches, even the brothels. And when at length he decides in despair to snatch a bicycle from outside a football stadium, he is seen and caught—and humiliated. De Sica watches him shuffle away disconsolately into the distance hand in hand with his small son, Bruno, who has in that moment of shame realized a new intimacy with his father. He can now share Antonio's grief, even if he cannot improve the situation, and to this extent the film ends on an optimistic note. "In Italy men often go out with their sons," says De Sica. "Children converse and argue with their father, become confidants, and very often become no longer children, but little men." Bruno is the key personality in *The Bicycle Thief*. Rome is seen through his eyes. Every shot not only describes the urban environment but also communicates the emotional pressures at work on Antonio and his son. De Sica's direct and unadorned approach to cinema is at its best here. The film is compassionate where it could be cynical; severe where it could be complaisant; sombre where it could be picturesque. Only one pro-

1948: Just before the robbery. THE BICYCLE THIEF.

fessional actor appears, in a minor role. Antonio was played by a metal worker who was unemployed a few weeks after the film was completed . . .

TREASURE OF SIERRA MADRE. United States. Script: John Huston from the novel by Bernard Traven. Direction: Huston. Photography: Ted McCord. Editing: Owen Marks. Music: Max Steiner. Art Direction: John Hughes. Players: Humphrey Bogart, Walter Huston, Tim Holt, Bruce Bennett, Barton MacLane, Alfonso Bedoya. Production: Warner Brothers (Henry Blanke). (126 mins.)

John Huston's film, which won three Oscars, confounded the fears of those in the cinema trade who felt that a picture without any women would be a disastrous failure. It is enlivened by Huston's rich sense of irony, and by his observation of men forced

1948: *Three men "on their uppers in Tampico, Mexico"—TREASURE OF SIERRA MADRE.*

1947: *The climax in the hall of mirrors.* **THE LADY FROM SHANGHAI.**

through circumstance and greed to live together (one thinks of other ill-assorted groups in his work, in *The Maltese Falcon,* or *Moby Dick*). Three men are on their uppers in Tampico, Mexico. Dobbs (Humphrey Bogart) is a captious beachcomber who begs openly from visiting Americans; Howard (Walter Huston) is a prospector belonging to an older generation, and his garrulous enthusiasm and talk of gold fire Dobbs and the young Curtin (Tim Holt). But when they reach the mountains, the pressures of loneliness and privation work inexorably on the men. The discovery of gold in a disused mine brings out the worst in Dobbs, who abandons Howard and then double-crosses Curtin. Huston watches this development with a derisive camera ("It's impersonal—it just looks on and lets them stew in their own juice," he says) and the final fiasco, as Dobbs is murdered for his shoes by some bandits who care nothing for the gold, gives the film a determinist humor rarely found in adventure stories of this kind. *Treasure of Sierra Madre* was indeed advertised as a Western, but the characterization is a good deal more intense than that, and one has to look back to *Greed* (see *1924*) to find a film laying comparable emphasis on the disintegration of people faced with unexpected wealth.

THE LADY FROM SHANGHAI. United States. Script: Orson Welles, from the novel by Sherwood King. Direction: Welles. Photography: Charles Lawton, Jr. Editing: Viola Lawrence. Music: Heinz Roemheld. Art Direction: Sturges Carne and Stephen Goosson. Players: Orson Welles, Rita Hayworth, Everett Sloane, Glenn Anders, Ted de Corsia, Gus Schilling, Erskine Sanford. Production: Columbia. (86 mins.)

Hunger and guilt are the two instincts which dominate not merely *The Lady from Shanghai* but also the other films of Orson Welles: a desperate craving for power on the one hand, and a resultant guilt complex on the other. Elsa Bannister (Rita Hayworth) and her crippled husband are vicious creatures who do not hesitate to exploit the naïve and hapless qualities of Michael O'Hara (the itinerant Irishman played by Welles himself). A leisurely yachting cruise leads to a preposterous murder design and a climax in an empty "Luna Park" where O'Hara, Elsa, and Bannister settle their accounts.

With this film, Welles shattered the myth of the good-hearted heroine in American cinema. Rita Hayworth (Welles's second wife) had become enshrined in *Gilda* two years previously. In *The Lady from Shanghai* Welles undermines her glamor, leaving her to die in the Magic Mirror maze instead of in the arms of the hero. Paradoxically, this is also Welles's wittiest film. O'Hara's mischievous Irish blarney lightens the tone, and the courtroom scene is rich in badinage and visual humor too.

Checklist of other important features

THE FALLEN IDOL. Britain. Director: Carol Reed. Ralph Richardson is magnificent as the timid embassy butler involved with a typist behind his wife's back and watched with adulation by the little boy in his charge.

KEY LARGO. United States. Director: John Huston. Humphrey Bogart as a disillusioned war veteran, and Edward G. Robinson as an ex-bootlegger on an offshore island after the war. Considerable tension, fine acting, but rather long-winded and theatrical in its bouts of talk.

LOUISIANA STORY. United States. Robert Flaherty's last film, sponsored by Standard Oil and emerging as a lyrical paean to nature and to human guile as represented in traditional terms by the Cajun boy in his boat and in modern scientific terms by the men who drill for oil in the Louisiana bayous.

THE NAKED CITY. United States. Director: Jules Dassin. A blonde is murdered in New York; the police investigation begins. This film records every move and every character with a degree of realism new to Hollywood in the late forties.

THE PIRATE. United States. Gene Kelly—posing as "the pirate"—and Judy Garland joust amorously with each other in the Caribbean. Vincente Minnelli's finest musical since *Meet Me in St. Louis.*

RED RIVER. United States. Director: Howard Hawks. Montgomery Clift and John Wayne as friends and rivals along the Chisholm Trail. A spirited Western, and a study of the deeper meanings of companionship.

LA TERRA TREMA. Italy. Luchino Visconti's renowned semi-documentary (dialogue in untranslated dialect) on injustice in a Sicilian fishing community. Flawed by its self-conscious, "arty" photography and its theatrical compositions.

UNFAITHFULLY YOURS. United States. Rex Harrison as the conductor who is beguiled into suspecting his wife's fidelity. Arguably the last instance of Preston Sturges's polished and economic humor.

THE WINSLOW BOY. Britain. Anthony Asquith's movie is concerned essentially with English spirit in the face of humiliation, and boasts a fine performance by Robert Donat as the thin-lipped, sarcastic, and rather vulnerable barrister. Based on the Archer-Shee case of a boy expelled from Royal Naval College for stealing a postal order.

Short films and Documentaries

VAN GOGH. France. Alain Resnais's "art films" are already classics of their kind. This one was awarded an Oscar in 1949 and reveals the brilliant montage which so characterizes all Resnais's work. It also conveys the creative continuity of Van Gogh the painter.

A DIVIDED WORLD (En kluven värld). Sweden. Director: Arne Sucksdorff. A jewel of a film about nature and its inexorable laws, conjured up out of a Swedish winter night and its shadows.

1948: Facts of Interest

Death of D. W. Griffith, Sergei M. Eisenstein, and Louis Lumière.

The Marx Brothers make their last film together, *Love Happy*.

The cinema is nationalized in Bulgaria, Hungary, and Rumania.

1949

THE THIRD MAN. Britain. Script: Graham Greene. Direction: Carol Reed. Photography: Robert Krasker. Editing: Oswald Hafenrichter. Music: Anton Karas. Art Direction: Vincent Korda. Players: Joseph Cotten, Orson Welles, Trevor Howard, Bernard Lee, Wilfrid Hyde White. Production: Carol Reed/London Films (Alexander Korda). (93 mins.)

If one thinks of levity as being the British cinema's abiding sin, then one will always be irritated by the films of Carol Reed. But *The Third Man* (like *Odd Man Out* (see *1947*) has more positive virtues than that. It is the highpoint of the British entertainment film between 1946 and 1958. Its picture of Vienna, conceived by Korda and given panache by the screenplay of Graham Greene, still looks valid, as Martins, a hack American novelist, tries to make sense of the inscrutable patterns of intrigue for which Harry Lime, his friend and a drug trafficker, is responsible. Not surprisingly, the moral lessons of *The Third Man* tend to be obscured by the accumulation of incidents and sinister characters. The clichés of melodrama abound, but the total spell continues to fascinate, a spell worked partly by the crystalline photography of Robert Krasker and the tantalizing, regretful zither music of Anton Karas. Orson Welles enjoys himself hugely as Lime, the smile slithering off his chalky face as a threat appears behind each suave comment. Reed's technical brilliance illuminates the climax in the city sewers: it becomes a mesmeric syncopation of wriggling shadows, churning water, and galloping footsteps, as the search for Lime gathers momentum. Alida Valli, playing the Czech actress in love with Lime, contributes a bitter sort of glamor that blends well with Joseph Cotten's wry, persistent performance as Martins. It is Welles, however, who most people will remember. He wrote his own part, and no other scene has quite the same bland menace as his conversation with Martins at the fairground, when he tries to justify his sale of human lives.

KIND HEARTS AND CORONETS. Britain. Script: John Dighton and Robert Hamer. Direction: Robert Hamer. Photography: Douglas Slocombe. Editing: Peter Tanner. Music: Mozart's "Don Giovanni." Art Direction: William Kellner. Players: Alec Guinness, Dennis Price, Joan Greenwood, Valerie Hobson, Audrey Fildes, Miles Malleson. Production: Ealing Studios. (106 mins.)

It was one of the tragedies of the British cinema when the BBC bought Ealing Studios in 1955 for just under a million dollars, for during the previous decade, under the guidance of Sir Michael Balcon, directors there such as Alexander Mackendrick, Henry Cornelius, and Charles Crichton were able to produce a series of caricatures of English life that remain among the funniest comedies on film. *Kind Hearts and Coronets* is the classic of this era, by virtue of its biting dialogue, its original theme, and superbly inventive incidents, and sterling performances from Dennis Price and Alec Guinness, which epitomize the English flair for understatement. The story is diabolical in its twists and turns. Louis Mazzini (Dennis Price) had for his mother a daughter of the Duke of Chalfont and for his father a disreputable Italian singer. When the family refuses to allow him to bury his mother in the ancestral vault, Mazzini sets out in revenge to eliminate the eight heirs who bar his way to the Dukedom. Alec Guinness interprets each relative with glee. His repertoire includes a suffragette who uses a balloon to attract publicity for her campaign, and is shot down by Mazzini; and a young buck who makes love in a punt beneath the sly shade of a lace umbrella (Mazzini sets the craft adrift and it vanishes with its occupants over a weir).

SHE WORE A YELLOW RIBBON. United States. Script: Laurence Stallings and Frank S. Nugent, from a story by James Warner Bellah. Direction: John Ford. Photography: Winton C. Hoch (Technicolor). Editing: Jack Murray. Music: Richard Hageman, Art Direction: James Basevi, Joe Kish. Players: John Wayne, Joanne Dru, John Agar, Ben Johnson, Harry

1949: The famous long last shot from THE THIRD MAN.

Carey Jr., Victor McLaglen, Mildred Natwick, George O'Brien. Production: Argosy Pictures (John Ford and Merian C. Cooper). (103 mins.)

The exploits of the United States cavalry have attracted Ford in many films (*Fort Apache, The Horse Soldiers, Sergeant Rutledge*). Nathan Brittles, the hero of *She Wore a Yellow Ribbon*, is a captain in the 7th Cavalry, only six days away from retirement when news arrives of Custer's death. Now he must try at all costs to prevent total war with the Indian tribes. He agrees with Chief "Pony that Walks" that they are too old for war. "But old men should stop war," he says, on behalf, one feels, of Ford himself, who has always lamented the clash between Yankee and Indian (cf. *Cheyenne Autumn*, 1964). Indeed

Brittles's farewell to the Chief is almost as moving as his last inspection of C Troop. The cavalry are compelled to charge through the Indian war camp by night because otherwise they would be overwhelmed the next day. They are dragged by duty to this hostile environment in the Southwest, but Ford shows that man is still exalted above the frowning outcrops of rock; that he is still capable of heroism, ambitions (Brittles dreams of pushing west in his retirement), and courtly love. Ford's beliefs were already old-fashioned when he made this film: he prefers justice and cameraderie to sex and degenerate behavior. As usual in his Westerns, scenes of dynamic action are punctuated with moments of amusement and sentimental reflection. Victor McLaglen offers an irrepressible portrait of the bibulous sergeant who

170

can fell seven men at a time, and the film is among the most handsome of Ford's productions, its warm colors recalling Frederick Remington's paintings of the west.

ON THE TOWN. United States. Script. Adolph Green and Betty Comden. Direction: Gene Kelly and Stanley Donen. Photography: Harold Rosson (Technicolor). Editing: Ralph E. Winters. Music: Leonard Bernstein and Roger Edens. Art Direction: Cedric Gibbons, Jack Martin Smith. Players: Gene Kelly, Frank Sinatra, Jules Munshin, Vera-Ellen, Ann Miller, Betty Garrett. Production: M-G-M (98 mins.)

With this exciting musical, Stanley Donen and Gene Kelly join Vincente Minnelli as masters of the song-and-dance film. *On the Town* uses real locations in New York as it follows three sailors during their twenty-four hours' leave in the big city. And despite this natural setting, scenes of fantasy are slipped effortlessly into the narrative—Vera-Ellen's exuberant athletics number, or the spotlit yearning by Kelly for his lost love near the end of the picture. One senses a new fluency—and a new wit—in the genre. Everyone seems to enjoy himself, even Alice Pearce as the unwanted, sniffling girlfriend. The girls have that rosy-cheeked glamor that makes forties' color look rather garish now, and it's perhaps inevitable that the musical film *par excellence* should be constructed and staged along circus lines, playing for the big climactic applause. Among the best songs are "Prehistoric Joe" (tap-dancing by Ann Miller), "Main Street," and "We're Going on the Town."

Checklist of other important features

LES AMANTS DE VÉRONE. France. Director: André Cayatte. A brave and passionate attempt to place the story of Romeo and Juliet in a modern setting, distinguished by the elegance of the décors and by the high level of acting (by Pierre Brasseur in particular).

CHAMPION. United States. Director: Mark Robson. Brash, sardonic look at big-time boxing, that shows the shabbiness and the corruption and the second-hand glamor that tempt an ingenuous champion like Kirk Douglas.

JOUR DE FETE. France. Jacques Tati arrives on the international screen, and his bumbling, subtly timed antics as the country postman establish him as one of the great film comedians of the postwar years.

MANON. France. Henri-Georges Clouzot's modern but somewhat academic version of "Manon Lescaut", using the last war and the shipment of Jewish refugees

to Palestine as its background, while the young lovers betray each other with their lack of moral courage.

ONLY A MOTHER (Bara en mor). Sweden. Director: Alf Sjöberg. One of the few Swedish films to tackle a social problem—the aimless, gypsy life of the

1949: A moment of solemnity in SHE WORE A YELLOW RIBBON

cotters in rural Sweden—*Only a Mother* has an outstanding portrayal by Eva Dahlbeck of the woman who cannot escape her lot.

PRISON (Fängelse). Sweden. Ingmar Bergman's first significant film, strongly aware of Strindberg in its depiction of the couple locked in squalor, self-pity, and quarreling.

LE SILENCE DE LA MER. France. Director: Jean-Pierre Melville. The forerunner of the French new wave of the late fifties. A quiet, haunting film about love during the French occupation, based on the short story by Vercors.

THEY LIVE BY NIGHT. United States. A promising début for Nicholas Ray. A sad, inexorable story of gangsters and the youth among them who tries to lead a fresh life with his girl.

TIGHT LITTLE ISLAND (Whisky Galore). Britain. Director: Alexander Mackendrick. 1943: a ship carrying 50,000 cases of whisky is wrecked off a thirsty Scottish isle. One of the most memorable of Ealing comedies, based on a novel by Compton Mackenzie, and shot entirely on the island of Barra in the Hebrides.

THE SET-UP. United States. Director: Robert Wise. An even better film about boxing than *Champion*. Robert Ryan as the ageing pugilist who runs foul of his local syndicate.

Short films and Documentaries

LE SANG DES BETES. France. Director: Georges Franju. A masterpiece among short films. It visits the abattoirs of Paris, where animals are slaughtered with a casual but ruthless efficiency. This is no mere undisciplined plea against cruelty to beasts; it is more a consistent statement of Franju's view that beauty and cruelty are never far apart.

1949: Facts of Interest

Death of Gregg Toland, the most gifted cinematographer of the period.

1950

SUNSET BOULEVARD. United States. Script: Charles Brackett, Billy Wilder, and D. M. Marshman Jr. Direction: Wilder. Photography: John F. Seitz. Editing: Doane Harrison and Arthur Schmidt. Music: Franz Waxman. Art Direction: Hans Dreier and John Meehan. Players: William Holden, Gloria Swanson, Erich von Stroheim, Nancy Olson, Fred Clark, Lloyd Gough, Jack Webb. Production: Paramount (Charles Brackett). (111 mins.)

Billy Wilder has delighted in dissecting certain portions of American life, and *Sunset Boulevard* is

1950: Gloria Swanson with Erich von Stroheim in SUNSET BOULEVARD.

173

his masterpiece. It probes right to the heartlessness of the Hollywood film industry, and ends with a dead writer floating at dawn in a private swimming pool. Joe Gillis (William Holden) is a struggling scriptwriter who becomes involved with Norma Desmond (Gloria Swanson), a star of the silent cinema. She lives in a vast mansion, her needs ministered by a statuesque butler (Erich von Stroheim) who is in fact her mentor, the director of her glorious youth. She refuses to acknowledge her loss of fame and beauty, and forces Gillis to write her the role of Salomé. The project is a disaster, and Norma Desmond rounds viciously on this lover who has shattered her dreams. Holden narrates the story in a beautifully laconic tone, and the intervening dialogue coruscates with repartee. Gloria Swanson delivers the line, "I *am* big, it's the pictures that got small," with an unforgettable blend of pride and scorn. Her mansion, with its bed in the shape of a gondola, and its stern barriers against the outside world, recalls Xanadu; and the luxury, combined with a fatal absence of responsibility, seduces Joe. Wilder's satirical approach gives way long before the end, so that, after so many years, the film assumes a curious, nagging intensity. It is as if Wilder were giving an ironic salute to the era of Norma Desmond as it fades irrevocably into the past.

RASHOMON. Japan. Script: Shinobu Hashimoto and Akira Kurosawa, from two stories by Ryunosuke Akutagawa. Direction: Kurosawa. Photography: Kazuo Miyagawa. Music: Fumio Hayasaka. Art Direction: So Matsuyama. Players: Toshiro Mifune, Masayuki Mori, Takashi Shimura, Machiko Kyo, Minoru Chiaki. Production: Daiei (Jingo Minoru/Masaichi Nagata). (88 mins.)

Though it is not Kurosawa's greatest film, *Rashomon* is superbly made and marks a significant stage in cinema appreciation. It won the Golden Lion at

1950: Toshiro Mifune as the bandit in RASHOMON.

Venice in 1951, and virtually introduced the Japanese cinema to the West. Kurosawa's approach is more Occidental than Ozu's or Mizoguchi's; for him, action rather than contemplation reveals the soul. His ubiquitous hero, Toshiro Mifune, plays here a bandit charged with raping a young woman and killing her husband in the forest. But there are four versions of the incident, told by a woodcutter who happened to be passing through the forest, by the injured girl herself, by her dead husband (speaking through a medium), and of course by the bandit. Kurosawa thus resorts to the prism as a means of reflecting the truth; each story yields a facet of reality but is distorted to a dubious degree.

Kurosawa's achievement depends on his analysis of human weakness. The forest is like a Garden of Eden, spoilt only by a man's transgressions. The elaborate sword fights between the bandit and the nobleman illustrate the various levels of fear and cowardice on which the film dwells. Each person in *Rashomon* is afraid of being humiliated. The most honest among them, the bandit, behaves the most unrestrainedly; and the most deceptive, the woman, behaves the most selfishly. Even the questioner, a commoner, acts uncharitably at the end, stealing the clothes of a baby he has found. The film closes as it begins, in a rain storm by the Kyoto Gate, and the woodcutter shuffles off with the baby, taking it home in an effort either to expiate his own guilt or to prove his humanity to the priest and the commoner who have sheltered with him. Despite its obsession with crime and guilt, *Rashomon* is a magnanimous film. Kurosawa's characters writhe and bend like puppets manipulated by fate, often unable to distinguish reality from illusion, truth from falsehood, and love from hate. But they *live* intensely, and their failings are universal.

THE YOUNG AND THE DAMNED (Los Olvidados). Mexico. Script: Luis Buñuel and Luis Alcoriza. Direction: Buñuel. Photography: Gabriel Figueroa. Editing: Carlos Savage. Music: Rodolfo Halffter, on themes by Gustova Pitaluga. Art Direction: Edward Fitzgerald. Players: Estela Inda, Miguel Inclán, Alfonso Mejía, Roberto Cobo, Hector López Portillo, Salvador Quiros. Production: Ultramar Films (Oscar Dancigers). (88 mins.)

Suddenly, after nearly twenty years in obscurity, Buñuel surfaces with a remarkable film in Mexico. *The Young and the Damned* is based on police records of juvenile delinquency, and has the same kind of innocuous prologue as *L'Age d'Or* (see *1930*). But no goodness endures to shine through the squalor, as it does in that superficially similar film, *Shoeshine* (see *1946*). Buñuel hitches his incidents to no optimistic, no rational, narrative form: where most directors cling to a moral outlook on life, he searches for the

1950: "The gregarious slums"—THE YOUNG AND THE DAMNED.

immoral and the surreal. Jaibo and Pedro are just two of the boys who eke out their existence in the gregarious slums of Mexico City, where the shabby Coca-Cola signs and the rutted roads betoken a misery dictated partly by climate, partly by conditions of labor.

"Only donkeys work," sneers Jaibo, who belongs to a generation that despises its elders' superstitions, without being able quite to escape their shadow. He kills ruthlessly and thoughtlessly. Like a pariah dog, he taints the whole community, and leads Pedro, younger and less depraved, astray from his mother and from an enlightened welfare officer. At the end Buñuel shows Pedro's dead body being dumped on a garbage tip by neighbors who are afraid even to tell the police of his murder, in case the universal guilt that hangs over the area should attach to them. The unmitigated cruelty of these final images is like a scream of protest. There is not one jot of sentimentality in *The Young and the Damned*. Nor is there any cynicism. There is just the bleak vision of a man convinced that life is hell on earth and that all men, consequently, are corrupt.

WAGONMASTER. United States. Script: Frank S. Nugent, Patrick Roper Ford. Direction: John Ford.

1950: WAGONMASTER—"enormous vistas and perspectives."

Photography: Bert Glennon, Archie Stout. Editing: Jack Murray. Music: Richard Hageman. Art Direction: James Basevi, Joe Kish. Players: Ben Johnson, Harry Carey Jr., Joanne Dru, Ward Bond, Charles Kemper, Alan Mowbray, Jane Darwell, Ruth Clifford. Production: Argosy Pictures / RKO (John Ford, Merian C. Cooper). (86 mins.)

John Ford's favorite place for filming has been Monument Valley, and in *Wagonmaster,* not his finest Western but still a lyrical achievement, he uses this location to accommodate enormous vistas and perspectives within the screen. The predominant feeling of distance and isolation gives a logic to the pioneering spirit of the Mormons who travel with their wagons towards their promised land around San Juan. It is a motley train; Ford has often been interested in just how harmoniously people deriving from disparate backgrounds and stirred by a common purpose (survival) can live together. The Mormons encounter an itinerant quack (Alan Mowbray) and his family. They are forced to accept a band of vicious outlaws as company. They are menaced by Indians. But even these anxieties pale beside the very business of negotiating the land. The huge, weird stone formations make human beings look like toy soldiers. The empty landscape drains to a faint echo the sound of the singing procession. Days of riding through the desert turn faces gaunt with hunger and thirst.

Wagonmaster is Ford's most *outdoor,* picaresque film, and it is founded on an admiration for the simple, clear-cut terms of the Western life, with a dance in the sun for the undeterred to compensate for the daily privations and dangers.

ALL THE KING'S MEN. United States. Script and Direction: Robert Rossen, from the novel by Robert Penn Warren. Photography: Burnett Guffey. Editing: Al Clark. Music: Louis Gruenberg. Art Direction: Sturges Carne. Players: Broderick Crawford, John Ireland, John Derek, Joanne Dru, Mercedes McCambridge, Anne Seymour. Production: Columbia. (109 mins.)

1950: The death of Willie Stark in ALL THE KING'S MEN.

Charles Foster Kane won publicity and influence through control of the press; Willie Stark (Broderick Crawford,) the bitter, small-town hick who looms over *All the King's Men,* escalates through the strata of American society by trading his political integrity for votes. Stark believes that good comes only out of bad, and sweeps nearly everyone along with his brand of frankness, ambition, and a habit of trampling on tradition. But his increasing use of blackmail and bribery leads inevitably to a violent end.

Rossen charts the progress of this grass-roots demagogue through the eyes of Jack Burdon (John Ireland), a disenchanted journalist who has a broken family background and whose allegiance is divided between the rich, conservative friends of his youth, and the Stark movement. But for once the director is not deeply interested in the emotional affairs of his characters. It is corruption that concerns him at every stage of the film. For power, Rossen demonstrates, corrupts not only its possessor but those around him too—Burdon for instance, and Sadie (Mercedes McCambridge), the laconic secretary who thrives on Stark's intoxicating progress to the Governorship. The feel of Kanona County, its quiet farmsteads contrasting with the crowded city, is still potent; the hushed-up scandals and the strong-arm tactics still disturb.

ORPHEUS (Orphée). France. Script and Direction: Jean Cocteau. Photography: Nicolas Hayer. Editing: Jacqueline Sadoul. Music: Georges Auric. Art Direction: Jean D'Eaubonne. Players: Jean Marais, Maria Casarès, François Périer, Marie Déa, Juliette Gréco, Edouard Dermit, Pierre Bertin. Production: André Paulvé / Les Films du Palais Royal. (112 mins.)

Like any paragon of the arts, Jean Cocteau never gave his whole attention to one medium. Celebrated as much for his poetry as for his novels, as much for his drawings as for his plays, he brought to the cinema a rare appreciation of its flexibility, its boundless possibilities of expression. In *Orphée* he sets the Greek myth in a Paris that seems to hover beyond time. Orphée (Jean Marais) is an inquiring but disillusioned poet who whiles away his hours at a café. Maria Casarès plays the Princess who acts as a minister of Death. She is fatally attracted by Orphée and when, in order to reendow him with life and happiness, she condemns herself, the myth of man's immortality is born. (Or, as a cynic might say of all Cocteau's work, the myth of the poet's special relationship with the other world is emphasized.) The mirror is the key emblem in this curious feat. A man is indistinguishable from his reflection in all but substance, just as the Princess's chauffeur (François Périer) and tame poet (Edouard Dermit) look as

1950: "The mirror is the key emblem" in ORPHEUS.

human after death as before it. The special effects are excellent and are blended into an atmosphere of unreality and dream that surely prefigures *Last Year in Marienbad* (see *1961*). Cocteau's supple camera flits from one location to another so ambiguously that one accepts events on their mythological level. The interrogatory dialogue is close to being absurd at times, and Cocteau lacks the sense of humor which his spiritual mentor, Georges Méliès, clearly possessed in his early cinema fantasies. But the application of pure style to the cinema is always engrossing, and Maria Casarès as the Princess is as mocking and beguiling as Cocteau must have wished.

TWELVE O'CLOCK HIGH. United States. Script: Sy Bartlett and Beirne Lay Jr., from their own novel. Direction: Henry King. Photography: Leon Shamroy. Editing: Barbara McLean. Music: Alfred Newman. Art Direction: Lyle Wheeler, Maurice Ransford. Players: Gregory Peck, Hugh Marlowe, Gary Merrill, Millard Mitchell, Dean Jagger, Paul Stewart. Production: 20th Century-Fox (Darryl F. Zanuck). (133 mins.)

The two films directed by Henry King in 1949–50 —*Twelve O'Clock High* and *The Gunfighter*—were not only the best of King's later career but also inspired Gregory Peck to give his most dedicated performances. Over the years the tough, exterior shell

177

Jean Cocteau.

of *Twelve O'Clock High* as a combat film has fallen away, leaving intact the clash of personalities at an American bomber base in England. General Savage (Peck) assumes command of 918 Group. The men have grown nervous with self-pity, under their all too kind colonel (Gary Merrill). Savage appears as an unwelcome martinet, brushing up discipline and curtailing leave. "Consider yourselves already dead," he snaps coldly to the pilots at briefing. Pride is the emotion he seeks to rouse in his men, and of course in the end he succeeds, although it is at the expense of his own health. Peck's characterization is excellent; fearlessness leavened with a sense of humor, and a personal involvement in the struggle against the Nazis. Dean Jagger as his adjutant also gives an intelligent performance, and King, apart from treating his characters so sympathetically, keeps events moving from the opening sequence, as the crippled bombers fly home after a daylight raid, to the collapse of the general as he is about to lead a crucial mission.

Checklist of other important features

ALL ABOUT EVE. United States. Director: Joseph L. Mankiewicz. Bette Davis at her peak as the middle aged actress exploited by the ruthless young Eve (Anne Baxter) on her way to fame. Mankiewicz's script is wittier and more cynical than his direction.

THE ASPHALT JUNGLE. United States. John Huston's outstanding gangster thriller, with his theme of disloyalty among thieves again to the fore.

LA BEAUTÉ DU DIABLE. France/Italy. Michel Simon, as an absent-minded *savant*, finds himself rejuvenated and transformed into Gérard Philipe in Clair's amusing variation on the Faust legend.

CRONACA DI UN AMORE. Italy. Michelangelo Antonioni's first feature—a dark tale of infidelity and murder, with each character a blueprint for the now familiar sufferers in Antonioni's world.

178

1950: Gregory Peck in TWELVE O'CLOCK HIGH.

THE FORBIDDEN CHRIST (Il Cristo Proibito). Italy. The only film made by the Italo-German novelist, Curzio Malaparte. A vigorous story of vengeance in southern Italy after the war, starring Raf Vallone.

THE GUNFIGHTER. United States. Director: Henry King. Gregory Peck as the reluctant fighter in what is usually termed the first "psychological" Western.

THE HEIRESS. United States. Director: William Wyler. Henry James's *Washington Square* brought coldly and forcefully to the screen, with performances of concealed power by Olivia De Havilland and Ralph Richardson.

INTRUDER IN THE DUST. United States. Director: Clarence Brown. A faithful, scrupulous film of William Faulkner's parable of the deep South. Hollywood's first successful study of the Negro problem.

LA RONDE. France. Hedonistic, nostalgic, sophisticated, *La Ronde* ranks high in the Max Ophüls canon, with lovers swinging from one pair of arms to another while Anton Walbrook stands by "love's roundabout" and orders the game.

SUNDAY IN AUGUST (Domenica d'Agosto). Italy. Director: Luciano Emmer. Rome in high summer. Everyone commutes to the beach at Ostia, and this film records the random happiness of five groups with an understanding humor and informality unusual in the Italian cinema at this time.

WINCHESTER '73. United States. Director: Anthony Mann. A crisp, impressive Western built around the story of the repeater that "won the West," with James Stewart and Shelley Winters.

Short films and Documentaries

BEGONE DULL CARE. Canada. Director: Norman McLaren. A completely abstract film, with lines contorting to the jazz music of the Oscar Peterson Trio; made in conjunction with Evelyn Lambart.

GUERNICA. France. Directors: Alain Resnais and Robert Hessens. A powerful cinematic exploration of Picasso's painting of the Spanish village bombed by Franco in 1937, accompanied by readings from Paul Eluard's poem on the disaster.

MIRROR OF HOLLAND (Spiegel van Holland). Netherlands. The life of the Netherlands reflected in the canals. The insubstantial shapes gradually take on a life of their own. The first short by Bert Haanstra—and a Grand Prix winner at Cannes.

1950: Facts of Interest

Death of Walter Huston and Al Jolson.
Cinerama Inc. is founded to develop the enlargement of the cinema screen.

1951

MISS JULIE (Fröken Julie). Sweden. Script and Direction: Alf Sjöberg, from the play by August Strindberg. Photography: Göran Strindberg. Editing: Lennart Wallén. Music: Dag Wirén. Art Direction: Bibi Lindström. Players: Anita Björk, Ulf Palme, Märta Dorff, Anders Henrikson, Lissie Alandh, Inger Norberg, Jan Hagerman, Ake Fridell. Production: Sandrew-Bauman (Rune Waldekranz). (90 mins.)

The marriage of theatre and cinema has seldom proved successful. Alf Sjöberg's screen version of Strindberg's *Miss Julie* is the only Swedish film to have won the Golden Palm at Cannes. The traits of sadism and masochism inherent in Scandinavian art are accentuated by Sjöberg's interpretation of a play that was wrung from its author's disastrous encounter with Siri von Essen—a countess while Strindberg was

1951: *Anita Björk as MISS JULIE.*

a servant girl's son. The brief love of Julie, the lady of the manor, and Jean, her father's footman, constitutes a fierce attack on a class system now supplanted by modern Swedish society. Sjöberg preserves the unbroken narrative flow of the play and also gives it an extra dimension by describing Julie's childhood (although this tends to release the emotions that on the stage are restricted to the sprawling kitchen set). The contrast between the count and his harridan of a wife helps to account for the uneasy blend of haughtiness and regret that fills the mature Julie. At certain moments, characters from different generations are seen in the same shot, so that contact with contemporary reality is never lost. Miss Julie sits musing in the lofty salon while the image she recalls—her mother carrying her in her arms—appears directly behind her. Humiliation and ambition, self-pity and self-loathing, pervade the film in equal measures. There is a furtive eroticism about the affair to which Sjöberg gives plastic form in such incidents as the quarrel between Julie and her fiancé, or the barn dance, where the contagious rhythm of the music matches the whirl of movement in the picture. Because he so transcends the stage, Sjöberg reaches the peak of his career with this angry, compulsive study of sexual frustration.

THE DIARY OF A COUNTRY PRIEST (Le Journal d'un Curé de Campagne). France. Script and Direction: Robert Bresson, from the novel by Georges Bernanos. Photography: Léonce-Henry Burel. Editing: Paulette Robert. Music: Jean-Jacques Grunenwald. Art Direction: Pierre Charbonnier. Players: Claude Laydu, Armand Guibert, Marie-Monique Arkell, Nicole Ladmiral, Jean Riveyre, Nicole Maurey, Antoine Balpêtré. Production: Union Genérale Cinématographique. (120 mins.)

Robert Bresson, the most severe and metaphysically inclined—with Dreyer and Bergman—of directors, has exerted considerable influence on younger French film-makers despite his frugal output: eight features

1951: THE DIARY OF A COUNTRY PRIEST—"an unassailable dignity."

in a quarter of a century. *The Diary of a Country Priest* is adapted from the book by Georges Bernanos. The young vicar senses an undercurrent of resentment to his work—to his very existence—in the village of Ambricourt. He assumes, with a kind of vicarious frustration, the misery of his parishioners, notably that of the countess, who has lost her son in infancy and is deceived by her husband.

Though long, the film has an urgent rhythm. Its scenes are terse and hasty (like the sentences in the novel), as if reflecting the priest's nervous struggle with the disease that is killing him. As his spiritual loneliness increases, so his pale features are bathed more and more in light from above, as if he were distinguished by grace from the hostile surroundings. Claude Laydu's is a face that, having once flinched from the enormity of human sin, can never smile or radiate pleasure again. As André Bazin has remarked: one must look in Bresson's faces "for an uninterrupted condition of soul, the outward revelation of an interior destiny." Yet Bresson the director is well aware of qualities that his priest lacks: the worldly conscience and strength of the older vicar of Torcy,

for example, or the mask of hearty goodwill Doctor Delbende shows to the world before committing suicide. Nor is the film morbid and masochistic, as critics have claimed, for the priest has a saving talent for bestowing peace on others, even if he remains restless and disconcerted himself. By calmly pruning away all extraneous detail, by choosing locations with grey skies and bare trees, Bresson arrives at an unassailable dignity, whereby the vulnerable priest's every movement is an act of preparation for his death, for his deliverance.

ILLICIT INTERLUDE (Sommarlek). Sweden. Script: Ingmar Bergman and Herbert Grevenius. Direction: Bergman. Photography: Gunnar Fischer. Editing: Oscar Rosander. Music: Erik Nordgren. Art Direction: Nils Svenwall. Players: Maj-Britt Nilsson, Birger Malmsten, Al Kjellin, Annalisa Ericson, Georg Funkquist, Stig Olin, Renée Björling. Production: Svensk Filmindustri. (96 mins.)

This is the first film showing Ingmar Bergman's ability to communicate intense pleasure and sadness

1951: The young lovers meet in ILLICIT INTERLUDE.

on a lyrical scale. Its story of a ballerina recalling her first love affair "across the long, grubby years" poses a problem and solves it triumphantly. For Marie (Maj-Britt Nilsson), this summer of happiness seemed unreal, too good to be true. But in her memories it is the horrid, dark existence following her lover's sudden death that assumes the lineaments of a nightmare. Thus the foreboding that distressed her in the past influences her consciousness as she returns on a sentimental journey to the island where she became infatuated with Henrik (Birger Malmsten). Only by re-living her anguish can she muster sufficient courage and tolerance to face the future. Love and self-knowledge are, after all, the two weapons Bergman gives his characters in the struggle with Death.

The sequences on the archipelago contain several indelible images: the stippled waters of the lake; the wild strawberry patch; Marie's uncle sitting wistfully at the piano. They express the brief idyll that summer can hold for the Scandinavians—mysterious, enchanting, and inexorably transient. But in the end, it is its emotional sophistication and validity, or perhaps above all Bergman's sincerity and extraordinarily sensitive technique, that save *Illicit Interlude* from drifting into oblivion with the scores of films about lost youth.

STRANGERS ON A TRAIN. United States. Script: Raymond Chandler, Czenzi Ormonde, from a novel by Patricia Highsmith, adapted by Whitfield Cook. Direction: Alfred Hitchcock. Photography: Robert

1951: Bruno searches for the lighter in STRANGERS ON A TRAIN.

183

Burks. Editing: William H. Ziegler. Music: Dimitri Tiomkin, Ray Heindorf. Art Direction: Ted Haworth, George James Hopkins. Players: Farley Granger, Robert Walker, Ruth Roman, Leo G. Carroll, Patricia Hitchcock. Production: Warner Brothers. (101 mins.)

Strangers on a Train can be termed the first film in Hitchcock's later and more fascinating period. Guy Haines is a skilled tennis player frustrated by his small-town wife and background. He sees in Ann Morton, a senator's daughter, an easy path to the society he craves, and Bruno Anthony, who "accidentally" meets him on a train, swims up from his subconscious. Like a genie, Bruno becomes the personification and executor of Guy's desires. So Guy murders his wife by proxy, as it were, *through* Bruno, and the cigarette lighter he leaves with him becomes a talisman of his guilt, of his involvement in the crime. The idea of Guy's killing Bruno's detestable father in return is only a dramatic device to show how remorselessly Guy is drawn down into the dark coils of the conspiracy against his better self. As so frequently in Hitchcock's work, the choice of milieux determines the suspense and the moral significance. The tawdry fairground is initially the ideal refuge for Bruno when he trails and murders Miriam; and at the end it is the "public place" where Guy struggles to escape from Bruno's malevolent influence and

to clear his name in the eyes of the world as well as his own conscience. Hitchcock's craftsmanship is impeccable throughout the film, not only in the crosscutting to create tension, but also in his registration of little quirks of behavior. Themes emerge here that are to predominate in later masterpieces like *Vertigo* (see *1958*), *Psycho* (see *1960*), and *The Birds* (see *1963*). The hints at sexual inadequacy and perversion (Bruno strangles women as a means of symbolic rape); or the conflict between darkness (Bruno who lives in the shadows) and light (Guy and his Washington sphere, tennis, parties, etc.). Certainly *Strangers on a Train* is considerably more than an insolent exercise in suspense.

THE LOST ONE (Der Verlorene). Germany. Script: Peter Lorre, Benno Vigny, Axel Eggebrecht. Direction: Peter Lorre. Photography: Vaclav Vich. Editing: Karl Otto Bartning. Music: Willi Schmidt-Gentner. Art Direction: F. Schroedter, K. Weber. Players: Peter Lorre, Karl John, Helmut Rudolph, Renate Mannhardt, Johanna Hofer, Lotte Rausch, Gisela Trowe. Production: Arnold Pressburger. (90 mins.)

The cinema is speckled with the attempts of celebrated actors to direct themselves. Peter Lorre, the acme of sardonic guilt in such films as *M, The Man who Knew too Much,* and *The Maltese Falcon,* returned to Germany in 1951 to make *The Lost One.*

1951: Peter Lorre (at right) in THE LOST ONE.

He uses the devices of the expressionist tradition to advantage, and his story of a research biologist working under the Nazis during the war is filled with shadows and a grey uselessness. Lorre's Dr. Rothe is a profound study of a man dragged to violence—to the murder of his fiancée and another woman who resembles her—not by any mental flaw but by his essential urge to survive beneath the Nazi régime (hence, one suspects, the frigid reception accorded the film in Germany). He remains superficially calm, as he learns that his fiancée has been passing his research material to London. But once he has killed her, he finds that fear quells all other feelings. He becomes a fugitive from his own crime; not, ironically, from arrest, for the authorities have condoned the incident. The discovery that he has been tricked by the Abwehr and that his victim was innocent rouses a surge of moral indignation in him. But he has to wait until the end of the war before he can be avenged both on Hösche, his evil genius from Hamburg days, and on himself. Most of the film consists of flashbacks, as Lorre relates his experiences to Hösche during a nocturnal drinking session in a refugee camp. One cannot forget his Dr. Rothe: the waxen features, the wary glance, the black overcoat, the look of chained desperation—all indicative of what Raymond Chandler termed, "the killers who are in love with death, to whom murder is a remote kind of suicide."

A PLACE IN THE SUN. United States. Script: Michael Wilson and Harry Brown, from the novel *An American Tragedy* by Theodore Dreiser. Direction: George Stevens. Photography: William C. Mellor. Editing: William Hornbeck. Music: Franz Waxman. Art Direction: Hans Dreier, Walter Tyler. Players: Montgomery Clift, Elizabeth Taylor, Shelley Winters, Anne Revere, Raymond Burr, Herbert Heyes, Keefe Brasselle, Shepherd Strudwick. Production: Paramount (George Stevens). (122 mins.)

The myth of a classless society in America was finally exploded by Dreiser's *An American Tragedy* in the twenties. George Stevens's film version is bereft of Dreiser's relentless cynicism. The depressing adolescence of Clyde Griffiths (renamed George Eastman in the film), and his even more harrowing experience in the condemned cell, are analysed abruptly, almost flippantly. The mechanics of the plot, which emerge gradually and with deliberation through Dreiser's loquacious prose, are too rudely disclosed in the script. The film evinces no feeling of waste and futility; it is a straightforward romance in the grand Hollywood tradition. On this level *A Place in the Sun* is imposing. Stevens illuminates his characters swiftly and economically (e.g. the shot of George sitting in his uncle's office, after he has arrived at the factory, bemused but ambitious). The

Elizabeth Taylor and Montgomery Clift in A PLACE IN THE SUN.

hero's diffidence at the Eastman party is also sharply observed, as he hovers awkwardly near one group after another, sharing their laughter with a false smile. Shelley Winters as Alice Tripp is ideally molded to the suffering factory girl who becomes the victim of George's desires: Alice is as imbued with class complexes as the Eastmans and their society friends. Her last conversation with George in the boat is given lurid power by Stevens, relying as he does at other crucial moments on the gigantic close-up and the weight of their physical surroundings on the players. A film, then, where an imaginative style coupled to the intensity of the original novel often overcomes a poor scenario.

Checklist of other important features

THE BROWNING VERSION. Britain. The misery of a punctilious and henpecked English schoolmaster (Michael Redgrave), described with sympathy by Terence Rattigan's script and with restraint by Asquith's direction.

THE BIG CARNIVAL. United States. Director: Billy Wilder. Kirk Douglas as the fiery journalist who unscrupulously manipulates a man's life in the Cliff Dwellings outside Albuquerque in order to restore his lost prestige in the world of journalism. Cynical, incisive, and utterly shameless.

EDUARD ET CAROLINE. France. Director: Jacques Becker. A sardonic, beautifully paced French comedy about a marriage near to failure, with Daniel Gélin as the ardent young pianist and Anne Vernon as his wife, adrift in Parisian high society.

THE MEDIUM. United States. Director: Gian-Carlo Menotti. "I consider this film as motion-picture perfection," wrote Jean Cocteau. With its weird mixing of opera and suspense, *The Medium* is a film impossible to classify, impossible to omit from any detailed survey of the cinema.

MIRACLE IN MILAN (Miracolo a Milano). Italy. Director: Vittorio De Sica. A quaint and sentimental fable about the exploitation of the poor, who are harried by the pressures of urban life. The corruption and dispossession of innocent folk has been the principal theme of the De Sica-Zavattini partnership.

LE PLAISIR. France. Director: Max Ophüls. Based on three short stories by Maupassant, told with Ophüls's irony and insight into character, as people seek pleasure from life desperately and almost grotesquely.

Short films and Documentaries

LES DÉSASTRES DE LA GUERRE. France. Director: Pierre Kast. The etchings of Goya come vividly and violently to life in this animated anti-war film.

GERALD McBOING BOING. United States. Director: Robert Cannon. One of the richest cartoons of the UPA vintage, featuring a little boy who "twangs" when he tries to talk.

LE SEL DE LA TERRE. France. Director: Georges Rouquier. As an observer of landscape Rouquier has few equals in the documentary field. This classic looks at the Camargue country near the mouth of the river Rhone.

1951: Facts of Interest

Death of Robert Flaherty.
Soviet film production at its lowest ebb—only six features completed.
Three-dimensional films are exhibited in Britain and the United States.

1952

LIVING or DOOMED (Ikiru). Japan. Script: Shinobu Hashimoto, Hideo Oguni, Akira Kurosawa. Direction: Kurosawa. Photography: Asakazu Nakai. Music: Fumio Hayasaka. Art Direction: So Matsuyama. Players: Takashi Shimura, Nobuo Kaneko, Kyoko Seki, Makoto Kabori, Kumeko Urabe, Yoshie Minami. Production: Toho (Shojiro Motoki). (143 mins.)

Several major directors have used the theme of life reviewed from the brink of death, and as Dr. Johnson commented, "When a man is to be hanged in a fortnight, it concentrates his mind wonderfully." Kanji Watanabe in *Living* is the Chief of his Citizens' Advice Bureau, the slave of a bureaucracy that looks on inertia as a virtue. Then he is told that he has incurable stomach cancer and, fired by panic and by the callous attitude of his son, he tries to wring some meaningful experiences from the short time left to him. He stumbles round the night spots of Tokyo, but he cannot steep himself in the artificial happiness offered by the bars and strip shows. He courts a girl from his office and she instills him briefly with energy and enthusiasm. His last action is to persuade the Deputy Mayor to transform a slum area into a playground. But the film does not thereby attack our moral conscience, for in Kurosawa's view each man is ultimately responsible for his own conduct. That the playground will be useful to others is incidental; the main thing is that its creation has meant something to Watanabe. The film could end with his death, but Kurosawa sidesteps sentimentality with a deliberate hiatus in the middle. Watanabe is indeed dead, but the scene switches to the funeral wake where, beneath his altar photograph, he is discussed by his family and colleagues. Their assessments, made less inhibited by *sake*, cast light on the dead man's personality from all manner of angles. A numbness steals over this part of *Living*, as first the mourners, and then the audience, realize that Watanabe's example will go unheeded. Suffering, like death, provokes all too personal a response. Restraint is the key element in Kurosawa's technique throughout the film: it is the tiny details, the facial expressions, that are so eloquent here.

UMBERTO D. Italy. Script: Cesare Zavattini. Direction: Vittorio De Sica. Photography: G. R. Aldo. Editing: Eraldo Da Roma. Music: Alessandro Cicognini. Art Direction: Virgilio Marchi. Players: Carlo Battisti, Maria Pia Casilio, Ileana Simova, Lina Gennari, Elena Rea, Memmo Cartenuto. Production: Rizzoli-De Sica-Amato. (88 mins.)

Another masterpiece about old age. The hero of *Umberto D* is based on De Sica's father, to whom this film of protest is dedicated. Domenico Umberto is a retired civil servant, living in a boarding house which, if it is not quite squalid, is certainly shabby and depressing. Domenico's face is troubled and reflects a life of respectability hardly maintained. He is reluctant to beg like most of his contemporaries. As he grows older and more impecunious, he finds himself politely discarded by his former acquaintances in the city. Only his dog is faithful, and only the maid in the boarding house shows any awareness of the pitiful limitations of his existence. De Sica describes the dramatic incidents in Domenico's life: his treatment in the hospital, where he lies bewildered in a vast ward; the loss of his dog and his desperate search for it in the abattoirs. Finally, resigned to destitution, his belongings sold, his pride offended, he tries to commit suicide—and fails lamentably. The way in which De Sica studies his hero's actions at this point is unforgettably sensitive. The old man starts to play with his dog in the park, and then the two of them, inseparable, disappear along an avenue. Umberto has reentered the world again. He has thrown off his despair because he cannot sink any lower. He has resolved to face life on its own terms. This film is sentimental and it is Latin. It is related with pathos and meticulous skill; and it will doubtless outlive all De Sica's other films.

1952: LIVING: "it is the tiny details, the facial expressions, that are so eloquent here."

1952: Carlo Battisti in UMBERTO D.

GOLDEN MARIE (Casque d'Or). France. Script: Jacques Becker and Jacques Companeez. Dialogue: Becker. Direction: Becker. Photography: Robert Le Febvre. Editing: Marguerite Renoir, Jacques Becker. Music: Georges Van Parys. Art Direction: J. A. D'Eaubonne. Players: Simone Signoret, Serge Reggiani, Claude Dauphin, Raymond Bussières, Gaston Modot, Dominique Davray. Production: Speva Films/Paris Films (Henri Baum). (96 mins.)

Jacques Becker, one of the most intelligent and discreet directors of his generation, was attracted by the past. His best period film remains *Golden Marie*, a story of *amour fou* in the Paris of 1904. Manda (Serge Reggiani), a carpenter's assistant, falls in love with the alluring Marie (Simone Signoret). He kills her escort in a fight and escapes with her to the country, where they enjoy a brief pastoral affair. Then Leca, leader of a gang of apaches, becomes jealous and tricks Manda into confessing his guilt to

1952: *GOLDEN MARIE: "the very incarnation of hedonism."*

the police. He is guillotined. To a certain degree all Becker's films are tragedies. But the gloom is relieved by a wit and a humanity that give his characters a cavalier quality and enable them to laugh contemptuously at life. The atmosphere of the 1900s is captured in the straw-hatted dandies who form Leca's gang, in the clumsy uniforms of the police, and in the unhurried pace of life in the streets and villages. Simone Signoret has never given a more confident performance. Her kindled eyes mock and tease the men who seek to court her. Her proud walk is the very incarnation of hedonism. The most gentle, the most affectionate moment of the film shows her watching a wedding in the little church of Joinville, with Manda standing awkwardly at her side. Her gaze softens, and in that instant one realizes just how evasive happiness can be. Becker is no sentimentalist; his lovers accept the dangers that transgression brings, and the end of *Golden Marie,* with the guillotine plunging down and dissolving to a vision of Marie and Manda dancing in the morning of their love, is controlled with unrivalled tact and regret.

VIVA ZAPATA! United States. Script: John Steinbeck, from the book *Zapata the Unconquerable* by Edgcumb Pichon. Direction: Elia Kazan. Photography: Joseph MacDonald. Editing: Barbara McLean. Music:

Alex North. Art Direction: Lyle Wheeler, Leland Fuller. Players: Marlon Brando, Anthony Quinn, Jean Peters, Joseph Wiseman, Arnold Moss, Lou Gilbert, Harold Gordon, Florenz Ames, Alan Reed, Margo. Production: 20th Century-Fox (Darryl F. Zanuck). (113 mins.)

Marlon Brando has taken many important roles in the cinema, but none quite so impressive and strangely eloquent as Emiliano Zapata, the hero of the Mexican revolution of 1910. President Diaz has been in office for over thirty years. Zapata leads the revolt to unseat him and to promote a just regime. He commands a natural respect; he is, as his father-in-law says, a man of substance without substance, a rancher without land. But when military success affords him the chance to wax fat, Zapata draws back from respectability and the trappings of control. He quits the Presidency and retires to the mountains, where he teaches the peasants to be afraid of no one. When he is finally lured to his death by the National Army, his supporters cannot believe that he is dead. The idea outlives the man.

Kazan achieves an authentic vision of Mexico and invests his film with a sense of gathering destiny. Zapata carries his comrades with him only to find them lacking in true temper. His shrewd, lusty Sancho Panza of a brother (Anthony Quinn) becomes a

1952: Anthony Quinn and Marlon Brando in VIVA ZAPATA!

animals, her own dog included. The farmer punishes his son brutally, and then signs the girl away to the authorities. At the close of the film she is seen crying pitifully for her mother in a throng of refugees.

If the story is concerned primarily with the relationship between children and their elders, Clément's theme is the irresponsible behavior of the Catholics in provincial France. Both families in the film are allegedly devout; and yet the children suffer simply because they display more reverence for the Christian cross than their elders. At the end, Paulette's sole chance of rehabilitation is destroyed through crassness and bigotry. Adults, the film persuades, are often unaware of their power to deprave. Clément's style reflects the contradictory elements that characterized this stage of the war; the uncompromising savagery of the first eight minutes contrasts with the serene romanticism of the children's conversations in field or barn. Brigitte Fosey combines felicitously the naïvety and suspicious reserve of the orphaned girl, and the guitar music of Narciso Yepes adds immeasurably to the impact of what is always a restrained, poignant, and humane film. It won an Oscar for Best Foreign Film in 1953.

Checklist of other important features

THE AFRICAN QUEEN. United States. Katharine Hepburn and Humphrey Bogart as polite but sarcastic lovers on board a rickety boat in East Africa. Directed by John Huston with a charm and a feel for the incongruity of the situation.

DEATH OF A SALESMAN. United States. Director: Laslo Benedek. A flamboyant but imaginative adaptation of Arthur Miller's play, with Fredric March as the demented salesman who sees his own decay mirrored in his son's behavior.

EL. Mexico. A study of jealousy bordering on para-

petty tyrant. Fernando Aguirre (Joseph Wiseman) arrives empty-handed but fanatical to beg Zapata's help in the beginning, and at the end is responsible for his leader's death. Brando, slumbrous, saturnine, close-eyed, gives a performance of the utmost simplicity. As Zapata he is forever chiding himself for his weakness, for his illiteracy, for the birthright that makes him dependent on his horse and his rifle. Kazan's work is full of men (Terry Malloy in *On the Waterfront*, Cal Trask in *East of Eden*) who rear up against oppression and have as their reward the discovery of their own insufficiencies, the revelation of their own corruptibility.

FORBIDDEN GAMES (Jeux Interdits). France. Script: Jean Aurenche, Pierre Bost, René Clément, and François Boyer from the latter's novel. Direction: Clément. Photography: Robert Juilliard. Editing: Roger Dwyre. Music: Narciso Yepes. Art Direction: Paul Bertrand. Players: Brigitte Fossey, Georges Poujouly, Lucien Hubert, Suzanne Courtal, Jacques Marin, Laurence Badie, André Wasley. Production: Robert Dorfmann/Silver Film. (102 mins.)

René Clément's masterpiece is, like much of his work, inspired by the last war. In the tottering France of June 1940, a tiny girl, Paulette, loses her parents during a Messerschmidt attack on a bridge. She is befriended by a boy, Michel, some years older than herself, but she cannot easily accept his peasant family. She tries simultaneously to express and to erase her regret for her parents by indulging with Michel in a furtive game of placing crosses on the graves of local

1952: Brigitte Fossey in FORBIDDEN GAMES.

190

noia in a newlywed man, to which Buñuel brings a typical combination of comedy and anti-Catholicism.

FIVE FINGERS. United States. Director: Joseph L. Mankiewicz. Although Michael Wilson's script is a shade too colorful, James Mason donates a suave portrayal of "Cicero," the spy who swindled and was himself swindled in Ankara in 1944.

THE GOLDEN COACH (La Carrozza d'Oro/La Carrosse d'Or). France/Italy. Drawn from a play by Prosper Mérimée. Renoir's excursion into the world of the commedia dell' arte is given stature by the subtle performance of Anna Magnani, as a Columbine with three mock suitors.

HIGH NOON. United States. Director: Fred Zinnemann. Gary Cooper as the marshal fighting against time and his own integrity. A major Western.

THE LIFE OF O'HARU (Saikaku Ichidai Onna). Japan. Kenji Mizoguchi's favorite film: a prostitute remembers the crucial episodes in her life. The successive deceptions, humiliations, and moments of hopefulness recur with inevitability but without monotony.

OTHELLO. Morocco. Orson Welles's elaborate orchestration of jealousy and suspicion, with the barbaric locations in North Africa giving the film an unexpected splendor.

THE QUIET MAN. United States. Director: John Ford. Galway as seen in color by the old master (his other Irish films include *The Informer* and *The Plough and the Stars*), with John Wayne and Victor McLaglen battling it out round the village amid a collection of local characters.

SINGIN' IN THE RAIN. United States. Directors: Gene Kelly and Stanley Donen. One of the best musicals of the fifties, with Kelly and Jean Hagen evoking the early days of the talkies with more than usual verve and élan.

A STREETCAR NAMED DESIRE. United States. Director: Elia Kazan. Of all the screen versions of plays by Tennessee Williams, this is probably the most accurate, celebrated for Marlon Brando's mumbling "Method" performance as Blanche Dubois's antagonist in New Orleans.

Short films and Documentaries

CHILDREN OF HIROSHIMA. (Gembaku no Ko). Japan. Director: Kaneto Shindo. A horrifying and passionate account of atomic destruction in Hiroshima and its lingering effects.

CRIN BLANC. Director: Albert Lamorisse. An absorbing childhood fantasy set in the Camargue where a fisherboy tames the white stallion at the head of the band.

HOTEL DES INVALIDES. France. Director: Georges Franju. A brilliantly edited attack on the concept and glorification of war that at first glance is an innocuous guide to the French War Museum in Paris.

NEIGHBORS. Canada. Norman McLaren won an Academy Award for this animated, live-action fable in which real characters jerk about, twenty-four times a second.

PANTA RHEI. Netherlands. Director: Bert Haanstra. A cinematic demonstration of Heracleitus's dictum that all things flow, extolling nature and revealing the sensuous undercurrents of life itself.

1952: Facts of Interest

Charles Chaplin takes his final leave of the U.S.A.
The first Cinerama film is shown, in which the images from three cameras are projected side by side with three projectors.

1953: Ingmar Bergman's THE NAKED NIGHT—"utter mortification."

1953

THE NAKED NIGHT (Gycklarnas afton). Sweden. Script and Direction: Ingmar Bergman. Photography: Sven Nykvist and Hilding Bladh. Editing: Carl-Olov Skeppstedt. Music: Karl-Birger Blomdahl. Art Direction: Bibi Lindström. Players: Harriet Andersson, Ake Grönberg, Hasse Ekman, Anders Ek, Gudrun Brost, Annika Tretow, Gunnar Björnstrand, Erik Strandmark. Production: Sandrews (Rune Waldekranz). (90 mins.)

A failure when it first appeared, *The Naked Night* has grown enormously in stature since 1953. Bergman's expressionist treatment, far from hampering the film, lends it an added density and macabre fascination. Like the majority of his early works, *The Naked Night* deals with a sullen man (Albert, the circus owner), and a woman (Anna, an equestrienne played by Harriet Andersson), bound together by instinct, loneliness, and self-betrayal. The friction between them reaches an intolerable pitch in a town in southern Sweden, where the circus pauses for a performance. Albert visits his former wife; Anna is seduced by Frans, an actor. A scarifying flashback at the beginning of the film yields a parallel for this story of debasement and remorse. Albert and Anna find themselves in a strange milieu: that of the theatre, with the footlights exposing their pathetic stances as they ask the producer for costumes. The exotic paraphernalia of the green-room mesmerize Anna and undermine her resistance to the malevolent, simpering Frans. Against these ornamental sessions, Bergman sets a series of scenes horribly bitter in their naturalism: Albert's encounter with his wife and his clumsy attempt to redeem his self-respect; or his fight with Frans in the sawdust ring that ends in utter mortification. Finally, as the troupe leaves at dawn, Albert is seen trudging along with Anna behind the caravans, with the melancholy whining of the circus music in the background. *The Naked Night* is not so enclosed a film as it appears. The characters struggle to move from one type of existence to another, but are drawn back inexorably into their narrow orbit.

They resemble all Bergman's heroes in that their aspirations fly beyond their capabilities. They cannot distinguish illusion from reality.

MR. HULOT'S HOLIDAY (Les Vacances de Monsieur Hulot). France. Script: Jacques Tati and Henry Marquet, with P. Aubert and J. Lagrange. Direction: Jacques Tati. Photography: Jacques Mercanton, Jean Mousselle. Editing: Baron, Bretoneiche, and Grassi. Music: Alain Romans. Art Direction: R. Briancourt, H. Schmitt. Players: Jacques Tati, Nathalie Paseaud, Louis Perrault, Michèle Rolla, Suzy Willy, André Dubois, Valentine Camax. Production: Cady-Films/Discina/Eclair-Journal. (90 mins.)

One of the cinema's most reticent comedians is Jacques Tati, who has made only four feature films in twenty years. Tati is the author, director, and leading actor of his comedies. His character of Mr. Hulot has proved to be an unusual mixture of the servile and the innocent. At heart he is an ordinary, unpretentious man—a normal being in a world of abnormality. He never indulges in gags himself, and yet he is often funnier and more mature than Chaplin. In *Les Vacances,* one first encounters Hulot in his coughing hen-house of a car, en route for the staid resort of St..Marc-on-Sea. The hotel staff are soon perplexed by this mysterious stranger who leaves doors open so that the resulting gusts of wind create havoc in the entrance lounge, and who plays raucous music when everybody else is quietly cheating at cards. His tennis serve is ferocious, and quickly denudes the court of opponents. At the climax of the holiday, he is trapped in a beach hut full of fireworks —at night—and chaos is complete. As in his later films, *Mon Oncle* (see *1958*) and *Playtime* (see *1967*), Hulot has a knack of provoking trouble without actually *causing* it. The hotel residents find themselves influenced by his absentmindedness, and are led into all kinds of stupid actions. Hulot's presence—elastic walk, mumbling speech, and overfilled pipe—tends to force these people to trip over their own petty

1953: Jacques Tati in his own comedy, MR. HULOT'S HOLIDAY.

conventions. Tati the director is always in evidence, too, compiling a soundtrack rich in humorous noises, and imparting to objects like a canoe the latent menace that paves the way for a Hulot catastrophe.

THE WAGES OF FEAR (Le Salaire de la Peur). France/Italy. Script: Henri-Georges Clouzot and Jérôme Géronimi from the novel by Georges Arnaud. Direction: Clouzot. Editing: Henri Rust, Madeline Gug, E. Muse. Music: Georges Auric. Art Direction: René Renoux. Players: Yves Montand, Charles Vanel, Véra Clouzot, Folco Lulli, Peter van Eyck, William Tubbs, Dario Moreno. Production: C.I.C.C./Filmsonor/Véra Film/Fono Roma. (156 mins.)

Clouzot's *The Wages of Fear* is among the finest suspense films ever made. Its tension derives as much from the interplay of characters as from the meticulous cutting and choice of locations. The first hour is devoted to a study of Las Piedras, a sprawling, unkempt town in South America, where a group of foreigners lie idle in the torpid heat. The community is like a prison, says Mario (Yves Montand): easy to enter but almost impossible to leave without money. He and three others, Jo, Luigi, and Bimba, predictably snatch at the chance to earn $2,000 apiece when a consignment of explosives has to be transported 300 miles to a blazing oil well. The two trucks follow the pipeline at a crawl; one spark or collision will detonate the nitroglycerine. A succession of hazards stretches courage and resourcefulness to the limit, and as the ageing Jo is wrenched into hysteria by the danger, Clouzot's camera observes the situation dispassionately, sliding this way and that in movements of discovery, revealing a broken pipe that splurges oil over the road in a fast-rising lake, or Bimba's shaving calmly just before his truck explodes. There are no concessions to sentiment, for in the aftermath of triumph, Mario plunges carelessly over a precipice, and the siren on his truck wails with appalling logic. Clouzot obviously admires the coarse comradeship that springs up of necessity between these doomed men; and he suggests that their deaths, though violent, are preferable to a slow decay in Las Piedras. "Nightmares follow me in real life," Clouzot has said, "I like to dream and remember my dreams."

194

The "hallucinatory tinge" of THE WAGES OF FEAR.

The Wages of Fear has precisely that hallucinatory tinge.

SHANE. United States. Script: A. B. Guthrie, Jr., from the novel by Jack Schaefer, with additional dialogue by Jack Sher. Direction: George Stevens. Photography: Loyal Griggs (Technicolor). Editing: William Hornbeck, Tom McAdoo. Music: Victor Young. Art Direction: Hal Pereira, Walter Tyler. Players: Alan Ladd, Jean Arthur, Van Heflin, Jack Palance, Brandon De Wilde, Ben Johnson, Emile Meyer, Elisha Cook Jr. Production: Paramount (George Stevens). (116 mins.)

Although its picture of the old West seems barely as authentic as John Ford's in *Stagecoach* or *My Darling Clementine*, George Stevens's *Shane* contains an unrivalled lyricism and simplicity of emotion. The color is used with imagination and an instinctive feeling for the locations. Shane (Alan Ladd) arrives at the Starretts' farm in Wyoming. He quickly earns the respect of the local folks as he helps them to frustrate the cattle baron, Rufe Ryker, who is threatening to drive them out of the valley. But he remains a remote figure. He is a kind of *ange purificateur;* he cannot stay at the farm he so plainly loves, because, having killed a man in the past, he is condemned to wander forever. Shane is the embodiment of all the ideals of the West—skill with his fists and his gun, tireless energy, quiet understanding, and a restrained dignity that makes him, in the eyes of young Joey, inimitable.

The grandeur of *Shane* lies in the sum of its parts, and admittedly not in its overall construction, which is uneasy. The uprooting of the stump with their axes by Shane and Starrett is a splendid kinetic symbol of cooperation. The brawl in the saloon is brilliantly shot and edited; an anthology piece. The final duel between Shane and Wilson is one of the finest in the genre. Jack Palance as the killer is an axiom. With his vulpine smile and clinical movements, he is the Lucifer of the West. Rich as *Shane* is in its details of settler life, it is sustained by the tension of the struggle between good and evil.

THE MEMBER OF THE WEDDING. United States. Script: Edna and Edward Anhalt from the story and play by Carson McCullers. Direction: Fred Zinnemann. Photography: Hal Mohr. Editing: William A. Lyon. Music: Alex North. Art Direction: Rudolph Sternad and Cary Odell. Players: Julie Harris, Ethel Waters, Brandon De Wilde, Arthur Franz, Nancy Gates. Production: Stanley Kramer. (91 mins.)

Nearly all Fred Zinnemann's films have been commanded by a central role, by a character in search of his place in society. His version of *The Member of the Wedding* never quite casts off its theatrical guise, but it boasts a heartfelt performance by Julie Harris. Rather foolishly, perhaps, the screenplay is based on the stage play and not on the story by Carson McCullers. The principal set is the kitchen of the ramshackle house where Frankie Addams (Julie Harris) lives with her colored nanny, Bernice (Ethel Waters), and her younger cousin John Henry (Brandon De Wilde). Frankie is perplexed beyond her adolescent years. When her brother announces his marriage she become petulant and frustrated; she tries to analyze her own emotions and to shuffle off her childish habits. Her father and her other relatives are maddeningly indifferent to her threats of flight after the wedding. Only John Henry's sudden and inexplicable death punctures her inferiority complex and permits her to realize her own identity.

Julie Harris's technique combines the best traditions of stage and screen acting. Her clear enunciation, and her constant appeal to some invisible audience, responds effectively to the large close-ups used by Zinnemann. She was twenty-six when she was making this film, and yet she ventures with uncanny assurance into the inquisitive personality of twelve year old Frankie, shifting cleverly from high spirits to moody skepticism.

Checklist of other important features

THE BAND WAGON. United States. Director: Vincente Minnelli. Fred Astaire and Cyd Charisse in the best musical of the year. Some magical numbers and several dashing color effects.

1953: *From George Stevens's SHANE.*

THE BIG HEAT. United States. Director: Fritz Lang. A brutal picture of the gangster underworld and the corruption it sows among the police. With Glenn Ford and Gloria Grahame.

THE BREAD OF LOVE (Kärlekens bröd). Sweden. Director: Arne Mattsson. An extraordinary memory of the Russian-Finnish war of 1939, with a patrol hemmed in by the enemy and by the all-pervasive snow, awaiting either starvation or death.

THE CRIMSON CURTAIN (Le Rideau Cramoisi). France/Italy. Director: Alexandre Astruc. A forty-five minute film of considerable style and atmosphere, set in the nineteenth century. A young cavalry officer falls in love with a mysterious girl in the house where he is quartered.

FROM HERE TO ETERNITY. United States. An army saga, based on the novel by James Jones and hovering around the Pearl Harbor disaster. The characterization is rather superficial, but the outbreaks of violence and hatred are handled well by Fred Zinnemann.

1953: *Julie Harris, Ethel Waters, and Brandon De Wilde in THE MEMBER OF THE WEDDING.*

GATE OF HELL (Jigoku-mon). Japan. Director: Teinosuke Kinugasa. One of the most beautiful of all color films—a feudal story unfolded with a formal grace and intensity that escape all but the greatest Japanese directors.

THE GREAT ADVENTURE (Det stora äventyret). Sweden. The most felicitous blend of fiction and documentary yet achieved by Arne Sucksdorff, a study of childhood life on a Swedish farm.

JULIUS CAESAR. United States. Director: Joseph L. Mankiewicz. John Gielgud's Cassius stands out in this dignified and flourishing conversion of play into film. With James Mason, Marlon Brando, Deborah Kerr.

LIMELIGHT. United States. Director: Charles Chaplin. A disappointing tribute to the British music hall by Chaplin, though his own performance as Calvero, the declining clown, is brilliant.

TOKYO STORY (Tokyo Monogatari). Japan. Director: Yasujiro Ozu. A masterpiece about a lonely old couple from the most domesticated of Japanese film-makers, whose quiet and warm observation supplants any hint of high-flown technique or melodrama.

I VITELLONI. Italy/France. Director: Federico Fellini. A look at some layabouts who drift round the bars and beaches of a seaside resort in winter; these men are rebellious, dissatisfied, spiritually starved, and Fellini watches them with compassion and subtlety.

UGETSU MONOGATARI. Japan. Kenji Mizoguchi's weird fable concerning potters and a mysterious princess has been overpraised, but the elegant compositions, the lyrical dialogue, and the historical verisimilitude, are undeniable.

Short films and Documentaries

LEONARDO DA VINCI, The Tragic Pursuit of Perfection. Britain/France. Director: Enrico Fulchignoni. A complete, perceptive study of the painter through his drawings, diagrams, and paintings.

UNICORN IN THE GARDEN. United States. Director: William Hurtz. A splendidly inventive UPA cartoon based on James Thurber's story about the domestic rupture averted by the appearance of the unicorn—in the garden.

1953: Facts of Interest

Death of Vsevolod Pudovkin, famous Soviet director.
The first film in CinemaScope, *The Robe,* is released by 20th Century-Fox.
Three-dimensional films appear in commercial cinemas.

1954

SENSO. Italy. Script: Luchino Visconti and Suso Cecchi d'Amico, from a short shory by Camille Boito. Direction: Visconti. Photography: G. R. Aldo and Robert Krasker (Technicolor). Editing: Mario Serandrei. Music: from Anton Bruckner's Seventh Symphony. Art Direction: Ottavio Scotti. Players: Alida Valli, Farley Granger, Massimo Girotti, Heinz Moog, Rina Morelli, Sergio Fantoni. Production: Lux Films. (120 mins.)

Against the backcloth of the Risorgimento and the crumbling of the old order in Italy, Visconti's masterpiece proceeds with all the majestic rhythm and the meticulous design of Grand Opera. It is a story of degradation; hardly a tragedy, for the lovers care little about the revolutionary ideals that fire those around them. Livia, the countess (Alida Valli) is ensnared by the suave masculinity of Franz Mahler (Farley Granger), an officer in the Austrian army. She bribes him to malinger so that they can remain together, but he spurns her shamelessly. She betrays him to the Commander and Franz is shot summarily for desertion.

Senso is probably the finest color film in the history of the cinema. The compositions have the deep-hued refulgence of Old Master paintings. The glimmering canals and decaying palazzos of Venice project unforgettably—and with romantic realism—the furtive pleasure and the fading resolution of the affair between the countess and her craven admirer. The battle of Custoza, at which Livia's cousin, a brave patriot, is wounded, begins with a formal advance by the infantry, and ends in chaotic retreat. Visconti brings to the film a sense of innate drama that resounds in the accompanying strains of Bruckner's Seventh Symphony. He lingers at the passing of an epoch, deploring the corruption and the hedonism, and yet admiring the elegance and the tranquillity of its civilization. *Senso* is great because Visconti's style is never indulgent. He describes the terrible progression of the lovers with a lucidity that often

1954: SENSO—"the countess and her craven admirer."

deserts him elsewhere in his work. When the countess flees deranged through the gloomy streets of Verona while Franz is dragged before the firing squad, it is as though Visconti had peeled away the pretense to display a loathsome foundation of hatred and desire.

SEVEN SAMURAI (Shichinin no Samurai). Japan. Script: Shinobu Hashimoto, Hideo Oguni, Akira Kurosawa. Direction: Kurosawa. Photography: Asakazu Nakai. Music: Fumio Hayasaka. Art Direction: So Matsuyama. Players: Takashi Shimura, Toshiro Mifune, Yoshio Inaba, Seiji Miyaguchi, Minoru Chiaki, Daisuke Kato, Ko Kimura. Production: Toho (Shojiro Motoki). (160 mins., originally 200 mins.)

198

1954: "The muddy compound where the fighting rages" in SEVEN SAMURAI.

Akira Kurosawa.

This was the most expensive film made in Japan up to 1954; and it is probably the most characteristic of Kurosawa's works. A small village is plundered annually by brigands and hires a group of samurai to defend it. Kurosawa's ample development of this narrative commands respect. Each samurai is given a distinctive, memorable personality, ranging from the phlegmatic Kâmbei (Takashi Shimura) to the volatile, reckless, but utterly engaging Kikuchiyo (Toshiro Mifune). Their fearlessness and their zest for battle inspire the villagers. The brigands, seen at the start of the film as invincible, gradually begin to appear vulnerable. The village and its environment hold a significance normally lacking in historical spectacles. There is the forest hillside, where the tree afford camouflage and the flowers permit a measure of romance when Kimura meets his girl. There is also the muddy compound where the fighting rages in the final reels of the film, and just as Kambei dictates the strategy of defense, so Kurosawa controls his camera placements and his cutting as the brigands hurtle into the village. And though these sequences are the most vivid in *Seven Samurai*, the entire film possesses an internal rhythm of its own—a tension roused not merely by the imminence of attack but also by the interplay of feeling between the samurai

199

themselves. They fight for three meager meals a day and for the sheer exhilaration of defeating the plunderers of society. It is scarcely surprising that Kurosawa so admires the cinema of John Ford or that *Seven Samurai* was re-made by John Sturges (under the title of *The Magnificent Seven*) in a Western setting.

THE ROAD (La Strada). Italy. Script: Federico Fellini, Ennio Flaiano, Tullio Pinelli, from a story by Fellini and Pinelli. Direction: Fellini. Photography: Otello Martelli. Editing: Leo Cattozzo. Music: Nino Rota. Art Direction: Mario Ravasco. Players: Giulietta Masina, Anthony Quinn, Richard Basehart, Aldo Silvani, Marcella Rovena, Lidia Venturina. Production: Carlo Ponti and Dino De Laurentiis. (104 mins.)

The spirit of Gelsomina prevails not only in *La Strada* but also in Fellini's *Lights of Variety, The Swindlers, Cabiria,* and even to a limited extent in *La Dolce Vita* (see *1959*), where Paola's image returns to haunt Marcello on the beach at dawn. For Gelsomina's stricken, clown-like face is the face of innocence, and Fellini describes how that innocence so angers and frustrates men that they must crush and humiliate it, until they realize that they have in fact destroyed their inner selves—that precious speck of goodwill that lies deep in every man. Gelsomina is virtually sold by her mother to Zampano, an itinerant charlatan, a creature of sullen brutality and commanding grunts. Gelsomina hovers in the margins of his life, eagerly discovering the world, as observant and as trusting as a child. Fellini's camera alights on her alone in dirty squares, or huddling miserably against the wind on a stretch of wasteland. Only "Il Matto" ("The Fool," played by Richard Basehart) comes close to understanding her, and when Zampano kills him, Gelsomina wilts and abandons her struggle. The final sequence, as Zampano learns long afterwards of her death, and staggers down to the twilit beach and claws the sand and sobs, as if he had lost an arm, is one of the most compulsive displays of emotion in Fellini's cinema. *La Strada* is filmed with an eye to visual distress that never falters. When "Il Matto" has been killed, the whole landscape seems to mourn with Gelsomina; the snowy fields and roads reflect her grief. When Zampano performs his strong man act for the last time, he paces round in an endless circle, his eyes cast down, and his numbed speech to the crowd conveys his mingled feelings of regret and guilt. And throughout this picaresque film, Nino Rota's famous tune comes and goes like romance or like a tantalizing ideal.

1954: Anthony Quinn and the pixy-faced Giulietta Masina in LA STRADA.

1954: Marlon Brando at the close of ON THE WATERFRONT.

ON THE WATERFRONT. United States. Script: Bud Schulberg, from articles by Malcolm Johnson. Direction: Elia Kazan. Photography: Boris Kaufman. Editing: Gene Milford. Music: Leonard Bernstein. Art Direction: Richard Day. Players: Marlon Brando, Eva Marie Saint, Lee J. Cobb, Karl Malden, Rod Steiger, Pat Henning, Leif Erickson, Arthur Keegan. Production: Horizon (Sam Speigel)/Columbia. (108 mins.)

When discussing this tribute to the moral and social conscience of a nation, many writers have confused non-conformity with Fascism. Terry Malloy (Marlon Brando), the callow docker whose brother Charley helps Friendly (Lee J. Cobb) to terrorize the waterfront, does not display the symptoms of megalomania. Like other Kazan heroes he lacks ambition; he is set apart from his companions only by profound reserves of disgust and personal pride. Edie (Eva Marie Saint), whose brother has been killed in suspicious circumstances, places her unsophisticated, waif-like personality at Malloy's disposal. Together they are alarmingly susceptible in a community founded on the survival of the fittest. Police, public commissioners, and priest alike are unable to destroy the power of the gangsters. But when Charley is murdered too, Malloy seeks revenge and is beaten up for his pains by Friendly's henchmen. As he struggles away through an avenue of dispassionate dockers, however, his eyes betray a glitter of pride. Thus the glorification of the individual that has angered Kazan's Marxist critics.

There is more than a patina of authenticity to the grimy dockland jungle where hooters moan in the background and pleasure is confined to the smoky cafés. Bernstein's remarkable music lashes the film along, and the cast is especially distinguished. Rod Steiger, Martin Balsam, and Eva Marie Saint have all developed since into major stars. Brando, gentle and disgruntled by turns, towers over the film, embodying much of the truculent idealism of Zapata.

201

Checklist of other important features

THE BAILIFF (Sansho Dayu). Japan. Slavery in eleventh-century Japan; another of Kenji Mizoguchi's tightly woven, poetical films. Restraint is the keynote here; each composition is charged with beauty and a peculiarly moving grace.

THE BAREFOOT CONTESSA. United States. Director: Joseph L. Mankiewicz. Ava Gardner as the Spanish dancer become Hollywood star and murdered by her wealthy husband. A kind of lush, romantic dossier maintained at a credible pitch by Humphrey Bogart as the world-weary director.

A GENERATION (Pokolenie). Poland. Director: Andrzej Wajda. The first film in a widely admired trilogy about Poland in wartime. It shows how young Stach and his comrades are gradually converted into bitter fighting machines, with love and devotion to a cause indissolubly linked.

KNOCK ON WOOD. United States. Directors: Norman Panama and Melvin Frank. Danny Kaye in his funniest film, a free-wheeling satire on psychiatry and the espionage game.

RIOT IN CELL BLOCK 11. United States. Director: Don Siegel. A prison drama distinguished by its documentary approach and its understanding of conditions in American prisons.

Short films and Documentaries

TIME OUT OF WAR. United States. Director: Denis Sanders. An interlude in the Civil War involving three soldiers. Only 23 minutes in length, but one of the cinema's greatest short stories, and one of its wisest interpretations of war.

1954: Facts of Interest

Death of Will Hays—initiator of the "Hays' Code."

1955

LOLA MONTES. France/Germany. Script: Max Ophüls, Annette Wademant, Franz Geiger, based on "La Vie Extraordinaire de Lola Montès," by Cecil St. Laurent. Direction: Max Ophüls. Photography: Christian Matras (CinemaScope and Eastmancolor). Editing: Madeleine Gug. Music: Georges Auric. Art Direction: Jean d' Aubonne, Willy Schatz. Players: Martine Carol, Peter Ustinov, Anton Walbrook, Ivan Desny, Will Quadflieg, Oskar Werner. Production: Gamma Films—Florida (Paris)/Oska Films (Munich). (90 mins; originally 140 mins.)

All Ophüls's talents reached their apogee in *Lola Montès,* which was drastically cut and reedited by its producers. Like another maimed work, Welles's *Othello,* it was shot at length (thirty-three weeks) in several different places: Nice, Bamberg, Austria, Munich ... It is still the greatest film yet made in the wide screen process. The film's first part and many of its later sequences are set in a gigantic circus, where Lola (Martine Carol) is on display as a symbol of degraded beauty, and the camera travels, here, there, and everywhere. It rises over chandeliers, follows performers round the spangled ring, swoops in for the ironic close-up, retreats suddenly to allow the full splendor of the spectacle to fill the screen. The colors and the soundtrack are as elaborately controlled as the décor. Throughout the film, as he relates in four major flashbacks the story of the gilded courtesan who has attracted Franz Liszt and King Ludwig of Bavaria among others, Ophüls remains the objective ringmaster. Lola is no better than an animal to be gazed at by the circus crowds. Ophüls often confided that he was intrigued not so much by Lola as by the reactions of the men who were dazzled by her superficial beauty. Peter Ustinov (the ringmaster here) wrote in an obituary that Ophüls was "like a watchmaker intent on making the smallest watch in the world and then, with a sudden flash of perversity, putting it up on a cathedral." In *Lola Montès,* the minutiae are gathered at last into a film of baroque splendor.

THE GIRL FRIENDS (Le Amiche). Italy. Script: Michelangelo Antonioni, Suso Cecchi d' Amico, Alba de Caspédès, from the story "Tra Donne Sole" by Cesare Pavese. Direction: Antonioni. Photography: Gianni Di Venanzo. Editing: Eraldo Da Roma. Music: Giovanni Fusco. Art Direction: Gianni Polidori. Players: Eleanora Rossi-Drago, Yvonne Furneaux, Gabriele Ferzetti, Madeleine Fischer, Valentina Cortese, Franco Fabrizi, Ettore Manni. Production: Trionfalcine (Giovanni Addessi). (104 mins.)

Cesare Pavese was a writer of much the same outlook as Scott Fitzgerald: the problems of assuaging boredom, of learning to live with monetary success on the one hand and artistic failure on the other color his novels, and *Tra Donne Sole* especially. Antonioni's film of this book is weighed down by some trite dialogue and sentimental situations, but it is very important by virtue of its narration. Antonioni's methods were not appreciated until the early sixties. Yet here he is already assembling his own film language. He relinquishes conventional editing in most scenes. Instead, he lets his characters betray themselves as he follows them discreetly with the camera. The environment of Turin becomes forceful and realistic as Antonioni dwells for a moment on some bystanders or an architectural outcrop before panning slowly round to discover his principal characters like aliens in this grey landscape.

Clelia (Eleanora Rossi-Drago) returns from Rome to her native Turin to launch a fashion salon. By chance she is drawn into a "group" of smart friends and finds herself face to face with the drab uselessness of their lives. Rosetta, prone to suicide, is desperately in love with Lorenzo, a painter who is troubled more than he admits by the success of his wife as a ceramist. Momina (Yvonne Furneaux), ignored by her husband, vents her despair on her acquaintances—insinuating, needling, admonishing, until it ends in tragedy. Lorenzo is already the typical Antonioni male, unable to comprehend the other sex and unaware that his egotism is so deeply wound-

1955: From Max Ophüls's LOLA MONTES.

1955: Franco Fabrizi, Ettore Manni, and Eleanora Rossi-Drago in THE GIRL FRIENDS.

ing to Rosetta, whose heart snaps like a straw as he tells her brusquely that he no longer needs her. Betrayal lies at the heart of Antonioni's cinema, and his bleak resignation accords precisely with Pavese's. When Momina enters a café with her friends and declares drily, "Tonight a miracle will happen—we'll have fun," one shudders as one laughs.

SMILES OF A SUMMER NIGHT (Sommarnattens leende). Sweden. Script and Direction: Ingmar Bergman. Photography: Gunnar Fischer. Editing: Oscar Rosander. Music: Erik Nordgren. Art Direction: P. A. Lundgren. Players: Ulla Jacobsson, Eva Dahlbeck, Margit Carlquist, Harriet Andersson, Gunnar Björnstrand, Jarl Kulle, Ake Fridell, Björn Bjelvenstam, Naima Wifstrand. Production: Svensk Filmindustri. (104 mins.)

Before this film was shown at Cannes in 1956, Ingmar Bergman was virtually unknown outside Sweden. Yet to some degree *Smiles of a Summer Night* is his most uncharacteristic achievement. Comedy has not featured prominently in the Swedish cinema since the days of Stiller. In this film, which revolves around a house party at the turn of the century, Egerman remarks sarcastically to his son (a theology student), "I thought comedy too worldly for a man of the Church," and the comment scores because one can never banish the thought that Bergman is a disenchanted artist, attached to the Strindberg tradition. But here the familiar threats are translated into puns,

the arguments become delightful repartee, frustration is disguised as pedantry. Tragedy, in a phrase, becomes farce. It is a film in which women assert their sophistication and their moral resilience. The men in *Smiles of a Summer Night* are spun to frustration in a web of civilized comportment. They cannot deny their pagan tendencies (and the film takes place during Midsummer night), but they cannot discard their masks—their code of civilized behavior—without appearing ridiculous. Only Frid and Petra, the groom and maid below stairs, can abandon themselves to the climate of eroticism. Throughout the film Bergman is in complete control of his material, and maneuvers his characters like elegant puppets among the sun-dappled lawns and rococo interiors. His dialogue sparkles with licentious wit, and, if the joke seems often to be at the expense of the director himself, it is because Bergman, more than almost any other film-maker of stature, is slyly aware of the illusion that he creates.

DEATH OF A CYCLIST (Muerte di un Ciclista). Spain/Italy. Script and Direction: Juan Antonio Bardem, from a story by Luis F. de Igoa. Photography: Alfredo Fraile. Editing: Margarita Ochoa. Music: Isidro Maiztegui. Art Direction: Enrique Alarcôn. Players: Lucia Bosé, Alberto Closas, Otello Toso, Carlos Casarvilla, Bruna Corra, Julia Delgado Caro. Production: Guion / Suevia / Gonzalez (Madrid) / Trionfalcine (Rome). (100 mins.)

1955: SMILES OF A SUMMER NIGHT—"the arguments become delightful repartee."

1955: Lucia Bosé in DEATH OF A CYCLIST.

Before *Death of a Cyclist*, too, was presented at the Cannes festival, the Spanish cinema was an unknown quantity (with the exception of Luis Berlanga's *Welcome, Mister Marshall!*, which had been co-scripted by Bardem). The first sequence is alarming and memorable. Two lovers run over a cyclist on a somber stretch of road and, in panic, leave him to die. She is the wife of a successful industrialist, he is a university lecturer owing his position to his brother-in-law. The accident shakes them profoundly, and Bardem moves in with his clever admixture of close-ups and attacking camera angles to record their fear and exasperation. A society blackmailer, Rafa, personifies their guilt, for Maria-José and Juan have to conceal their love from her husband as well as their crime from the police. They try feverishly to shed their self-deception, but whereas Juan reassesses his career objectively, and is prepared in the end to confess, Maria-José has too much to lose—reputation, wealth—for her to behave so rationally. Selfish motives encourage her, like nearly everyone in the film, to sidestep the real issues involved. Bardem not only illustrates how a crime of chance leads inevitably to a crime of premeditation, but also hints at the unrest and corruption running through Spanish society. The students' demonstration is clearly provoked by more than Juan's failing to pass a girl in the annual exams. And the accident only awakens Juan's dormant dissatisfaction with his life. "I belong to a time when there were

too many symbols," he says before resigning from the university. These discordant elements are suggested in the soundtrack (where in one instance a single piano note plucks at the lovers' conscience) and in the feverish rhythm of the film itself. Bardem leaves each scene just when the psychological tension is at its height; a dangerous style, and one which, although applied effectively here, has led the Spanish director to excessive and inevitable melodrama in his later films.

A STAR IS BORN. United States. Script: Moss Hart, based on a screenplay by Dorothy Parker, Alan Campbell, and Robert Carson, from a story by William A. Wellman and Robert Carson. Direction: George Cukor. Photography: Sam Leavitt (CinemaScope and Technicolor). Editing: Folmar Blangsted. Music: Harold Arlen, with lyrics by Ira Gershwin and Leonard Gershe. Art Direction: Malcolm Bert. Players: Judy Garland, James Mason, Jack Carson, Charles Bickford, Tom Noonan, Lucy Marlow, Amanda Blake. Production: Transcona Enterprises—Warner Brothers. (150 mins.)

Innumerable articles, even books, have been written about the mystique of the star system. Sometimes Hollywood itself has produced the penetrating analysis—films like *Sunset Boulevard* (see *1950*), *The Big Knife* (see *below*), and *Inside Daisy Clover* come to

James Mason and Judy Garland in A STAR IS BORN.

mind. But George Cukor's re-make of *A Star is Born* is ultimately the most likeable of all, because it accepts—it shares—with a kind of nerve-wracked joy, the grease paint illusion that it mocks. There are moments of satire at the beginning, when stars arrive for a charity evening, but the tone of the script thereafter is compassionate and melodramatic. Norman Maine (James Mason) discovers a singer, Esther Blodgett (Judy Garland); and these two stars pass in their courses, one in decline, the other in the ascendant. As Esther's career prospers at the Niles Studio, so Maine's evaporates. He is egocentric and a womanizer; he drinks depressively. At the Academy Award ceremony he pleads embarrassingly for a job, and Esther reveals her true worth, by nursing him and supporting him and, after his selfish suicide, choosing to keep his name in defiance of Hollywood's notoriously short memory. Cukor's film has a sense of occasion; it revels in the potentialities of the wide screen; it turns the garish colors of the film industry to dramatic effect; and the musical numbers prove that Miss Garland has that "little something extra" that Ellen Terry defined as star quality. It is her triumph, and to see and hear her singing "It's a New World" to Maine in the motel is to experience Hollywood romance at its artificial best.

STELLA. Greece. Script and Direction: Michael Cacoyannis, from a play by J. Cambanelis. Photography: Costa Theodorides. Music: Manos Hadjidakis. Art Direction: Yanni Tsarouchi. Players: Melina Mercouri, Georges Foundas, Aleko Alexandrakis, Sofia Vembo. Production: Millas Film. (94 mins.)

Just as the Spanish cinema attracted international attention with *Death of a Cyclist*, so the Greek cinema was revealed with *Stella*. Michael Cacoyannis worked in England between 1939 and 1950, and in

the sixties he has made a number of English language co-productions. But his most characteristic and vibrant work has reflected Greek society and tradition. *Stella* is dominated by the burning *joie de vivre* of Melina Mercouri, who plays the star singer at a tawdry taverna in Athens. She wants to celebrate her energy and her freedom, and to see every man kneeling at her feet in admiration. "Oh love is like a glass of sparkling wine, Enjoy it while it lasts," runs the bouzouki song, and Stella will allow neither the bourgeois morals of Aleko, her suitor, nor the selfish desire of Milto, the footballer, to brook her liberty. She obeys her impulses without pausing to calculate the risks and when, in a community governed by harsh and inflexible customs, she refuses to come to her wedding, she could not care less if it means death. There is an echo of classical Greek tragedy as black tones creep into the final scenes and the lovers approach each other across a square at dawn. This stylization has tended to spoil many of Cacoyannis's subsequent films. But here the unashamed passion of Stella's life makes the immaturities of technique seem trivial.

1955: STELLA—"an echo of classical Greek tragedy."

Checklist of other important features

ANIMAL FARM. Britain. Directors: John Halas and Joy Batchelor. The first full-length cartoon to be made in Britain, full of invention and persuasive animal "voices" (by Maurice Denham).

BAD DAY AT BLACK ROCK. United States. Director: John Sturges. Spencer Tracy as the one-armed citizen who arrives at a desert township and neatly disposes of its terrorist (Robert Ryan). This film uses the wide screen intelligently.

THE BIG KNIFE. United States. Director: Robert Aldrich. A compelling adaptation of Clifford Odets' play about an embittered star, thrashing ineffectually within the Hollywood machine. With Jack Palance.

THE BLACKBOARD JUNGLE. United States. Director: Richard Brooks. One of the first taut, violent films about American schools and delinquency. Glenn Ford as the teacher has never found a role more perfectly suited to his image of integrity and quiet resolution.

BLACK TUESDAY. United States. Director: Hugo Fregonese. A superbly shot melodrama with Edward G. Robinson as the racketeer who breaks out of prison just prior to his execution.

EAST OF EDEN. United States. Director: Elia Kazan. One of James Dean's few film roles—as Cal, Steinbeck's outsider who rebels against his father and his brother around Monterey in 1917. Distinguished playing by Julie Harris.

KILLER'S KISS. United States. First, low-budget film by a former "Life" photographer, Stanley Kubrick, destined to become one of America's best directors. A short story of love and jealousy in a squalid area of New York City, told in flashback and containing possibly the most vicious boxing match yet shown on the screen.

KISS ME DEADLY. United States. A searing, atrocious Mike Hammer thriller tersely presented by Aldrich with all his nightmarish skill.

MARTY. United States. Director: Delbert Mann. A low-budget picture chiefly distinguished by Paddy Chayefsky's screenplay concerning the Italian area in Bronx. Winner of the Grand Prix at Cannes.

THE NIGHT OF THE HUNTER. United States. Director: Charles Laughton. Scripted by James Agee, this haunting film about a psychopathic preacher (Robert Mitchum) and his lust for money is told in a stream of uncanny, expressionist images.

PATHER PANCHALI. India. Marks the début of India's greatest director, Satyajit Ray, and is close to a masterpiece. Apu discovers the world as a child while his family struggles to make ends meet.

LA POINTE COURTE. France. A couple reexamine their marriage after four years, in an isolated French fishing village. A highly sophisticated début by Agnès Varda, one of the few woman directors of talent to emerge since the war.

RICHARD III. Britain. The best of Laurence Olivier's three Shakespeare films. An altogether dramatic, and largely cinematic rendering of the play, with an imposing cast and a fine score by William Walton.

SHIN HEIKE MONOGATARI. Japan. Director: Kenji Mizoguchi. A marvellous color recreation of medieval Japan, focusing on the clash between the soldier monks and the samurai.

THE SWINDLERS (Il Bidone). Italy. The most merciless of Fellini's works, a portrayal of confidence tricksters who prey on other people's illusions, only to be the more inexorably disillusioned themselves.

YANG-KWEI-FEI. Japan. The last film of importance by Mizoguchi; set in the eighth century, it relates the story of a humble girl raised to be the mistress of the Emperor of Japan, and a fragile, elegiac tone runs through the tragedy.

Short films and Documentaries

NIGHT AND FOG (Nuit et Brouillard). France/Italy. Director: Alain Resnais. Commissioned to mark the tenth anniversary of the liberation of the concentration camps by the Allies, Night and Fog is one of the greatest of documentaries. In a stunning combination of color (for the present-day sequences) and black-and-white (for the library footage), the film re-creates the harsh terror of Auschwitz and reminds us of a universal responsibility for this catastrophe. Night and Fog is lucid, objective, and yet profoundly concerned; one cannot say the same for many films on this topic.

BLINKITY BLANK. Canada. Director: Norman McLaren. An experiment in intermittent animation, with synthetic sounds scratched directly on the film.

THE RED BALLOON (Le Ballon Rouge). France. Director: Albert Lamorisse. A little boy and a strange and wonderful balloon that pursues him round Paris. Nothing more and nothing less inhabits this delightful fairy tale which won many honors in its year.

RYTHMETIC. Canada. Director: Norman McLaren. Numerals jostle with each other, forming sums and equations in a strict arithmetical balance in one of McLaren's intelligent cartoons.

1955: Facts of Interest

Death of James Dean.
The International Confederation of Art Cinemas is founded, linking specialist houses all over Europe.

1956

THE BURMESE HARP (Biruma no Tategoto). Japan. Script: Natto Wada, from a story by Michio Takeyama. Direction: Kon Ichikawa. Photography: Minoru Yokoyama. Music: Akira Ifukibe. Art Direction: Takashi Matsuyama. Players: Rentaro Mikuni, Shoji Yasui, Tatsuya Mihashi, Taniye Kitabayashi, Yunosuke Ito. Production: Nikkatsu Company. (116 mins.)

This is the first part of a trilogy of war films directed by the versatile Kon Ichikawa. It is a requiem for the Japanese defeat in Burma, grave rather than sentimental, noble rather than sordid. In 1945 a unit of men struggle over the mountains towards the Thailand border. But they are captured by the British. The war is finished. Mizushima, favorite among the troops for the songs he plays on his harp, is parted from his friends, and is appalled by the corpses that he sees everywhere. His initial reaction is instinctive: he burns a few bodies on a hillside to drive away the vultures. He retrieves a dead man's family photo. But soon the atmosphere of death overwhelms him, and he becomes a Buddhist monk at Mudon, burying his companions and refusing to go back to Japan. Ichikawa's pronounced humorous streak enlivens the early scenes, but his respect for the situation introduces a mystical note that finds its visual equivalent in the temples around Mudon. Mizushima finds himself profoundly in sympathy with the placid *modus vivendi* of the Burmese. "Whatever you do is useless," a priest tells him, "Burma is Burma, Burma is Buddha's country." The dignity of Mizushima's letter to the unit, read aloud by the captain as their ship sails towards Japan, lingers like an echo after the film ends. Mizushima represents a hostage to the war dead, a token of hope and vision in the face of catastrophe.

ATTACK. United States. Script: James Poe, from a play, "Fragile Fox," by Norman Brooks. Direction: Robert Aldrich. Photography: Joseph Biroc. Editing: Michael Luciano. Music: Frank DeVol. Art Direction: William Glasgow. Players: Jack Palance, Eddie Albert, Lee Marvin, Robert Strauss, Richard Jaeckel, Buddy Ebsen, Strother Martin. Production: The Associates and Aldrich Company. (104 mins.)

Robert Aldrich, among Hollywood's most skillful exponents of violence and chilling conflict, uses World War II as a setting for *Attack,* a biting study of disloyalty, cowardice, and incompetence. Lt. Koster (Jack Palance) knows that his company commander, Cuny (Eddie Albert), is unreliable, febrile, and dependent on drink. Morale is low, as the troops near the end of the war along the German border. Then a breakthrough brings them into combat again, and Koster is sent forward with his platoon to occupy a small, ruined town. It is crawling with Nazis. Koster loses nearly all his men and staggers back in a rage to kill Cuny, who has failed to give him fire support. But, in the face of an enemy attack, he postpones his vengeance too long.

Aldrich seems disinclined to denigrate war itself. Koster, after all, performs his job with utter callousness. The colonel (Lee Marvin), and the sycophantic Cluny would be as corrupt in any other walk of life. But the hostile environment—the vulnerable buildings, the desolate town, the suspicious silence before the Nazis open fire—pares down the men's reserves of friendship and tolerance, until animosity takes control. The optimism of the last scene, as the General hears the story, is in contrast to the astringent flavor of the bulk of the film. Besides, the situation has already closed like a steel trap around the hapless Koster. He is the real anti-hero, who only Aldrich can fathom so well.

BEYOND A REASONABLE DOUBT. United States. Script: Douglas Morrow. Direction: Fritz Lang. Photography: William Snyder. Editing: Gene Fowler Jr. Music: Herschel Burke Gilbert. Art Direction: Carroll Clark. Players: Dana Andrews, Joan Fontaine, Sidney Blackmer, Philip Bourneuf, Shepherd Strudwick, Arthur Franz. Production: RKO Radio. (80 mins.)

1956: Communal singing in THE BURMESE HARP.

1956: Jack Palance in ATTACK.

Fritz Lang worked in Hollywood for over twenty years. His first American film was *Fury* (see *1936*), and his last was *Beyond a Reasonable Doubt*. This low-budget thriller is about a novelist, Dan Garrett, who agrees to become the guinea pig in an attempt to halt the career of the District Attorney, who has already sent apparently innocent men to the chair. Garrett is encouraged by his fiancée's father, Austin Spencer, who is publisher of the local paper and an opponent of capital punishment, to plant evidence suggesting that he strangled a nightclub dancer in a ravine outside the town. During his trial, and after his conviction, Garrett is forced to experience the degradation of the criminal, and Lang returns here to the mood of *You Only Live Once* (see *1937*), fascinated as he is by the contagiousness of guilt. Indeed, although the final scenes assert that Garrett really *did* kill the dancer, one is left with the inescapable and illogical feeling that the crime has been assigned by events to a basically innocent man.

Beyond a Reasonable Doubt is constructed with precision and flexibility. Lang keeps the narrative moving so swiftly that tiny clues to the outcome of the film tend to pass unnoticed, and at certain decisive moments he can accelerate his pace to achieve an effect of numbed shock (the sudden death of Austin Spencer, for example). Personalities are treated much more sympathetically here than in Lang's German period; they are no longer puppets manipulated by fate, but emotional people who are uncertain of their feelings and their affections. And if *Beyond a Reasonable Doubt* seems implausible on a naturalistic level, its twists and turns are perfectly adapted to the unpredictable responses of its characters.

THE FORTY FIRST (Sorok Pervyi). U.S.S.R. Director: Grigori Chukhrai. A tale of desert island romance during the Russian revolution, with Chukhrai's colorful and rugged style signalling a brief new flowering of Soviet cinema.

GERVAISE. France. Director: René Clément. A raucous, savage adaptation of Zola's *L'Assommoir*, about a steeplejack and his crippled wife (Maria Schell), who plunge deeper and deeper into the drunken squalor of nineteenth-century Paris.

INVASION OF THE BODY SNATCHERS. United States. Director: Don Siegel. A thoughtful science-fiction thriller, intelligently scripted by Daniel Mainwaring. Starring Kevin McCarthy, Dana Wynter.

GIANT. United States. Director: George Stevens. Three generations of Texans from the pages of Edna Ferber are exhaustively analyzed in this film, which includes the last performance by James Dean and one of the best of her career by Elizabeth Taylor.

UN CONDAMNÉ A MORT S'EST ÉCHAPPÉ. France. A painstaking and psychologically gripping account of an escape from prison. Robert Bresson's first film for five years.

THE KILLING. United States. Director. Stanley Kubrick. A tense, ably directed parable on greed, as a gang raids the Teller's office on the day of a big race.

THE LAST HUNT. United States. Director: Richard Brooks. An unusual Western, with Robert Taylor as the demented buffalo hunter, intent on wiping out every herd in South Dakota.

THE MAN WITH THE GOLDEN ARM. United States. Director: Otto Preminger. An angry film about a drug addict (Frank Sinatra), which never flinches in its gaze at the agony and the sordidness to which such men are condemned by their own weakness.

THE SEARCHERS. United States. Arguably the last of John Ford's great Westerns, where private concerns are more important than the conventional issues of the genre. Filmed in Monument Valley.

1956: Sidney Blackmer and Dana Andrews in BEYOND A REASONABLE DOUBT.

Checklist of other important features

BABY DOLL. United States. Director: Elia Kazan. An absorbing, never subversive study in morals and racial feeling written by Tennessee Williams and introducing Carroll Baker as the teenage wife.

Short films and Documentaries

THE PICASSO MYSTERY (Le Mystère Picasso). France. Director: Henri-Georges Clouzot. The most revealing documentary to date on Picasso's methods, themes, and painting devices.

211

REMBRANDT, PAINTER OF MAN (Rembrandt, Schilder van de Mens). Netherlands. Director: Bert Haanstra. Concentrating on about sixty paintings by Rembrandt, this impeccable documentary relates the artist's life to his work more movingly than one would think possible.

THE SILENT WORLD (Le Monde du Silence). France. Director: J.-Y. Cousteau. A masterpiece among underwater documentaries, distinguished by its camerawork (Edmond Séchan and Louis Malle), and by its poetic rhythm.

A SUNDAY IN PEKING (Dimanche à Pékin). France. An idiosyncratic report on life in China, typical of Chris Marker's work. He has been called the cinema's first essayist.

TOGETHER. Britain. Director: Lorenza Mazzetti. A 50 minute study of two deaf and dumb worker friends in the East end of London, pathetic, ironic, understanding, and finally tragic.

TOUTE LA MÉMOIRE DU MONDE. France. A dreamlike exploration of the National Library in Paris which foreshadows much of Alain Resnais's later work in the cinema.

1956: Facts of Interest

Death of Alexander Dovzhenko, Soviet director, and of Kenji Mizoguchi, for some the finest Japanese film-maker.

1957

THE SEVENTH SEAL (Det sjunde inseglet). Sweden. Script and Direction: Ingmar Bergman. Photography: Gunnar Fischer. Editing: Lennart Wallén. Music: Erik Nordgren. Art Direction: P. A. Lundgren. Players: Max von Sydow, Gunnar Björnstrand, Nils Poppe, Bibi Andersson, Bengt Ekerot, Ake Fridell, Inga Gill, Erik Strandmark, Gunnel Lindblom, Inga Landgré. Production: Svensk Filmindustri. (95 mins.)

Bergman's masterpiece is as imposing a milestone in world cinema as Goethe's *Faust* is in literature. Nowhere else is Bergman's work so universal and so eloquent. It is clear that only within an allegorical, historical framework could the many ideals and emotions of *The Seventh Seal* be compressed. The knight who returns from the Crusades and travels home through a plague-stricken Sweden embodies the aspirations and inadequacies of modern man. The events he witnesses and the people he meets give at last a pattern and a meaning to his wasted life. Jöns (Gunnar Björnstrand) tempers his lord's optimism with a coarser, more hedonistic attitude, and a sense of rough justice that favours the exploited clown, Jof, rather than the malevolent seminarist Raval, whose hypocrisy had launched the knight on his expedition a decade earlier. But then each character in the film wears, like a pierrot or a harlequin, his sentiments on his sleeve, and contributes a portion of human experience ranging from the tender to the farcical. Bergman's pictorial imagination draws its strength from the medieval frescoes of Dalarna where Death—as in the film—plays chess with his victims. In unforgettable sequences, such as the procession of the flagellants and the burning of the witch, Bergman invests horror with an exquisite feeling of release, the Totentanz against a baleful sky dissolving to a sunlit shore and the "Holy Family" moving slowly away in their wagon, sheltered by love from the Apocalyptic threat. Max von Sydow as the knight gives a majestic performance.

THE HOUSE OF THE ANGEL (La Casa del Angel). Argentina. Script: Leopoldo Torre Nilsson, Beatriz Guido, Martin Rodriguez Mentasti, from the novel by Beatriz Guido. Direction: Torre Nilsson. Photography: Aníbal González Paz. Music: Juan Carlos Paz. Players: Elsa Daniel, Lautaro Murúa, Guillermo Battaglia, Jordana Fain. Production: Argentina Sono Film. (73 mins.)

Leopoldo Torre Nilsson's sixth film, *The House of the Angel*, is among his best. Its brevity is perhaps explained by the director's rigid discipline in paring away all superficial scenes and events. The story is of a young girl, whose life is blighted by her mother's puritanical insistence on her growing up at once free of sin and in ignorance of the facts of life. Not surprisingly, she throws herself into the arms of the first handsome man—a political deputy named Pablo—who pays attention to her. But he does not marry her, and she is condemned to live alone with her ageing father in the "house of the angel," locked in a claustrophobic limbo until her death.

Torre Nilsson's style is undoubtedly eclectic. The harsh fear of evil betrays an admiration for Bergman; the perennially perverse children confirm a knowledge of Buñuel's work; and the subjective, furtive camera movements are strongly reminiscent of Welles and Hitchcock. Yet this approach does succeed well when applied to the distasteful, equivocal type of story in which Beatriz Guido (the director's wife) excels. There is a disturbing parallel between Pablo's life and Anna's. Each is an individual imprisoned in a gigantic social framework. Morality is paramount, in private and public spheres. Pablo's career is ruined because his father's skulduggery is uncovered by a rival deputy, and Anna's puberty ends in violence because of her mother's bigoted attitudes. This bold characterization extends to others in the cast. Anna's extrovert sisters, her superstitious nanny ("even as children men have got the devil in them"), and her strait-laced mother, are all alive and credible. They

1957: *THE SEVENTH SEAL. Death appears on the shore.*

1957: *THE SEVENTH SEAL. The travelling players.*

1957: *From THE HOUSE OF THE ANGEL.*

are viewed through the young girl's eyes, and one feels pity for Anna because, like other Torre Nilsson heroines, she can only come to terms with life by shedding her inhibitions and experiencing the bitterest disillusion. With Anna, the disillusion is too shattering, and she retreats still further beyond the reach of the few adults who care for her.

TWELVE ANGRY MEN. United States. Script: Reginald Rose. Direction: Sidney Lumet. Photography: Boris Kaufman. Editing: Carl Lerner. Music: Kenyon Hopkins. Art Direction: Robert Markell. Players: Henry Fonda, Lee J. Cobb, Ed Begley, Martin Balsam, E. G. Marshall, Jack Warden, John Fiedler, Jack Klugman. Production: Orion-Nova (Henry Fonda, Reginald Rose). (96 mins.)

The cross-fertilization of talent between television and cinema proved to be an extremely fruitful process in the American film world during the fifties. Franklin Schaffner, John Frankenheimer, Martin Ritt, and Delbert Mann were among the directors who moved to Hollywood after an outstanding career in television, and Sidney Lumet's *Twelve Angry Men*—deriving, incidentally, from a teleplay—can be regarded as the most successful marriage between the two media. A youth is seemingly guilty of murder; only Henry Fonda, as Juror No. 8, is unhappy about the evidence. By a combination of reason, insistence, and lucid demonstration, he gradually shifts the embedded vindictiveness of his colleagues on the jury. *Twelve Angry Men* is a film that exalts the individual, the man who dares to stand up against eleven sweating jurors and flatly disagree with them, not because he has any evidence that will contravert their opinions but simply because his instinct warns him that a decision is being made automatically rather than considerately. Lumet preserves the claustrophobia of the jury room by declining to take his cameras outside, even to illustrate Fonda's arguments and surmises. To resort to flashbacks would not only put the audience ahead of the jury—it would also dispel the frustration that is generated among the jurors because they do not *know* the facts. Lumet has never improved on this hermetic film; and Henry Fonda's integrity has rarely served a role so well.

THE BRIDGE ON THE RIVER KWAI. Britain. Script: Pierre Boulle from his own novel. Direction: David Lean. Photography: Jack Hildyard (Technicolor). Editing: Peter Taylor. Music: Malcolm Arnold. Art Direction: Donald M. Ashton. Players: Alec Guinness, William Holden, Jack Hawkins, Sessue Hayakawa, James Donald, Geoffrey Horne, Andre Morell. Production: Horizon/Columbia. (161 mins.)

In the past twelve years David Lean has made only three films—*The Bridge on the River Kwai, Lawrence*

of Arabia (see *1962*), and *Doctor Zhivago*—each celebrating in epic terms the destiny of a man thrusting his head against convention. *The Bridge on the River Kwai* still looks the most virile of the three, and includes an unusually serious performance by Alec Guinness as Colonel Nicholson. He and his battalion are captured by the Japanese in 1943. Colonel Saito (Sessue Hayakawa) determines to bring British protocol to its knees. Nicholson, a peculiar blend of courage and masochism, is badly beaten and then locked in a tiny hut beneath the full glare of the sun. But he survives with a fearless upper lip, and maintains his men's morale by working on the Burma–Siam railway, constructing a bridge that (with his quixotic turn of mind) he hopes will last 600 years.

As the bridge nears completion, so an Allied commando unit approaches its objective, and Nicholson's tenacity is frustrated. "Madness, madness," says the army doctor, as the little name-board from the bridge floats ironically downstream after the explosion. But Lean has shown that it was not mere folly; that Nicholson's men are much more sensibly employed than the commandos who kill and are killed on their way through the jungle; and that the Colonel's loyalty to principle is in fact every bit as logical as it may appear ludicrous. *The Bridge on the River Kwai* is long and expensively produced. It represents the peak of the film industry's effort to entertain the declining audiences of the period.

EDGE OF THE CITY. United States. Script: Robert Alan Aurther. Direction: Martin Ritt. Photography:

1957: Sessue Hayakawa and Alec Guinness in the sun in BRIDGE ON THE RIVER KWAI.

1957: Sidney Poitier and John Cassavetes in EDGE OF THE CITY.

Joseph Brun. Editing: Sidney Meyers. Music: Leonard Rosenman. Art Direction: Richard Sylbert. Players: John Cassavetes, Sidney Poitier, Jack Warden, Kathleen Maguire, Ruby Dee, Robert Simon, Ruth White. Production: M-G-M (David Susskind). (85 mins.)

Martin Ritt is another American director who came to the cinema via television (although he had acted in Cukor's *Winged Victory* in 1944, and had produced several plays in the forties). *Edge of the City* is the first of his socially conscious films—with *No Down Payment* (also 1957) and *Hud* (see *1963*) to follow. Axel (John Cassavetes) is an army deserter with an unhappy family background, who has assumed a guilt complex for the death of his brother. He finds a job as a freight handler in the New York train yards, alongside Tommy (Sidney Poitier), a Negro who takes him in hand and tries to show him that life can be good. Axel's search for self-respect is hampered by a vicious foreman in the yard. "In this world," he is told, "there are two sorts. There are the men and there are the lower forms," and when he fights the

foreman in a tense duel with freight hooks, he finds that Tommy sacrifices his life for him.

Despite the predictable pattern of its story, which ends with Axel's dragging his enemy to justice, *Edge of the City* is commendable for its sophisticated attitude towards the color problem. Tommy is not a deferential underdog like the majority of Negroes in films. His role is purposeful and uninhibited. His lack of resentment is conspicuous in the grim atmosphere of the railyard—and in the American cinema of the fifties.

Checklist of other important features

THE CRANES ARE FLYING (Letyat Zhuravli). U.S.S.R. Director: Mikhaïl Kalatazov. One of the most dynamic Soviet films of the decade, flawed only occasionally by overemphasis, and reaching a tender intensity in its love scenes, as a girl (Tatiana Samoilova) and her fiancé are separated by war.

A FACE IN THE CROWD. United States. Director:

Elia Kazan. Budd Schulberg's rivetting story of Lonesome Rhodes, the ingenuous hick raised to the stature of a TV idol, aided and finally condemned by Patricia Neal as the radio reporter.

FEAR STRIKES OUT. United States. Director: Robert Mulligan. An incisive film about the father–son relationship that is set in the world of league baseball and contains Anthony Perkins's first major performance.

FUNNY FACE. United States. Director: Stanley Donen. A musical based subtly on the thirties' show with tunes by Gershwin. Fred Astaire and Audrey Hepburn recapture some of the Hollywood musical's freshness and unabashed charm, helped by Ray June's glossy photography.

KANAL (or They Loved Life). Poland. Director: Andrzej Wajda. The Warsaw uprising is on the brink of defeat; a company's stragglers try to survive in the sewers. The second part of Wajda's trilogy, and based on a true incident.

A KING IN NEW YORK. Britain. A silver-haired Chaplin as the dethroned monarch at the mercy of American show business.

A MATTER OF DIGNITY (To Telefteo Psemma). Greece. Many would regard this as Michael Cacoyannis's most penetrating film about Greek life. Walter Lassally contributes some brilliant camerawork.

NIGHTS OF CABIRIA (Le Notti di Cabiria). Italy/France. Director: Federico Fellini. Giulietta Masina as the genial, gullible, irrepressible prostitute whose simplicity reveals the human society around her as vicious and insensitive.

THE OUTCRY (Il Grido). Italy. Director: Michelangelo Antonioni. Steve Cochran miscast as the Italian factory worker who stumbles through the grey Po valley in search of peace of mind. Antonioni's uncompromising diagnosis of the malaise, however, makes the film a near masterpiece.

RUN OF THE ARROW. United States. Director: Samuel Fuller. An offbeat Western, starring Rod Steiger as a Yankee captured by Indians after Appomattox, with an outstanding music score by Victor Young.

SAIT-ON JAMAIS. France/Italy. Director: Roger Vadim. A characteristically complicated study of decadence in a wintry Venice by Roger Vadim, discoverer of Brigitte Bardot (who does not play in the film).

A SUNDAY ROMANCE (Bakaruhában). Hungary. Director: Imre Fehér. A provincial love affair between serving maid and aristocrat during World War I. Impeccable period detail, and an ironic, yet tolerant, taste in the direction.

SWEET SMELL OF SUCCESS. United States. Director: Alexander Mackendrick. Clifford Odets's script embraces extremes of cynicism and sophistication in this crisp dossier of corruption in New York journalism, with Burt Lancaster and Tony Curtis excellent as a million-reader columnist and his slavish henchman.

3:10 TO YUMA. United States. Director: Delmer Daves. An economical Western noted for its psychological conviction and the tense passage of hours as Van Heflin attempts to keep Glenn Ford, the outlaw, under lock and key.

THE THRONE OF BLOOD (Kumonosu-jo). Japan. A Japanese screen version of "Macbeth," with the medieval setting brought vigorously to life by Kurosawa's unparalleled technique.

THE TIN STAR. United States. Director: Anthony Mann. Anthony Perkins plays a greenhorn sheriff trying to come to terms with "bounty man" Henry Fonda in another of Mann's classic Westerns.

WILD STRAWBERRIES (Smultronstället). Sweden. For many this is Bergman's masterpiece, probing as profoundly and as dispassionately as it does into the life of a rather egotistical old Professor as he travels to Lund to receive an honorary degree.

THE WITCHES OF SALEM (Les Sorcières de Salem). France. Director: Raymond Rouleau. A brooding, atmospheric version (scripted by Sartre) of Arthur Miller's play ("The Crucible") about the seventeenth-century witch-hunt in Salem.

THE WRONG MAN. United States. Alfred Hitchcock diverts from his usual thriller technique to film the true story of Manny Balastrero, the bass-fiddler arrested for a crime he never committed.

Short films and Documentaries

FLEBUS. United States. Ernest Pintoff's intellectual and acutely funny cartoon made for Terrytoons.

LA JOCONDE. France. Director: Henri Gruel. A Grand Prix-winning satire about the Mona Lisa and her legend, using animated cut-outs of the painting in the Louvre.

LES MISTONS. France. Director: François Truffaut. A strikingly outrageous observation of adolescent problems that combines irony with lyricism, not altogether successfully.

RODIN'S HELL (L'Enfer de Rodin). Director: Henri Alekan. A distinguished art film which looks boldly and also mesmerically at Rodin's bronzes, linking them to Dante's vision of hell, to the accompaniment of the extraordinary music of Jacques Lasry.

1957: Facts of Interest

Deaths of Humphrey Bogart, Oliver Hardy, Louis B. Mayer, Max Ophüls, and Erich von Stroheim.

1958

ASHES AND DIAMONDS (Popiol i Diament). Poland. Script: Jerzy Andrzejewski and Andrzej Wajda, from the novel by Andrzejewski. Direction: Wajda. Photography: Jerzy Wojcik. Editing: Halina Nawrocka. Music: Filip Nowak and the Wroclaw Rhythm Quartet. Art Direction: Roman Mann. Players: Zbigniew Cybulski, Ewa Krzyzewska, Waclaw Zastrzezynski, Adam Pawlikowski, Jan Ciecierski, Arthur Mlodnicki. Production: KADR Group / Film Polski. (105 mins.)

In the context of national cinema, the late fifties belong to the Poles just as the mid-sixties belong to the Czechs. Andrzej Wajda, a graduate of the famous film school at Lodz, has proved the most thoughtful and exciting talent of this new generation in Poland.

Ashes and Diamonds is the third part of his trilogy devoted to the struggle against war. It is May, 1945. The Nazis have surrendered unconditionally. But the atmosphere is not entirely joyful. There is the prospect of civil war between the Nationalists, the underground fighters typified by Maciek (Zbigniew Cybulski), and the Communists, led by Szczuka, the ageing party secretary. The brilliant opening ambush beside a chapel, where sacrilege and massacre go hand in hand, sets the tone of postwar frustration and inefficiency. Maciek tries fruitlessly to break the habit of killing, and grasps at a few hours of happiness and contemplation with a barmaid (Ewa Krzyzewska). Others are affected differently. Andrzej, Maciek's superior, abandons the quest for heroism, and leaves

1958: ASHES AND DIAMONDS. Maciek and the girl he loves.

1958: *ASHES AND DIAMONDS. The death scene.*

for his youth. Apu fondles a fern, which reminds him of the fern he used to transfer from book to book; he casts away the sheets of his novel on a hillside at dawn, and the music of Ravi Shankar reaches a pitch of indescribable melancholy. But at last he is reunited with his little son, and the meeting gives him vitality and joy with which to face the future. Thus the wheel has turned full circle, and the trilogy closes with Apu carrying his child, just as it began with his grandmother rocking him in his cradle. Ray's films all proceed at a leisurely pace, but their imagery is so imaginative, and their sparse conversations so eloquent, that one can only submit to the serene spell they exert.

1958: *THE WORLD OF APU—"a pitch of indescribable melancholy."*

the town after the abortive assassination attempt. Kotowicz, the aristocrat, celebrates the peace grandiloquently at a banquet.

The pessimism and the humor, the patterns of darkness and light, are reflected in Wajda's organization of space and symbolic settings. Flaming glasses of vodka stand for lost comrades; a statue of Christ hangs upside down in the rubble of a church; fireworks brighten the sky as Maciek shoots Szczuka. In these baroque surroundings men take on a futile, fragile splendor. But while the revellers applaud the last Polonaise, Maciek plunges out to his death in the morning sunlight. He is the corpse of an old, unwanted Poland, and Wajda has given his night of procrastination a meaning and a universality that cannot date.

THE WORLD OF APU (Apur Sansar). India. Script and Direction: Satyajit Ray, from a novel by Bidhutibhustan Bandapadhaya. Photography: Subrata Mitra. Editing: Dulal Dutta. Music: Ravi Shankar. Players: Soumitra Chatterjee, Sharmila Tagore, Shapan Mukherjee, S. Aloke Chakraverty. Production: Satyajit Ray. (106 mins.)

Satyajit Ray's trilogy of films about Bengali life represents one of the peaks of achievement in film art. *Pather Panchali* (see *1955*) is a product of Ray's spare time between 1952 and 1955, and focuses on the formative years of the young Apu, protected and chided by his mother and sister while his father struggles to earn a living. *Aparajito* (*The Unvanquished*) deals with the adolescence of Apu after his father's death, and with his discovery of learning. *The World of Apu* is even more impressive, for its hero is now a man, able for the first time to register love and tragedy in their proper perspective. He marries, writes a novel, and then loses his wife in childbirth. Bitterly hurt, he staggers away into the countryside, and, in a series of haunting images, Ray expresses his nostalgia

VERTIGO. United States. Script: Alec Coppel and Samuel Taylor from the novel *D'Entre les Morts* by Boileau and Narcejac. Direction: Alfred Hitchcock. Photography: Robert Burks (Technicolor). Editing: George Tomasini. Music: Bernard Herrmann. Art Direction: Hal Pereira, Henry Bumstead, Sam Comer, and Frank McKelvey. Players: James Stewart, Kim Novak, Barbara Bel Geddes, Tom Helmore. Production: Paramount (Alfred Hitchcock). (128 mins.)

Hitchcock's peculiar gift has always been to provoke a sense of *involvement* in his audience. In *Vertigo*, there are classic instances of this: the prowling automobile drives through San Francisco, Scottie's dreams near the middle of the film, the vertiginous shots of stairways and streets a score of storeys down. Scottie (James Stewart) is the innocent drawn into a nightmare of intrigue and mental disturbance. Stewart's protuberant look of inquiry has never been quite so apposite and persuasive; it conceals a vulnerability that can rear up under stress. Scottie is attracted by

1958: Kim Novak and James Stewart in VERTIGO.

Madeleine (Kim Novak), introduced as his old friend Elster's wife; she is fey and remote; she is the accomplice in a murder plot and when, a long while after the crime, Scottie discovers her again, brunette instead of blonde, named no longer Madeleine but Judy, she tries to deny to herself the realization that Scottie is not in love with *her* but with an idealized version of her—with a dream. But Scottie sees in Judy the chance to cure his haunting, to erase the events of the past by tracing over them . . .

The pattern of the film is immaculate. Hitchcock so often and so wisely resists the temptation to use flashbacks to illustrate Madeleine's fantasies. The unreal impinges on the real, the abnormal on the normal, in such mesmeric sequences as the stroll in the forest. Herrmann's music slides cunningly from lingering rhythms of regret into dark, macabre chords. *Vertigo* contains some of Hitchcock's most poignant moments, as when Madeleine exclaims on the beach, "Oh, Scottie, I'm not mad—and I don't want to die!" And yet until the very last minute the old master is ready with an image of terror that freezes the blood.

PATHS OF GLORY. United States. Script: Stanley Kubrick, Calder Willingham, Jim Thompson, from a novel by Humphrey Cobb. Direction: Kubrick. Photography: Georg Krause. Editing: Eva Kroll. Music: Gerald Fried. Players: Kirk Douglas, Ralph Meeker, Adolphe Menjou, George Macready, Wayne Morris, Richard Anderson, Joseph Turkel. Production: Bryna (Kirk Douglas). (85 mins.)

Thoroughbred films about World War I have appeared rarely since the thirties. *Paths of Glory* was shot on location in Germany and remains Kubrick's most pitiless, virulent work. Kirk Douglas gives authority and a tight-lipped desperation to Colonel Dax, the French officer who opposes his superiors when they court-martial three innocent men after the GHQ has ordered a suicidal attack. The mastery of the situation that Kubrick establishes in the opening minutes, with the General's submitting to bribery and then walking through the trenches dispensing platitudinous encouragement to the soldiers, is never relaxed. Any departure from the pose of duty is construed as treason, and patriotism, which Samuel Johnson termed "the last refuge of a scoundrel," affords the excuse for sadism, cowardice, and blackmail. The sunlight streaming across the marble floors and lofty rooms of a chateau mocks the inhumanity of the court-martial, an obdurate travesty of justice that has no ear for reason or compassion. Kubrick's technique has a cold glitter: the camera is used unflinchingly like a weapon, darting into close-up to capture the indignation on an officer's face, advancing relentlessly at eye level towards the stakes against which the condemned men will be shot, or sweeping across the slopes to describe the wholesale slaughter of a division. The cutting from scene to scene is so tellingly shot that it becomes a kind of visual shorthand. Only at the end is emotion allowed to enter the film, when Dax's men listen in numbed silence to a German girl prisoner who sings to them of love in war.

ORDERS TO KILL. Britain. Script: Paul Dehn, from an original story by Donald C. Downes. Direction: Anthony Asquith. Photography: Desmond Dickinson. Editing: Gordon Hales. Music: Benjamin Frankel. Art Direction: John Howell. Players: Paul Massie, Irene Worth, James Robertson-Justice. Eddie Albert, Lillian Gish, Leslie French. Production: Lynx Films (Anthony Havelock-Allan). (111 mins.)

A war background and the problem of personal honor enter into Anthony Asquith's masterpiece, *Orders to Kill*. The story concerns an ex-pilot (Paul Massie) who, sent to Paris in 1944 to kill a traitor, is mentally ruined by the ordeal. He turns to drink, and only regains his poise when he realizes that his is not such an individual guilt after all. "The two moral points that arise from the film," says Asquith, "are that there is really no difference between dropping a bomb and killing an innocent man, and that you're just as likely to kill an innocent person with a bomb as you are with your hands."

Orders to Kill is one of the most persuasive of British films. It is a thriller that contributes a portrait of its leading character as profound as M in Fritz Lang's film or Johnny McQueen in *Odd Man Out*. Massie's playing is excellent, veering from the youthful flippancy of his approach to training in England, to his impassioned remorse when he has killed his victim Laffitte. Irene Worth gives a bitter, gallant performance as the Resistance agent, and Eddie Albert is unexpectedly sensitive as the American commander. Asquith's technical command, too

1958: After the abortive attack—PATHS OF GLORY.

often expended on whimsical and sentimental material in the past, brings to the film an enduring glitter and resolution. His compositions—the close-up of the blood-stained hand at the start, the terrifying illusions of "The Tunnel of Love" in which Massie has to kill dummy Nazis, the inspired shots of his hiding Laffitte's money in the Montparnasse cemetery—are characteristic of the self-effacing talent first glimpsed in the twenties.

NAZARIN. Mexico. Script: Luis Buñuel and Julio Alejandro, from the novel by Benito Pérez Galdós. Direction: Buñuel. Photography: Gabriel Figueroa. Editing: Carlos Savage. Art Direction: Edward Fitzgerald. Players: Francisco Rabal, Marga Lopez, Rita Macedo, Ignacio Lopez Tarso, Ofelia Guilmain, Luis Aceves Castañeda. Production: Manuel Barbachano Ponce. (94 mins.)

"If Christ came back, they'd crucify Him all over again," Buñuel has remarked, and in *Nazarin* he reveals himself once more as an atheist still struggling to justify his rejection of Catholicism. Nazarin is a priest at the turn of the century whose quixotic goodness opposes him to church and police alike. He is spurned like the plague wherever he goes. "What's your life worth? You on the good path, I on the bad path . . . we're both useless," he is told by a church thief. At the end, desperate for food and drink, he is forced to accept charity. "Dios sè lo paga," he mutters in gratitude like any other Spanish beggar, and his loss of faith is signalled with a thunder-

1958: Paul Massie, sent to Paris to kill a traitor, in ORDERS TO KILL.

223

ous drumming on the soundtrack. For, in Buñuel's eyes, Nazarin is the dupe of a false and effete vision of mankind: he is defeated, as Viridiana (see *1961*) is defeated, but as a result he begins to see that man is more important than a divine image, and that masochistic saintliness is as dangerous as the inquisitorial attitudes of the clergy. But there is no dwelling on an effect. *Nazarin* proceeds simply and lucidly like a fable, a fable illustrated with brimstone imagery—a brawl to the death between two women, a lewd dwarf's lusting after a prostitute, or Nazarin shuffling along in a chain gang.

Checklist of other important features

LE BEAU SERGE. France. Claude Chabrol's first film and the sign for the arrival of a whole group of new directors in the French cinema—the "nouvelle vague." This film, with its rural setting and sharp characterization, still looks imposing.

BRINK OF LIFE (Nära livet). Sweden. The nearest to a documentary ever made by Ingmar Bergman, about three women in a maternity hospital and their problems and disappointments.

THE DEFIANT ONES. United States. Director: Stanley Kramer. Two convicts, one black, one white, escape from a prison transport. But they are chained together . . . A sturdy, strident, film about race relations.

I WANT TO LIVE! United States. Director: Robert Wise. Susan Hayward in her Oscar-winning role as the woman condemned to the gas chamber in San Quentin, directed with documentary terseness and achieving a memorable tension.

THE LEFT HANDED GUN. United States. Director: Arthur Penn. A striking portrayal of Billy the Kid (Paul Newman) as the illiterate outlaw finds himself unable to match his legend. The anti-romantic Western par excellence.

THE LOVERS (Les Amants). France. A lyrical night of love at a country house is the centerpiece of Louis Malle's famous study of the haute bourgeoisie and their bored amorality.

MURDER BY CONTRACT. United States. Director: Irving Lerner. An outstanding B-feature, shot in eight days, that deals with a young assassin's fatal aversion to women and scares as much by virtue of its editing and soundtrack as by the performance of Vince Edwards.

MY UNCLE (Mon Oncle). France. Director: Jacques Tati. Another hilarious installment in the life of Mr. Hulot, confronted this time with all the ferocious complexity of modern scientific gimmicks.

ROOM AT THE TOP. Britain. With this adaptation of John Braine's novel about an ambitious Yorkshireman, Jack Clayton began a fresh phase in the British cinema, the characteristics of which were to include realism, uninhibited sexual relationships, and an emphasis on the class struggle.

LE TÊTE CONTRE LES MURS. France. Director: Georges Franju. A disquieting attack on the intolerance and lack of sympathy inherent in society, focused on an asylum where doctors crush any attempt at self-expression.

TOUCH OF EVIL. United States. Orson Welles's uneven, but brilliantly-made film about corruption on the Mexican border and the conflict between morality and justice that finally undoes Hank Quinlan, the police chief played by Welles himself.

Short films and Documentaries

GLASS. Netherlands. Bert Haanstra's witty, absorbing, sensitive vision of the glass-maker's art, edited to perfection.

THE LITTLE ISLAND. Britain. Arguably the most impressive cartoon of the last decade, a satirical fantasy in which Truth, Beauty, and Goodness fail to live amicably together, animated by the twenty-four-year-old Canadian, Richard Williams.

TWO MEN AND A WARDROBE. Poland. A cruel and amusing fable in which Roman Polanski casts a wry glance at society's callousness and defectiveness as two men stumble out of the sea with a large wardrobe and try in vain to leave it in a nearby town.

1958: Facts of Interest

The "free cinema" movement reaches its height in Britain, led by directors such as Lindsay Anderson, Tony Richardson, and Karel Reisz.

1959: HIROSHIMA MON AMOUR—the lovers in the café.

1959

HIROSHIMA MON AMOUR. France/Japan. Script: Marguerite Duras. Direction: Alain Resnais. Photography: Sacha Vierny, Michio Takahashi. Editing: Henri Colpi, Jasmine Chasney. Music: Giovanni Fusco, Georges Delerue. Art Direction: Esaka, Mayo, Petri. Players: Emmanuelle Riva, Eiji Okada, Bernard Fresson, Stella Dassas, Pierre Barbaud. Production: Argos Films/Como Films/Daiei Motion Pictures/Pathé Overseas (Samy Halfon). (91 mins.)

Alain Resnais was already celebrated as a documentary film-maker (see *1955* for *Night and Fog*), when he made *Hiroshima Mon Amour* from an original scenario by Marguerite Duras. Here the avant-garde in literature and the avant-garde in cinema joined hands in the most startling film to emerge from France since the war. The plot embraces the emotions of a woman of thirty-four who, because the brutal war evidence at Hiroshima evokes her first love affair, confesses her tragedy to a Japanese architect. Love grows between them; but she refuses to sacrifice herself to it. She claims that forgetfulness is a stronger force and that she will forget the Japanese just as she has forgotten her first lover—a German soldier shot on Liberation Day—and as the people of Hiroshima have banished their memory of the atomic explosion in 1945.

Resnais imparts tremendous force to these feelings by his use of environment—the war museum at Hiroshima, the procession of schoolgirls carrying doves for peace, the café overlooking the river where dawn brings a sad equilibrium to the lovers' relationship. The revolutionary style of the film is compounded of dexterous editing, music that is aligned unforgettably to each situation, and flowing shots that involve the spectator in the drama. The private loss and the public tragedy fuse. Perhaps the most imperishable quality of *Hiroshima Mon Amour* is that, within all the staggering audacity and beauty of its composition, it remains a plaintive and very moving love story. It has influenced scores of films in the last eight years.

THE LADY WITH LAP DOG (Dama s sobachko) U.S.S.R. Script and Direction: Josif Heifitz, from the story by Anton Chekhov. Photography: Andrei Moskvin, D. Meschiev. Editing: S. Derevimsky. Music: N. Simonian. Art Direction: B. Manevitch, I. Kaplan. Players: Ya Savvina, Alexei Batalov, Ala Chostakova, N. Alisova, D. Zebrov. Production: Lenfilm Studios. (90 mins.)

Not often has a work of fiction been so faithfully transplanted to the screen as Chekhov's short story, *The Lady with Lap Dog*. It is the achievement of the veteran Soviet director Josif Heifitz, whose first film appeared in 1929. In Yalta, that spa so beloved of the Russian aristocracy during the nineteenth century, a married man is entranced by a young woman, who is also married. Both know that to pursue their love would be fatal, but emotions prove too strong, and they come together again in Moscow. The ending is equivocal, for one of Chekhov's cardinal rules was that an author should remove both the beginning and the end of his stories. The music matches precisely the elegiac mood of the love sequences, and the locations add immensely to the film. When Anna and Dimitri wander into the mountains, they hardly speak;

"The elegiac mood" of THE LADY WITH LAP DOG.

but the scene is charged with all the grandeur, tranquillity, and nostalgia of Chekhov's description. Then, winter in Moscow: the period atmosphere crystallized in a few shots of incredible depth and detail, with the onion minarets twinkling white with snow, and the balloons of a street-seller billowing up on one side of the busy thoroughfare. In stark contrast to this is the little home town of Anna, with its bare streets and gloomy fences. The cinema possesses few works of comparable elegance and restraint.

BREATHLESS (A Bout de Souffle). France. Script and Direction: Jean-Luc Godard, from an idea by François Truffaut. Photography: Raoul Coutard. Editing: Cécile Decugis. Music: Martial Solal. Players: Jean-Paul Belmondo, Jean Seberg, Daniel Boulanger, Jean-Pierre Melville, Liliane David, Henri-Jacques Huet. Production: SNC/Georges de Beauregard. (87 mins.)

This first film by one of the most widely discussed

directors of the sixties retains, on account of its time and attitude, a certain importance in world cinema. Michel (Jean-Paul Belmondo) is a con man who models himself on Bogart and kills and steals for the fun of the affair. In Paris he disturbs the life of an American girl friend, Patricia (Jean Seberg), who eventually betrays him to the police. Godard dedicates the film to Monogram Pictures to emphasize his admiration for the American gangster genre, and already the traits that are to distinguish his work are clearly visible: the illogical, "jumpy" editing, the inconsequential snatches of dialogue, the excellent use of Paris as a background to the story, and the childishness of the concept if not of the actual events. Certain scenes, such as the amusing interview given by an author to reporters at Orly airport, are witty in themselves. For Godard's cinema is governed by the *episode*. His heroes and heroines flit from one physical situation to another—in most instances, to death or to love-making. His significance lies in his uncompromising and affectionate recording of all that

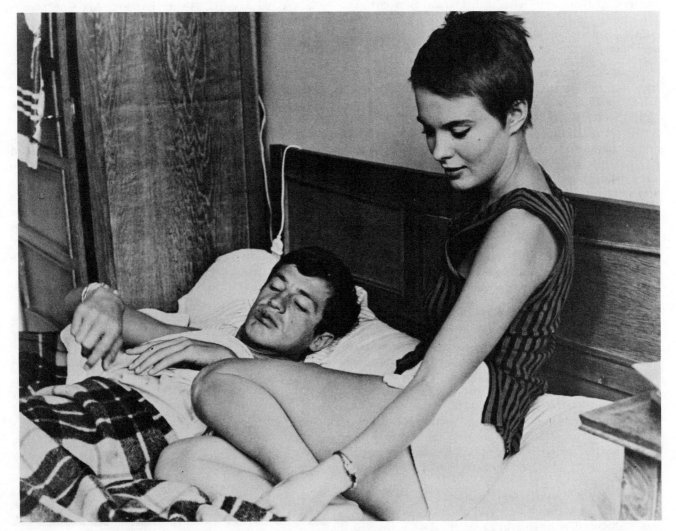

1959: The long central sequence of BREATHLESS, with Jean Seberg and Jean-Paul Belmondo.

is garish and pretentious and expendable in our age.

SOME LIKE IT HOT. United States. Script: Billy Wilder and I.A.L. Diamond. Direction: Wilder. Photography: Charles Lang Jr. Editing: Arthur Schmidt. Music: Adolph Deutsch. Art Direction: Ted Haworth. Players: Marilyn Monroe, Tony Curtis, Jack Lemmon, George Raft, Pat O'Brien, Joe E. Brown, Nehemiah Persoff. Production: Ashton/Mirisch (Billy Wilder). (120 mins.)

Billy Wilder, content to let the spectator chuckle privately at the sly innuendoes of *Sunset Boulevard* (see *1950*), sharpens his comic genius to the point of burlesque in *Some Like it Hot,* giving the film an outrageous, hectic tone admirably suited to the period —1929, with jazz and bootlegging in full swing. Joe (Tony Curtis) and Jerry (Jack Lemmon) are unemployed musicians who just happen to witness the St. Valentine's Day massacre and must flee for their lives. They dress up as girls and join a female jazz band en route for Miami Beach—with all the hilarious and often satirical results that the imagination of Billy Wilder and I.A.L. Diamond can conjure up. The gags progress with a smoothness that masks the iron discipline Wilder wields over the film. The female impersonation is exploited for all it is worth, and takes on an extra dimension of wit when Joe "changes back" into a playboy yachtsman, explaining to a wide-eyed Marilyn Monroe in an impossible Cockney accent how girls leave him frigid. Wilder's utterly shameless attitude toward sex is, appropriately, geared to the final line, as Joe E. Brown, the polygamous millionaire who has been courting Jerry, replies, "Well, nobody's perfect!" to his "bride's" desperate admission that he is a man. In these grotesque circumstances, even the cold-blooded slaying of George Raft and his henchmen at the dinner table exudes a certain sardonic humor. *Some Like it Hot* belongs to the handful of really memorable American comedies.

BALLAD OF A SOLDIER (Ballada o Soldate). U.S. S.R. Script: Valentin Yoshov and Grigori Chukrai. Direction: Chukrai. Photography: Vladimir Nikolayev and Eva Saveleva. Editing: M. Timofeieva. Music: Mikhail Ziv. Art Direction: B. Nemechek. Players: Vladimir Ivashov, Shanna Prokhorenko, Antonina Maximova, Nikolai Kruchkov, Ievgeni Urbanski. Production: Mosfilm Studios. (92 mins.)

Grigori Chukhrai is one of the more lyrical talents to come from the Soviet Union during the last generation, although *Ballad of a Soldier* remains his least sophisticated and most immediately captivating film. Chukhrai wanted to deal with the emotional experience of his own generation, who had been dragged into war straight from school, and to whom the fleeting opportunities of leave meant more than the battles.

1959: SOME LIKE IT HOT—in the Miami hotel.

Alyosha is a nineteen-year-old signalman who contrives to knock out two tanks and wins a six-day respite from the fighting in which to visit his mother and repair the family roof. Delays and misfortunes prevent him from staying more than a few minutes at home, but he learns about life on the journey. He meets a girl, Shura, and falls in love a little. He takes a present to a comrade's wife—and finds her living with another man. Although Chukhrai lays much emphasis on the theme of the journey, with the train puffing over the steppes and through the birch woods towards Georgievsk, his film is really a series of incidents. One marvels at the natural humor and the unadorned sentiment more perhaps than at the fluency of the technique. Most moving of all is Alyosha's reunion with his mother, which as they realize that they have nothing to talk about, that the conventional responses are superfluous, has the impact of a dying fall.

1959: *From BALLAD OF A SOLDIER.*

SUDDENLY LAST SUMMER. Britain. Script: Gore Vidal and Tennessee Wiliams, from the play by the latter. Direction: Joseph L. Mankiewicz. Photography: Jack Hildyard. Editing: Thomas G. Stanford. Music: Buxton Orr and Malcolm Arnold. Art Direction: Oliver Messel. Players: Elizabeth Taylor, Katharine Hepburn, Montgomery Clift, Albert Dekker, Mercedes McCambridge. Production: Sam Spiegel (Horizon British). (114 mins.)

Perhaps only Joseph L. Mankiewicz has captured on film the depravity and repression that stock the theatre of Tennessee Williams. *Suddenly Last Summer* is based on a one-act play first performed in 1958. It revolves round a characteristically nasty revelation—that the late Sebastian Venable was a homosexual as well as a rather flowery poet, and that his sister and even his mother lent their protection by procuring for him. A young brain surgeon stumbles on this family secret as he treats the sister Kathie (Elizabeth Taylor), for presumed insanity.

Although the action is restricted mainly to the Venable home, Mankiewicz films his subject in such a way as to let the décor and the encounters between the characters inspire memory and hatred. The garden, with its carnivorous plants and Polynesian heads, is both beautiful and hideous, like its owner, Violet Venable (Katharine Hepburn). Miss Hepburn's glacial voice, perpetually on edge, and rigid smile enrich this part enormously. She speaks of skies "filled with savage, devouring birds," and of carving "each day like a piece of sculpture," with her beloved son Sebastian. It is a climactic moment when she is denounced as a murderer by Kathie: all the film's suspense has been carefully husbanded to achieve this *frisson*.

Checklist of other important features

ANATOMY OF A MURDER. United States. Director: Otto Preminger. James Stewart as the lawyer set to defend an army lieutenant on a murder charge, with Lee Remick as the sexy wife. Complex, ambivalent in its conclusions, and beautifully made.

THE BRIDGE (Die Brücke). West Germany. Director: Bernhard Wicki. A brave, almost masochistic, exhumation of the last days of Hitler's campaign, as seven schoolboys, barely trained, are sent fatally to the front.

CHANCE MEETING. Britain. A bright and limpid film, perhaps the most successful (certainly the least pretentious) film Joseph Losey has made in London, its tale of double-crossing among the nouveau riche reflecting some alarming attitudes.

THE COUSINS (Les Cousins). France. Only the cynical and mistrustful prosper in Claude Chabrol's world. Here Charles comes to Paris fresh from the provinces, and is disillusioned, corrupted, and killed by the city.

FACE OF A FUGITIVE. United States. Director: Paul Wendkos. A "B" Western that stands out for its lucid narrative and its visual imagination, as Fred MacMurray waits in Tangle Blue for the evidence that will identify him as a wanted man to arrive.

FATE OF A MAN (Sudba Chelvieka). U.S.S.R. Director: Sergei Bondarchuk. The director plays the leading role here, as a village carpenter whose life is ruined by the war, and he reveals an acute talent for expressing anguish in visual terms. One of the great films about World War II.

FIRES ON THE PLAIN (Nobi). Japan. Director: Kon Ichikawa. Another superb war film, avoiding gratuitousness in its treatment of the barbarism and unrelieved suffering of troops in retreat.

THE 400 BLOWS (Les Quatre Cents Coups). France. François Truffaut makes his début with a personal and humorous study of a young boy misunderstood and mal-treated by everyone, from his parents to his school teacher.

GENERAL DELLA ROVERE (Il Generale della Rovere). France/Italy. Director: Roberto Rossellini. A study of blackmail and its unexpected results, as the Nazis force Vittorio De Sica, already a charlatan, into posing as a patriotic general. Persuasive.

LOOK BACK IN ANGER. Britain. Director: Tony Richardson. A biting and authentic film version of John Osborne's notorious play about one disgruntled Englishman.

LOTNA. Poland. Director: Andrzej Wajda. A meditative, nostalgic film about the disappearance of cavalry from modern warfare and the effect a single horse, named Lotna, has on its successive owners in a Polish regiment.

PICKPOCKET. France. A thief's loneliness and desire to escape from the society he despises. Robert Bresson's treatment is masterly as always—ascetic, elliptical, endowing every tiny action with spiritual weight.

THE SAVAGE EYE. United States. Directors: Ben Maddow, Joseph Strick, Sidney Meyers. A terrifying, grotesque glimpse of urban life and solitude that shocks every inch of the way, thanks to its *cinéma vérité* style and despite its portentous commentary.

STARS (Sterne). Bulgaria/East Germany. Director: Konrad Wolf. An intense yet restrained story of the love of a German soldier for a Jewish girl during World War II.

THE SWEET LIFE (La Dolce Vita). Italy/France. Federico Fellini's devastating report on Italian high society, whose frustration, disenchantment, and unfulfilled aspirations are suggested in Marcello, the journalist who moves from crisis to crisis and from party to party.

Short films and Documentaries

GIUSEPPINA. Britain. Director: James Hill. A ravishing sponsored film, set in Italy, which shows how enlightened this branch of the cinema can be.

MOONBIRD. United States. Two youngsters have an adventure in their garden at night; John Hubley's cartoon style is unique, all watery, insubstantial figures and strangely drawling voices.

VOLCANO (Aux Rendez-vous du Diable). France. Director: Haroun Tazieff. The most startling documentary of its kind—an exploration of the world's major volcanoes which took eleven years to complete.

WE ARE THE LAMBETH BOYS. Britain. Director: Karel Reisz. Another industrial sponsor, Ford, enabled a director to flex his talent on a study of a youth club in London's East End.

1959: Facts of Interest

Japan leads world film production with 493 features.
The U.S.S.R. makes more shorts (750) than any other country.
Moscow holds its first International Film Festival.
Death of Charles Vidor, Cecil B. DeMille, Jean Grémillon, and Preston Sturges among directors, and of Gérard Philipe, Errol Flynn, Victor McLaglen, Lou Costello, Paul Douglas, and the inimitable Kay Kendall among players.

1960

L'AVVENTURA. Italy/France. Script: Michelangelo Antonioni, Elio Bartolini, Tonino Guerra. Direction: Antonioni. Photography: Aldo Scavarda. Editing: Eraldo Da Roma. Music: Giovanni Fusco. Art Direction: Piero Poletto. Players: Monica Vitti, Gabriele Ferzetti, Lea Massari, Dominique Blanchar, Renzo Ricci, James Addams. Production: Cino del Duca, Produzione Cinematografiche Europe, Société Cinématographique Lyre. (145 mins.)

Michelangelo Antonioni was virtually unknown when he brought *L'Avventura* to the Cannes Festival in 1960. Those minor masterpieces, *Le Amiche* (see *1955*) and *Il Grido* (see *1957*), had not excited vast enthusiasm. But *L'Avventura* is such a modern and yet such a timeless film that the passing years have given it enormous stature. The theme: emotional rashness and misjudgments among the Italian *nouveaux riches*. A yachting party loses one of its members, a girl, Anna, discontented mentally (not physically) with her fiancé, Sandro. An abortive search for her dwindles to lassitude in face of a new and more studied relationship—between Sandro and Claudia (Anna's best friend).

L'Avventura does not take people and events at their external value, and attempts to register the tensions that underlie the banal conversations and the idle promenades. Antonioni impresses because he tends to "write" more with his images than with his dialogue. Comment is oblique, as in the novels of Scott Fitzgerald (whose *Tender is the Night* this film resembles). The final twenty minutes are brilliant, with their pregnant silences as Claudia trips along corridors and through the vast public rooms of a sleeping hotel in search of her lover; the dawn sky conveying the melancholy of the situation as she accepts that Sandro has been unfaithful; and the close-ups of her hand as she hesitates before stroking his head in token of understanding and pity. As the heroine of *L'Avventura*, Monica Vitti stands revealed as the most axiomatic and alluring of contemporary actresses.

THE HOLE (Le Trou). France/Italy. Script: Jacques Becker, José Giovanni, and Jean Aurel, from a novel by José Giovanni. Direction: Becker. Photography: Ghislain Cloquet. Editing: Marguerite Renoir. Music: none. Art Direction: Rino Mondellini. Players: Michel Constantin, Jean Keraudy, Philippe Leroy, Raymond Meunier, Marc Michel. Production: Play Art/Filmsonor (Paris)/Titanus (Rome). (123 mins.)

This is the story of a vain attempt to escape from the Santé prison in Paris in 1947. Roland, Geo, Manu, and Monseigneur are four tough convicts planning to dig through the floor of their cell, when Gaspard, who is accused of murdering his wife with a shotgun, is flung in with them. They trust him. He digs with them. And at last he betrays them. Cooperation is all; one man's weakness can doom the others. Becker uses this orthodox subject to express his wonderful love of mankind, his grasp of its psychology, and his high esteem for the moral, as opposed to the material, victory. *The Hole* shows four strong men fighting for their freedom just as simply and methodically as they fold cardboard boxes in their cells. They are like restless animals, and they must not be contained. When the men are filing through a bar or smashing away at concrete, the camera lingers on the work, lovingly watching, creating the impression that Becker behind it is striving to help the escape. The world of Jacques Becker is one in which every minute detail is vital and worth experiencing. *The Hole* is a compelling comment on humanity in harness as well as a work of suspense, and consequently it is among the finest escape films of all time.

PSYCHO. United States. Script: Joseph Stefano, from the novel by Robert Bloch. Direction: Alfred Hitchcock. Photography: John L. Russell. Editing: George Tomasini. Music: Bernard Herrmann. Art Direction: Joseph Hurley. Players: Anthony Perkins, Janet Leigh, Vera Miles, John Gavin, Martin Balsam, John McIntire. Production: Paramount (Alfred Hitchcock). (109 min.)

1960: Monica Vitti after the night on the island in *L'AVVENTURA*.

1960: *Violence among prisoners in* THE HOLE.

1960: PSYCHO—"black objects (like the patrolman's sunglasses) seem more opaque and menacing than usual."

In Hitchcock's cinema, vulnerability leads inexorably to voyeurism and thence to violence. *Psycho* lures its audience into a vortex of horror from which only the final shot grants issue. The story of Marion Crane (Janet Leigh), the girl who steals $40,000 and spends a last, fatal night at the Bates Motel, is trite, but

Alfred Hitchcock.

Hitchcock invests his symbols of latent chaos—the "old dark house," the stuffed birds—with such subjective power that one is stunned into complicity with events; one shares vicariously Norman Bates's moment of anxiety as Marion's car pauses before sinking irrevocably into the swamp; one participates in the murder of Arbogast as the camera pursues him down the stairs; one feels *physically* the bird-like frailty of Norman's head as Hitchcock stares up at his neck and jaw. Guilt is on this occasion transferred not to a character in the film but to the spectator, who is committed immediately Marion decides to abscond with the money.

Herrmann's string music again plays an intense role in this process of identification, these murders by proxy. The film is bathed in a dusky light so that black objects (like the patrolman's sunglasses) seem more opaque and menacing than normal. And through Anthony Perkins's puckered, mobile features Hitchcock projects an image of humanity clamped in its private trap of frustration and anguish. This is not only Hitchcock's greatest film; it is the most intelligent and disturbing horror film ever made.

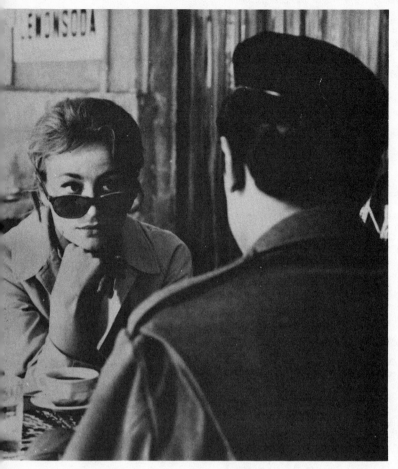

ROCCO AND HIS BROTHERS (Rocco e i suoi fratelli). Italy/France. Script: Luchino Visconti, Vasco Pratolini, Suso Cecchi D'Amico, inspired by Giovanni Testori's "Il Ponte della Ghisolfa." Direction: Visconti. Photography: Giuseppe Rotunno. Editing: Mario Serandrei. Music: Nino Rota. Art Direction: Mario Garbuglia. Players: Alain Delon, Renato Salvatori, Annie Girardot, Katina Paxinou, Roger Hanin, Paolo Stoppa, Suzy Delair, Claudia Cardinale, Max Cartier. Production: Titanus (Rome)/Les Films Marceau (Paris). (180 mins.)

Visconti's *Rocco* recalls the realism of his first film, *Ossessione* (see *1942*). The events and personalities are typical of Italian lower-class society, and Visconti imposes a pattern on these humble, violent lives, with flamboyant assurance, so that the film has strong affinities with Greek tragedy. Looming over the drama like some harridan from Sophocles is Katina Paxinou as the mother—ambitious, venomous, and effusive, in many ways the architect of disaster. Rocco (Alain Delon) is one of her four sons. The family migrates to Milan from southern Italy. They hope to make a new and lucrative life in the city. But Simone, the crudest of the brothers, lusts after Nadia, a prostitute (Annie Girardot), and the rivalry between him and Rocco for the girl's affections leads to moral degradation and murder. After the first hour of the film the background of Milan loses its significance; the characters dominate the screen. Rocco himself is depicted as a saintly figure whose tremulous love for Nadia contrasts with the animalistic grovelling of Simone. And Nadia is the seed of corruption, diabolically elegant and seductive. Yet, in that unforgettable sequence on the roof of Milan cathedral, one feels a twinge of sympathy for her, as Rocco rejects her out of selflessness, and consigns her to Simone— and to death. As a grandiose study of love and violence, *Rocco* surpasses all Visconti's recent work in the cinema.

Checklist of other important features

THE CONCRETE JUNGLE (The Criminal). Britain. Possibly the best British crime film of the decade, with director Joseph Losey delving deep into the sinister and precarious relationship between warder and prisoner.

THE KNIGHTS OF THE TEUTONIC ORDER (Krzyzacy). Poland. Director: Aleksander Ford. One of the very few European spectacular films that measures up to Hollywood's scale—a reconstruction of the medieval struggle between Poland and the Teutonic Knights, made on the 550th anniversary of the Battle of Grunwald.

MODERATO CANTABILE. France. Dismissed as pretentious by a majority of critics, Peter Brook's film, based on a novel by Marguerite Duras, is still intensely personal, splendidly acted (by Jeanne Moreau), and photographed with fluency.

MOTHER JOAN OF THE ANGELS (Matka Joanna od Aniolow). Director: Jerry Kawalerowicz. Demons at work in a Polish nunnery. A tale of harsh and peculiar dimensions told in a series of black and white scenes that confirm Kawalerowicz's enormous talent.

PLAYING AT LOVE (Les Jeux de l' Amour). France. Director: Philippe De Broca. One of the few accomplished French comedies of the past twenty years, with Geneviève Cluny and Jean-Pierre Cassel having one lover's row after another in their cluttered antique shop. There is an entrancing score by Georges Delerue.

SATURDAY NIGHT AND SUNDAY MORNING. Britain. Director: Karel Reisz. The film that, for many, heralded a renaissance in the British cinema. The coarse ambitions of Arthur Seaton (Albert Finney) were typical of a group of films and novels in the sixties. "What I want is a good time. All the rest is propaganda."

SHOOT THE PIANO PLAYER (Tirez sur le Pianiste). France. François Truffaut creates a quixotic Paris where a shy, self-effacing pianist (Charles Aznavour) finds his life enveloped in comedy and tragedy. A triumph of limpid technique and idiosyncratic wit.

THE SIGN OF LEO (Le Signe du Lion). France. Director: Eric Rohmer. A man without money in the hot idleness of a Paris summer. Rohmer charts his decline with sternness and dispassion.

SPARTACUS. United States. Director: Stanley Kubrick. Spartacus, the gladiator (Kirk Douglas), leads a rebellion and follows it through too far. Superlative acting by Peter Ustinov and Laurence Olivier suggests the twin qualities of pre-Christian Rome, mannered servility on the one hand, and arrogant ambition on the other.

THE TRIALS OF OSCAR WILDE. Britain. Director: Ken Hughes. Peter Finch makes a surprisingly good Wilde in this altogether excellent study of the poet and his downfall in turn of the century London.

THE UNFORGIVEN. United States. John Huston's first real Western, alive with memorable pictures, and with a telling performance by Lillian Gish as the step-mother of an unhappy half-caste girl (Audrey Hepburn).

THE VIRGIN SPRING (Jungfrukällan). Sweden. A stark excursion into medieval legend that contains some of the most tender and some of the most obscene sequences ever made by Bergman.

Short films and Documentaries

THE DREAM OF WILD HORSES (Le Songe des Chevaux Sauvages). France. Director: Denys Colomb de Daunant. A weird and hallucinating impression of the horses of the Camargue, ending in a brilliantly-photographed sequence in slow motion.

PRIMARY. United States. Directors: Richard Leacock, Robert Drew, Don Pennebaker, Al Maysles. This account of one of John Kennedy's elections marks an important point in the progress of documentary films. Its rough and ready yet wholly intimate style has influenced many *cinéma-vérité* directors since.

THE RUNNING JUMPING AND STANDING STILL FILM. Britain. Director: Richard Lester. An abstract concoction of "goonery" by Peter Sellers, Spike Milligan and others that was never intended for distribution and in the end was nominated for an Academy Award.

1960: Facts of Interest

Death of Mack Sennett, Clark Gable, Victor Sjöström, and Bretaigne Windust.

A major strike by actors in Hollywood disrupts production.

Some sixty seven directors make their début in France between 1959 and 1960, thus constituting the "nouvelle vague."

1961

LAST YEAR IN MARIENBAD (L'Année Dernière à Marienbad). France/Italy. Script: Alain Robbe–Grillet. Direction: Alain Resnais. Photography: Sacha Vierny. Editing: Henri Colpi, Jasmine Chasney. Music: Francis Seyrig. Art Direction: Jacques Saulnier. Players: Delphine Seyrig, Giorgio Albertazzi, Sacha Pitoëff, Pierre Barbaud, Françoise Bertin, Luce Garcia-Ville, Héléna Kornel, Jean Lanier. Production: Terra-Film / Films Tamara / Films Cormoran / Précitel / Como-Films / Argos-Films / Cinétel / Silver-Films / Cineriz (Rome). (94 mins.)

From a swift and unpredicted relationship between Alain Resnais and Alain Robbe-Grillet, among the leading avant-garde novelists in France, was born one of the strangest, most cerebral films of the sixties. One has to show one's interpretation immediately when one summarizes the "plot." A man, X (Giorgio Albertazzi), appears to be persuading a woman, A (Delphine Seyrig), that she is due to give him her love, which she has promised a year ago in the same or a similar place. Eventually, either by virtue of the man's cogency, or because of the woman's conviction that she would do well to leave her present life with her rather minatory guardian, M (husband? brother?), the couple depart together.

All this is set in an ornate hotel, which the camera explores with an insistent rhythm, passing under glittering, prehensile chandeliers and candelabra, moving slowly down empty corridors and along dark galleries like a somnambulist, keeping pace the while with the monotonous voice of X on the soundtrack. The formal gardens, where the characters are rooted in statuesque poses, contribute to the feeling of inhumanity and intellectual anxiety. The film could conceivably survive without Robbe-Grillet's stilted and pompous dialogue; it would be worthless, however, without Resnais's peerless pictorial flair. *Last Year in Marienbad* is a demonstration of Louis Delluc's dictum that "a good film is a good theorem." But it is a curiosity of the cinema, possessing a maddeningly enigmatic irrelevance, like the paintings of Salvador Dali or the novels of James Joyce.

THE NIGHT (La Notte). Italy/France. Script: Michelangelo Antonioni, Ennio Flaiano, Tonino Guerra. Direction: Antonioni. Photography: Gianni Di Venanzo. Editing: Eraldo Da Roma. Music: Giorgio Gaslini. Art Direction: Piero Zuffi. Players: Jeanne Moreau, Marcello Mastroianni, Monica Vitti, Bernhard Wicki, Maria Pia Luzi, Vincenzo Corbella. Production: Nepi-Film (Rome) / Sofitedip / Silver-Films (Paris). (121 mins.)

Jeanne Moreau and Marcello Mastroianni in THE NIGHT.

The pattern of our lives, according to Antonioni, is dictated by materialism and the pressure of external forces. In *The Night*, even more than in *L' Avventura*, the surroundings overwhelm and diminish the personalities. Giovanni Pontano (Marcello Mastroianni) and his wife Lidia (Jeanne Moreau) gradually become aware of the paralysis that has enveloped their marriage. It is a painful discovery that emerges from a sultry afternoon and an all-night party. The high, futuristic buildings of Milan seem to encroach implacably on this couple. He is a successful novelist whose inspiration is deserting him; she remembers the one true lover in her life, Tommaso, who dies from cancer during the film. At the alfresco party,

1961: A typical grouping from LAST YEAR IN MARIENBAD.

Alain Resnais.

each of them seeks adventure in the arms of another partner. But in the dawn they stroll away together, mindful of the true situation. "If I want to die tonight," says Lidia, "It's because I no longer love you," and Giovanni, resorting to the only kind of persuasion he knows, covers her with kisses while the camera tracks away like an embarrassed witness.

The Night is Antonioni's most rigorous film. Its action is concentrated into less than twenty four hours. Even in those scenes that drip on inexorably, Antonioni is observing his characters with a sharpness and lucidity rare in the modern cinema. A disquietude hangs over the situation, as if man was at last beginning to realize how he has let his emotions atrophy and be outpaced by scientific progress. He no longer understands the world in which he exists; he no longer understands his partner. Egotism, sexual laxity, and lack of communication are the maladies Antonioni is determined to diagnose in this ambiguous and desolate masterpiece.

1961: AN AUTUMN AFTERNOON: Hirayama with his daughter in Ozu's quiet and moving masterpiece.

AN AUTUMN AFTERNOON (Samma No Aiji). Japan. Script: Kogo Noda, Yasujiro Ozu. Direction: Ozu. Photography: Yushin Atsuta (Agfacolor). Editing: Yoshiyashu Hamamura. Music: Takanobo Saito. Art Direction: Tatsuo Hamada. Players: Chishu Ryu, Shima Iwashita, Nobuo Nakamura, Ryuji Kita, Shinichiro Mikami, Keiji Sada. Production: Shochiku. (113 mins.)

Ozu's characters tended to age as he himself grew older. In *An Autumn Afternoon* they are mainly men in their fifties still liable to adjust their modus vivendi. There is Hirayama, an auditor and a widower, who lives with his younger son and his daughter. There is Kawai, who advises his old school friend to find a husband for the girl. There is Horie, a contemporary of them both, who has just married a very young woman and relishes the situation. These good-natured folk meet regularly to drink *sake* and to laugh over college memories. But the story in any film by Ozu is always simple and even pedestrian. Melodramatics and climaxes are foreign to him, for his men are not of the kind who shake the world or seek to reform it. Responding to their Buddhist traditions, they come to terms with the inevitability of human existence, and it is this process—this discovery of a route through life—that Ozu describes with such unhurried precision. Although the film is concerned primarily with a fading generation, the pressures and trappings of urban life in the sixties are not ignored. Factory smoke billows outside Hirayama's office window. A portable television set stands discreetly in the background at Kawai's house. Ozu has pared away his style until merely the blank, unmoving stare of the camera remains—and suffices—to observe the domestic conversations and intrigues that the film consists of; while the dialogue, carefully prepared for months in advance, is never pompous or unnatural. This incredibly serene but sophisticated approach banishes sentimentality from *An Autumn Afternoon*. The warm colors, the mellow humor, and the plaintive music, confirm Ozu's great sympathy for his men. Hirayama is sad as he drinks alone after his daughter's wedding, and yet one senses that the sudden and entrancing sight of her arrayed for the ceremony earlier in the day has compensated his spirit and inspired him to understand the world just one degree more.

VIRIDIANA. Spain/Mexico. Script: Luis Buñuel, Julio Alejandro. Direction: Buñuel. Photography: José F. Aguayo. Editing: Pedro del Rey. Music: from Handel's "Messiah". Art Direction: Francisco Canet. Players: Silvia Pinal, Francisco Rabal, Fernando Rey, Margarita Lozano, Victoria Zinny, Teresa Rabal, José Calvo, Joaquín Roa. Production: Uninci S.A. / Films 59 (Madrid) / Gustavo Alatriste (Mexico). (91 mins.)

The debasement of ideals is a chronic theme in Buñuel's work. *Viridiana*, which shared the Grand Prix at Cannes in 1961, was banned by Franco's government in Spain. Because its leading figure is a demure young girl rather than a doubting priest, Buñuel's blasphemy is thrown into more savage relief than ever. Summoned from her monastery to nurse her transvestite uncle, Don Jaime, she finds herself surrounded by superstition and immorality. When,

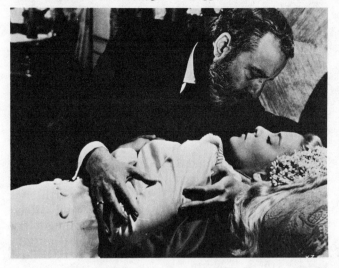

Luis Buñuel.

in his frustrated desire for her, Don Jaime commits suicide, Viridiana renounces her intention to take the veil and prepares to atone for what she believes to be her responsibility . . . She converts the decrepit house into a refuge for the halt and the blind, while Don Jaime's illegitimate son Jorge (Francisco Rabal) proceeds to reconstruct the estate. But one evening the beggars occupy the mansion's private rooms and indulge in an unruly, anarchic feast. Assaulted and shocked, Viridiana at last acquiesces in the disharmony. This is, for Buñuel, a triumphant conclusion. Like so many of his heroes, Viridiana has discovered a life of the senses, and has abandoned the traditional morality with which she has been hedged in as a novice.

Viridiana is infested with symbols. They abound both in the dialogue (a beggar speaks of Holy Water that infects worshippers with syphilis), and in the imagery (the pocket knife in the shape of a cross, the masturbatory handles of a skipping rope). The climate of superstition aroused by these symbols gives the film an elusive quality. Does Don Jaime indeed rape Viridiana? Is she at the end to be Jorge's complaisant mistress? Has the pop music of the last scene really replaced the Hallelujah Chorus that rings out above the beggars' orgy? These are questions that imply that Buñuel is, after thirty years of atheistic protest, still fighting to escape the shadow of the Church.

SHADOWS. United States. Direction: John Cassavetes. Photography: Erich Kollmar. Editing: Len Appelson and Maurice McEndree. Music: Charles Mingus. Players: Lelia Goldoni, Ben Carruthers, Hugh Hurd, Anthony Ray, Rupert Crosse, Tom Allen, Dennis Sallas. Production: Cassavetes-McEndree-Cassel. (81 mins.)

John Cassavetes filmed *Shadows* during 1958 and 1959 for about $40,000. It was shot on 16mm and a tape recorder was used to pick up the direct sound. At the end there were between ten and twelve hours of footage which Cassavetes edited down to feature length over a nine-month period, selecting significant moments and passages from the many improvised stretches of dialogue. *Shadows* was shown in London in 1960 and opened in New York in 1961. It influenced many directors as far as the details of its production were concerned, but what looks vital about it now is the grimy truth of its observation. For *Shadows* is about a Negro family that, in Cassavetes's words, "lives just beyond the bright lights of Broadway": Ben, Hugh, Tom and the others—New Yorkers trying to get a purchase on the fringes of stable society and compromising all the time for fear of losing that precarious chance. The ragged strips of dialogue and the spontaneous fights are just stages in their instinctive search for pleasure and status. Ben, the mulatto, haunts the film more than anyone; a hunched-up embodiment of melancholy, a jazz musician without a job, drifting away into the city night as the film closes. If there is sympathy in *Shadows*, there is also resignation. Happiness shines briefly for Tony and Lelia in Central Park, but soon they too are drawn back into a pattern of inarticulateness and high-strung recriminations. There is a form to *Shadows*, there is even a central crisis when Tony discovers that Lelia is a half-caste; but it is the film's coarse, consistent texture that counts, its unabashed stare at the seamier side of metropolitan life, and its rejection of the platitudes of Hollywood cinema.

THE MISFITS. United States. Script: Arthur Miller. Direction: John Huston. Photography: Russell Metty. Editing: George Tomasini. Music: Alex North. Art Direction: William Newberry, Stephen Grimes. Players: Marilyn Monroe, Clark Gable, Montgomery Clift, Eli Wallach, Thelma Ritter, James Barton, Estelle Winwood. Production: Seven Arts/United Artists. (125 mins.)

This was the last film completed by Marilyn Monroe before she committed suicide in 1962. She was far more than a dumb cover blonde. She exemplified much of the anxiety and confusion of life in the sixties. As she talks in her slightly gasping manner, her lips melt into intimacy and her eyes stare refulgently

SHADOWS (1961)—a brief moment of happiness for Tony and Lelia.

1961: THE MISFITS. "The convulsive struggle with the stallion."

at some private hallucination beyond her listener. Arthur Miller's original and highly-charged screenplay for *The Misfits* inspired not only Huston but also the players to work at an extraordinarily high level of awareness. The friction in the film comes from two opposing experiences of life. Roslyn (Marilyn Monroe) and Gay (Clark Gable) have an affair after both have secured divorces in Reno. In the margins of the romance Guido and Perce share a disenchantment with their lot. Like everyone who comes to Reno, Gay is a tired fugitive. He knows he has outlived his time. He is still involved with the cowboy things that thrilled him in his youth, but they have changed around him. Roslyn, at the other pole, is fleeing from the men who have exploited her susceptibilities. She cares for every living creature in sight. "We're all dying, aren't we?" she asks Guido breathlessly while they dance, snapping her fingers to the rhythm in an effort to dismiss the sadness. In the marvellous scene on the resert flats at the end, her misgivings and Gay's jubilation collide. Roslyn suffers as the mustangs are rounded up, and she dashes away in the truck and screams helplessly at the men, writhing alone on the landscape like a horse toiling against the ropes—a symbol of Gay's capacity for inflicting pain in spite of himself. But his convulsive struggle with the stallion in the dusk is an anthology piece; Gay makes virility really seem a virtue here. If the characters in *The Misfits* are unstable, the film is not. Huston's technique sets their predicament firmly in the unfamiliar environment of Nevada, each image at the house in the hills suggesting a peace that Gay and Roslyn are, in their different ways, trying to grasp.

Checklist of other important features

ACCATTONE. Italy. Director: Pier Paolo Pasolini. Accattone is a likeable pimp whose outbursts represent some of the most virile and bitter charges against society in the Italian cinema.

L'ASSASSINO. Italy/France. Director: Elio Petri. A disturbing study in guilt as an antique dealer is accused by mistake of the murder of his mistress and patron.

BANDITS AT ORGOSOLO (Banditi a Orgosolo). Italy. Director: Vittorio De Seta. A brilliantly photographed, quasi-documentary about a shepherd in the Sicilian mountains who is slowly forced to retaliate when his flock disappears.

CLEAR SKY (Chistoie Nebo). U.S.S.R. Within the framework of a war film, Grigori Chukhrai probes surprisingly deeply into the meaning and extent of democracy in Stalinist Russia.

CLEO FROM 5 TO 7 (Cléo de 5 à 7). France/Italy. Director: Agnès Varda. A story of anguish and bittersweet despair in Paris, as a young blonde singer faces the prospect of death from cancer.

DIVORCE—ITALIAN STYLE (Divorzio all'Italiana). Italy. Director: Pietro Germi. Marcello Mastroianni is consistently funny as the Sicilian baron bored to distraction by his wife and trying desperately to bypass the national divorce laws.

THE HAND IN THE TRAP (La Mano en la Trampa). Spain/Argentina, and SUMMER SKIN (Piel de Verano). Argentina. Two more studies of corrupt South American aristocracy by Leopoldo Torre Nilsson. Both plots are superficially banal, but both are deftly and exotically handled.

THE HUSTLER. United States. One of the peaks in Robert Rossen's career; a purposeful examination of the world of the pool-shooters, with Paul Newman as the young hustler locked in combat with the champion (Jackie Gleason) and his gambling manager, who is given a haunting, ruthless strain by George C. Scott.

THE ISLAND (Hadaka no Shima). Japan. Director: Kaneto Shindo. Seldom has the fight for subsistence been more ascetically described than in this tightly sprung film. There is no dialogue. A man and his wife fetch water from the mainland in order to tend their island's plants and so earn a precarious source of food.

THE JOB (Il Posto). Italy. A delightful first film by Ermanno Olmi. Observation—sometimes satirical, sometimes sardonic, always engaging—is *The Job's* prime quality; not so much its story of a diffident young man in search of employment.

LOLA. France/Italy. Comedy and pathos mingle in Jacques Demy's first feature film, about a cabaret dancer in Nantes and her sentimental education.

THE LONG ABSENCE (Une Aussi Longue Absence). France/Italy. Director: Henri Colpi. Georges Wilson and Alida Valli in a slow, beautiful, and sincere tragedy about amnesia and lost love. From a story by Marguerite Duras.

ONE EYED JACKS. United States. Director: Marlon Brando. A brooding, ornate Western built by Brando around his own outlaw figure, bent on revenge and immolation in Mexico.

THROUGH A GLASS DARKLY (Sasom i en Spegel). Sweden. The first of Ingmar Bergman's trilogy of "chamber" films, with a cast of four characters preying on one another's weaknesses on a lonely Baltic island.

WEST SIDE STORY. United States. Directors: Robert Wise and Jerome Robbins. A celebrated stage musical transferred to the screen with considerable success, starring Natalie Wood and Richard Beymer.

Short films and Documentaries

THE APPLE. Britain. Director: George Dunning. One of the best cartoons, hinting, behind its humorous drawing, that most of us are driven by complexes and frustrations.

THE FAT AND THE THIN (Le Gros et Le Maigre). France. Director: Roman Polanski. A moral about the master-servant relationship and the way to survive in a sadistic world can easily be construed in this classic short.

HAPPY ANNIVERSARY (Heureux Anniversaire). France. Pierre Etaix lives in a world stuffed with gags. Here he plays the ardent husband snarled up in traffic while his wife waits more and more impatiently at home on their wedding anniversary.

RUPTURE. France. Another Etaix comedy. He tries to write a letter to his beloved, but everything he touches is hostile, even pen and paper.

1961: Facts of Interest

Death of Gary Cooper.

1962

JULES AND JIM (Jules et Jim). France. Script: François Truffaut and Jean Grualt, from the novel by Henri-Pierre Roché. Direction: Truffaut. Photography: Raoul Coutard. Editing: Claudine Bouche. Music: Georges Delerue. Players: Jeanne Moreau, Oskar Werner, Henri Serre, Vanna Urbino, Marie Dubois, Boris Bassiak, Sabine Haudepin. Production: Les Films du Carrosse/S.E.D.I.F. (105 mins.)

The spirit of rebellion, mischief, and bawdiness in Truffaut's first two features, *The 400 Blows* and *Shoot the Piano Player* (see *1959* and *1960*), is tempered in *Jules and Jim,* his greatest film. The story begins in 1912 and traces the love of first Jules and then his close friend Jim for Catherine (Jeanne Moreau), who punishes them both with a typically headstrong and malicious gesture at the end. The film oscillates violently between merriment and gloom, for Catherine regards the world as rich enough to be cheated—and, despite her grasshopper mind, she wins. For Jules, who unfortunately believes in fidelity in marriage, she is a little of mother, daughter, and wife. Jim, the graver and more diffident, admires Catherine as a creature of instincts and liberal emotions. She brings an undeniable elegance to the friends' ramshackle life in Paris, and during World War I she remains a focus of attention for them both.

The chiselled sentences of Roché's novel are matched admirably in the film by Truffaut's own vigorous, short-hand style, and by the infectious zest of Delerue's music. Indeed only Truffaut seems to be the rightful heir to Jean Renoir. When asked about the attributes needed by a director to make worthwhile, satisfying films, he replied, "Sensitivity, intuition, good taste, and intelligence are the main ones. A little of each of these will yield very little, but a great deal of any one of them will make an appealing film, and a lot of all four will make a masterpiece." *Jules and Jim* has these qualities in abundance.

THE TRIAL (Le Procès). France/Italy/Germany. Script and Direction: Orson Welles, from the novel

1962: Exuberance in Truffaut's JULES AND JIM.

by Franz Kafka. Photography: Edmond Richard. Editing: Yvonne Martin, Denise Baby, Fritz Mueller. Music: Jean Ledrut, and the "Adagio" by Albinoni. Art Direction: Jean Mandaroux. Players: Anthony Perkins, Orson Welles, Romy Schneider, Suzanne Flon, Elsa Martinelli, Jeanne Moreau, Akim Tamiroff. Production: Paris Europa Productions (Paris) / FI-C-IT (Rome) / Hisa-Films (Munich). (120 mins.)

In the prologue to *The Trial,* Welles comments, "It has been said that the logic of this story is the logic of a dream—of a nightmare." This sets the tone for one of the most remarkable films of the sixties. Joseph K (Anthony Perkins), the clerk who is arraigned and condemned for an undisclosed offence, stands—in Welles's eyes—for a society that is to blame for the

Anthony Perkins screams at the Court in THE TRIAL.

ghastly knots into which it has tied itself. He is gullible, and convinced of his inferiority. He is an insignificant speck in a bureaucratic community (illustrated with a breathtaking shot of hundreds of typists at work in a vast exhibition hall). He is tempted and bewildered by the women he meets—Miss Burstner in his own apartment block, Leni, the Advocate's assistant, or Hilda who works at the court. He is prevented from meeting those people responsible for his fate; he is always fobbed off with the accessories to the Law. And when at last he takes to flight, he emerges in a cathedral, where the Advocate demonstrates his guilt to him in allegorical terms. Outside, the executioners squat and wait...

The monstrous perspectives of the Gare d'Orsay (the principal location for the film), the vistas of imprisoned glass, the iron stairways and myriad corridors combine to form a symboïic background that is an equivalent of the labyrinthine ways and mournful buildings of Kafka's Prague. The noble chords of Albinoni's "Adagio," detached from the action and opposed to the stuttering montage, lend a sound of inevitability to the film. Welles shows in *The Trial* that expressionism is still a ferociously effective style in the cinema, and he uses it to emphasize that the omniscient State is as potential a danger as it was in 1925, when Kafka's book was first published.

THE SEA (Il Mare). Italy. Script: Giuseppe Patroni Griffi and Alfio Valdarini. Direction: Patroni Griffi. Photography: Ennio Guarnieri. Editing: Ruggero Mastroianni. Music: Giovanni Fusco. Art Direction: Pierluigi Pizzi. Players: Umberto Orsini, Françoise

Prévost, Dino Mele, Gianni Chervatin, Celestino Cafiero, Renato Scala. Production: Gianni Buffardi. (110 mins.)

This outlandish beacon of a film illuminates 1962 with the cold light of a masterpiece by Antonioni. But if Giuseppe Patroni Griffi (more widely known in Italy for his work in opera) has been influenced by Antonioni, he brings to *Il Mare* an unconventional flair for cinematography. His camera dwells on three people who have run emotionally aground on Capri during wintertime. An actor, an elegant woman, and a sullen boy. Each seems to be escaping from a nameless past; each hopes to cleanse his spirit in this limbo of sky and sea and mental solitude; each looks eagerly to one of the others for security. By refusing to furnish details of their regular lives, Patroni Griffi succeeds in directing one's attention specifically to their behavior on the island, their frustrated arguments and egocentric desires. Brooding clouds and violent rain weigh on these refugees from society. The hotels and the cafés are deserted. The opening shots of the actor arriving on board a pleasure ferry bare of passengers and trappings strike a note of boredom and loneliness that is sustained to the end. In this forsaken environment, vanity and magniloquence can be seen as the repellent traits that they are, and Fusco's high-pitched music trembles, and files the nerves, in the intervals of disengagement.

THE KNIFE IN THE WATER (Noz w Wodzie). Poland. Script: Jerzy Skolimowski, Jakub Goldberg, and Roman Polanski. Direction: Polanski. Photography: Jerzy Lipman. Editing: Halina Prugar. Music: Krzysztof Komeda. Players: Leon Niemczyk, Jolanta Umecka, Zygmunt Malanowicz. Production: ZRF "Camera", Warsaw / Film Polski. (94 mins.)

After the glories of the late fifties, the Polish cinema began a recession, prompted and symbolized by the death of Andrzej Munk in 1961. Since then only two major directors have come from Paland, Roman Polanski and Jerzy Skolimowski. *The Knife in the Water,* directed by Polanski with dialogue by Skolimowski, is a modern variation on the theme of the eternal triangle. Andrzej, a middle aged journalist, and Christine, his wife, are constrained to take a young boy aboard their yacht for a Sunday's cruise. At first considerately and then on purpose, Andrzej uses the boy's earnest obedience to demonstrate his immaturity. Like a boxer he scores points calmly and confidently, humiliating his young rival with petty tricks and remarks. But his complacence is gradually undermined by his wife's ambiguous attitude towards their guest, who flaunts his masculinity in a small way too. Inevitably, there is a quarrel, and in a taut climax at dawn the boy feigns drowning and returns to seduce Christine. Polanski's ability to trap emotions in his imagery is seen at its best in this film. The

1962: Françoise Prévost in THE SEA.

1962: THE KNIFE IN THE WATER—"inevitably, there is a quarrel."

three companions on the boat are dissociated from the rest of humanity in the lonely lake district. Polanski watches them unblinkingly from one cunning camera set-up after another, waiting for the men to betray their flaws. Like Genêt and Kafka, he records his characters' behavior as he sees it, not straining to stretch their skirmishes out along a motive, but rather sensing instinctively how they react to challenges within their lives.

ticated of Buñuel's films. In *The Exterminating Angel*, twenty guests congregate at a Mexican mansion for dinner. But, despite the enforced gaiety, there is a queer tone to the party. The servants, all save the butler, feel impelled to leave the house. Then, as no one offers to leave, and the dawn approaches, the host grows apprehensive. The guests slump in sleep like gypsies in the salon, and are still there after an impromptu breakfast.

1962: THE EXTERMINATING ANGEL.

THE EXTERMINATING ANGEL (El Angel Exterminador). Mexico. Script: Luis Buñuel, from a scenario by him and Luis Alcoriza, adapted from the play "Los Náufragos de la Calle de la Providencia," by José Bergamín. Direction: Buñuel. Photography: Gabriel Figueroa. Editing: Carlos Savage Jr. Music: extracts from Paradisi, Scarlatti, and Gregorian chants. Art Direction: Jesús Bracho. Players: Jacqueline Andere, José Baviera, Silvia Pinal, Augusto Benedico, Luis Beristain, Antonio Bravo, Claudio Brook. Production: Gustavo Alatriste. (93 mins.)

Violence is rarely absent from even the most sophis-

These people are literally—or rather spiritually—immured. It seems impossible to cross the threshold of the room. The characters react differently to the Kafka-esque situation. As the days lengthen, a man dies. A pair of lovers stab themselves to death in a closet. Slowly and inexorably the veneer of good manners slips away from the smartly-dressed guests. The butler chews paper to stave off his hunger. Some of the women become deranged. Outside, even a brigade of sappers fails to penetrate the building. The progression towards the ironic climax, when the prisoners escape and give thanks in a nearby church, is wonderfully limpid. Buñuel works for most of the time within a single set, and avoids all the lapses into fantasy that could so easily ruin this strange fable. *The Exterminating Angel* is a savage commentary on human society, and it is typical of Buñuel that only the lambs can wander unimpeded through the invisible wall that surrounds the guests.

THÉRÈSE DESQUEYROUX. France. Script: François Mauriac and Claude Mauriac, from the novel by the former. Direction: Georges Franju. Photography: Christian Matras. Editing: Gilbert Natot. Music: Maurice Jarre. Art Direction: Jacques Chalvet. Players: Emmanuèle Riva, Philippe Noiret, Edith Scob, Sami Frey, Jeanne Perez, Lucien Nat. Production: Filmel. (109 mins.)

Georges Franju made his reputation as a director of short films during the fifties. Since he ventured into feature films the results have been uneven. *Thérèse Desqueyroux,* however, is based on the grave and rational novel by François Mauriac, and Franju's ideas about guilt and innocence find an ideal setting among the pine forest estates of the Landes. Thérèse seeks marriage as a refuge more than a possession. She suffers from a creeping inferiority complex. She is attracted to her husband's fragile young sister, Anne, and her jealousy of Anne's love for Azévédo is given much emphasis by Franju. His camera searches out the essential symptoms of her decline—the vanity, deep-seated beneath a meek exterior, her hypochondria, Bernard's brutish misunderstanding of her motives for trying to poison him.

Franju's investigation of conformist habits and repressions is incisive, and he alludes to passions and complexes that ripple beneath the religious façade of the family. The visual subtlety of the film underlines the solitary existence of Thérèse at Argelouse, summery days with Anne being replaced by persistent rain, as the house assumes the dimensions of a prison; and seldom has a piano score seemed so eloquent as Maurice Jarre's does here. Its smooth harmonies express the resignation of a woman—and a director—who believes that life is one long struggle against overwhelming odds.

Checklist of other important features

BARON MUNCHHAUSEN (Baron Prasil). Czechoslovakia. Director: Karel Zeman. A lively and diverting combination of cartoon and puppetry techniques with painted backgrounds (inspired by Gustav Doré) that recalls Méliès in its richness of invention and its respect for fantasy.

THE DREADED MAFIA (Salvatore Giuliano). Italy. Director: Francesco Rosi. Rosi's most widely known film lays bare the roots of organized banditry and accentuates the latent antagonism between the north and south of Italy, though it needs to be seen again and again before the precisely calculated patterns of movement and subversion assume their disturbing logic.

THE ECLIPSE (L'Eclisse). Italy/France. Director: Michelangelo Antonioni. Lassitude has given way to an inner confusion in Antonioni's world, but underneath it is another study of failing emotions, and Vittoria (Monica Vitti) is outstripped by the "sick hurry" and "divided aims" of urban life.

ELECTRA (Elektra). Greece. Director: Michael Cacoyannis. An over-formal, but dramatically gripping

Edith Scob and Emmanuèle Riva in THÉRÈSE DESQUEYROUX.

attempt to film Greek tragedy. Irene Papas is outstanding in the title role, and the photography of Walter Lassally is the best of the year.

EVE. France/Italy. Director: Joseph Losey. No director can pinpoint egocentricity so excruciatingly as Losey. In this maimed masterpiece, set in Venice, a harlot (Jeanne Moreau) steals the soul of a Welsh novelist (Stanley Baker), who in his turn has stolen fame from his dead brother.

LAWRENCE OF ARABIA. Britain. Director: David Lean. Brilliant camerawork records every facet and line of the desert that so bewitched Lawrence, even if Robert Bolt's script makes the hero himself too flamboyant and overdramatizes his exploits.

LONELY ARE THE BRAVE. United States. Director: David Miller. Dalton Trumbo's screenplay gives intelligence and candor to this offbeat "Western," in which cowboy Kirk Douglas finds himself out of place in modern society.

THE MIRACLE WORKER. United States. The story of young Helen Keller's fight to beat blindness and deafness with the often unappreciated aid of Annie Sullivan (Anne Bancroft), directed with a fine sense of humanity by Arthur Penn.

NINE DAYS OF ONE YEAR (Devyat' Dney Odnogo Goda). U.S.S.R. Director: Mikhaïl Romm. A remarkably tight, gripping film about problems of science and private life in the Soviet Union, with Alexei Batalov as the nuclear physicist who is so obsessed by his work that he neglects his wife.

RIDE THE HIGH COUNTRY. United States. Director: Sam Peckinpah. Randolph Scott and Joel McCrea tempted out of retirement for a complex and inspiring Western.

THAT CAT! (Az príjde Kocour). Czechoslovakia. Director: Vojtech Jasny. A delightful Czech whimsy that makes unusual use of color in its picture of a small provincial town.

THE TRIAL OF JOAN OF ARC (Le Procès de Jeanne d'Arc). France. Robert Bresson's austere treatment of Joan's interrogation and death lasts only sixty five minutes, but the stark bones of the story give it the unadorned power one associates with this film-maker.

Short films and Documentaries

THE BATH HOUSE (Banya). U.S.S.R. Directors: Sergei Yutkevitch, Anatoli Karanovitch. A brilliant puppet film version of the Mayakovsky satirical play.

THE FLYING MAN. Britain. Director: George Dunning. An experiment in the cartoon form, where insubstantial figures dance about the screen and mutate in almost abstract patterns of color.

PLAY. Yugoslavia. Director: Dušan Vukotić. A children's fantasy in animated style.

THE HOLE. United States. In all John Hubley's cartoons the message is more important than the form. Here two men talk of nuclear catastrophe.

INCIDENT AT OWL CREEK (Au Coeur de la Vie). France. Director: Robert Enrico. Oscar-winning episode from a film based on Ambrose Bierce's Civil War stories. A soldier about to be hanged imagines himself escaping and meeting his girl again.

THE NOSE (Le Nez). France. A grey, haunting film of Gogol's short story, mounted on Alexandre Alexeïeff's "pin screen," with its one million pins casting shadows across a board.

1962: Facts of Interest

Marilyn Monroe apparently commits suicide.
No fewer than 718 foreign films are released in the U.S.A.

1963

8½ (Otto e Mezzo) Italy. Script: Federico Fellini, Ennio Flaiano, Tullio Pinelli, Brunello Rondi, from a story by Fellini and Flaiano. Direction: Fellini. Photography: Gianni Di Venanzo. Editing: Leo Cattozzo. Music: Nino Rota. Art Direction: Piero Gherardi. Players: Marcello Mastroianni, Claudia Cardinale, Anouk Aimée, Sandra Milo, Rossella Falk, Guido Alberti, Barbara Steele, Madeleine Lebeau, Jean Rougeul, Edra Gale. Production: Angelo Rizzoli. (138 mins.)

The age of the *auteur*—the man who writes and directs his films in order to convey a personal vision—has provoked the cinematic testament: Cocteau's works, for instance, or Bergman's. But the problems of the creative conscience are not usually so aggressively and dazzlingly pursued as they are in *8½*. Guido is an extension of Fellini himself, forty three years of age, irresolute in his choice of characters and finding that his own life slowly and inexorably impinges on the film he is about to shoot. He is at once at home and afraid in the turbulent circus that commercial film-making comprises; he is distracted by his chocolate-box mistress and by his astringent wife. He is confused by sporadic memories of his Catholic childhood. The two most impressive women in this climate of sexual fallibility, the monstrous Saraghina and the beneficent Claudia, represent the poles of his yearning, and also the familiar comic and hallucinatory extremes of Fellini's world. The sparkling whites and charcoal blacks of *8½* reflect the division between fantasy and reality in Guido's experience, and only in the concluding scene, when all his friends and colleagues parade on the sands, does he seem as

8½: The fantasy in the underpass at the start of the film.

8½: The director (Marcello Mastroianni) with his wife (Anouk Aimée).

decisive as he is in his dreams. He is reconciled, like Fellini himself, to his faults. Whereas at the beginning he tries desperately to escape from a subterranean mass of cars and faces, at the end he is eager to join the circle of society, with all its disparate figures. Fellini's greatness is his ability to sublimate these complexes and flights of imagination; his art is that of a funambulist, depending for its success less on grace than on an intuitive panache and a mastery of illusion.

THE SILENCE (Tystnaden). Sweden. Script and Direction: Ingmar Bergman. Photography: Sven Nykvist. Editing: Ulla Ryghe. Music: Johann Sebastian Bach's "The Goldberg Variations." Art Direction: P. A. Lundgren. Players: Ingrid Thulin, Gunnel Lindblom, Birger Malmsten, Jorgen Lindström, Hakan Jahnberg. Production: Svensk Filmindustri. (95 mins.)

The exalted hopes and the magniloquent failures so characteristic of Bergman's vintage films (those made between 1955 and 1959) are absent from *The Silence*. A gathering disenchantment with the restless ideals of his youth has accompanied Bergman's in-

Ingmar Bergman.

1963: THE SILENCE—"degradation and perdition."

252

creasing ascendancy over the medium. Only degradation and perdition are open to Ester and Anna, the two sisters (?) who arrive in a weird, oppressive city, and find themselves trapped in their hotel just as they are ensnared by their own vindictive jealousy. Bergman is no longer concerned with the problems of religion and faith. *The Silence* is important because it concentrates so intensely on the difficulties of personal communication in modern society, callous as that society is. This feeling of alienation is emphasized by the incomprehensible language of Timoka; the bizarre and faintly sinister troupe of dwarfs; the dead furnishings of the hotel; and the hints of a war beyond the private world of the two women. But apart from these abstract and resonant symbols, *The Silence* is held in a rigid balance by the conflict between Ester and Anna—between moral judgment and physical instincts, between inhibition and indulgence, between mind and body. There was a stage when Bergman regarded God as the quintessence of love; but in this film there is no love, no authentic human sympathy; and when at the end the boy Johan mouths the few words Ester has written down for him, he is like a member of a new civilization, learning to live from the very beginning.

WILL O' THE WISP (Le Feu Follet). France/Italy. Script and Direction: Louis Malle, from the novel by Pierre Drieu La Rochelle. Photography: Ghislain Cloquet. Editing: Suzanne Baron. Music: Erik Satie. Art Direction: Bernard Evein. Players: Maurice Ronet, Léna Skerla, Yvonne Clech, Hubert Deschamps, Bernard Noël, Jeanne Moreau, Alexandra Stewart. Production: Nouvelles Editions de Films/Arco Film. (110 mins.) Also known as THE FIRE WITHIN.

The most eclectic of the postwar generation of French film-makers has been Louis Malle. In each of his films he has attempted to master a new style and a fresh brand of subject matter. *Le Feu Follet* holds many affinities to the latter days of Scott Fitzgerald, and the film is shot through with a languorous, insidious melancholy. Alain Leroy (Maurice Ronet) is resting in a sanitarium after a nervous breakdown. He is young and wealthy, and has decided to commit suicide. He travels to Paris to see his society acquaintances for the last time. Arid memories hang about their apartments. Alain laughs and gets drunk in their company, but in none of them does he evoke the warmth or sympathy that might dissuade him from taking his life. Each passes judgment on him, either to his face or behind his back. The words of his farewell note—"I have killed myself because you have not loved me"—suggest the isolation that has afflicted not only Alain but also Jill in *A Very Private Affair* and Florence in *Lift to the Scaffold* (two of Malle's earlier films).

Le Feu Follet is narrated with unerring control and sophistication. Alain is accused of trying to behave like an adult but his anguish is so acutely registered that the intellectual conversations are boring, embarrassing, and often humiliating. Erik Satie's clear and piercing piano notes sustain the mood of solitude and stress the gulf that yawns between Alain and the suave, feckless inhabitants of the Boulevard Saint-Germain. Suicide suddenly seems inescapable. The pictures of Marilyn Monroe on the bedroom wall take on a quite unsensational logic.

THE PASSENGER (Pasazerka). Poland. Script: Zofia Posmysz-Piasecka, Andrzej Munk. Direction: Munk, completed by Witold Lesiewicz. Photography: Krzysztof Winiewicz. Editing: Zofia Dwornik. Music: Tadeusz Baird. Art Direction: Tadeusz Wybult. Players: Aleksandra Slaska, Anna Ciepielewska, Jan Kreczmar, Marek Walczewski, Maria Koscialkowska. Production: Kamera Unit (Wilhelm Hollender)/Film Polski. (62 mins.)

This legless giant of a film underlines, more than any obituary could, the loss suffered by the Polish cinema when Andrzej Munk was killed in 1961. If he had made nothing else (and there are those who think highly of *Eroica*), *Passenger* would ensure him a major place among postwar directors. Munk died while engrossed on the picture, and the Kamera Unit assembled the sequences that had already been shot. An elegant German woman, Lisa, is travelling on a sea cruise. At Southampton she sees a girl coming aboard who resembles uncannily the Polish girl, Marta, she had commanded at Auschwitz fifteen years earlier. Her *émigré* husband inquires about her anxiety, and Lisa tells him (in flashback) a varnished version of the truth. Then, in a lengthier flashback, she recalls the relationship as it really was—that of a mistress watching over her slave. One can only conjecture as to the outcome—perhaps the new passenger is just a

1963: LE FEU FOLLET (WILL O' THE WISP)—*"Suicide suddenly seems inescapable."*

1963: Anna Ciepielewska in THE PASSENGER.

double of the Polish prisoner, and Lisa's guilty conscience is responsible for her anguish. The prologue and the epilogue consist of stills on a square screen. They seem torn from life as they repeatedly congeal the fear, pain, dislike, and curiosity aroused in Lisa by the new arrival. Munk would in all probability have concluded the film on an ambivalent note, and the unfulfilled scenes on the liner might well have deepened and extended the dramatic impact. The flashbacks are the fibre of *The Passenger* as it now exists, and Munk's, cool, somber appraisal of the concentration camp somehow gives the impression of a nightmare recollected in tranquillity. His understanding of the psychological skirmishing between the two women is even more remarkable. Lisa regards her *protégée* with a kind of feline sadism blended with admiration for the nobility and meekness of the Polish girl. It says much for Munk's compassionate treatment of his characters that both Marta and Lisa remain in the mind as sympathetic figures.

HANDS OVER THE CITY (Le Mani sulla Città)

Italy. Script: Francesco Rosi, Raffaele La Capria, Enzo Provenzale, Enzo Forcella. Direction: Rosi. Photography: Gianni Di Venanzo. Editing: Mario Serandrei. Music: Piero Piccioni. Art Direction: Massimo Rosi. Players: Rod Steiger, Guido Alberti, Carlo Fermariello, Salvo Randone, Dany Paris, Angelo D'Alessandro. Production: Galatea (Lionello Santi). (105 mins.)

In 1962 Francesco Rosi, the supreme film journalist of the period, made *Salvatore Giuliano,* a startling polemic on the Mafia in Sicily. But *Hands over the City* is a more ruthless and lucid study of social turbulence. Naples is controlled, claims Rosi, as firmly by the *camorra* (political groups in the City Council) as Sicily has been by the Mafia since the war. Nottola (a brilliant portrait by Rod Steiger, who speaks the language as though he were a born Neapolitan) is a building tycoon who pursues profit unscrupulously when it comes to replacing hovels with luxury flats. He is shrewd, volatile, and lavish with his money so that he can maintain a sécure foothold in the Council

junta. He becomes the center of a scandal when one of his buildings collapses, and Rosi shows with bitter objectivity how, far from suffering for his capitalistic sins, Nottola merely changes his political colors and, at the end of the film, is free to speculate once more.

While the bustle and confusion of Naples surge to life in the photography of the late Gianni Di Venanzo, the core of *Hands over the City* takes place in the Council chamber, where frenetic clashes between Left and Right are maneuvered to subtle advantage by the leader of the Center party (Salvo Randone), who believes that "the greatest sin is to be defeated." These scenes are enriched with bursts of trenchant dialogue. His opponents stab away at the position of Nottola, and yet have to acknowledge finally that he is still the master. But Rosi's protest lingers, unquenched. The film is shot in documentary style as if artifice could not withstand the restless spirit of inquiry that animates Rosi's work and gives it that sharp, three-dimensional quality.

THE SERVANT. Britain. Script: Harold Pinter, from the novel by Robin Maugham. Direction: Joseph Losey. Photography: Douglas Slocombe. Editing: Reginald Mills. Music: John Dankworth. Art Direction: Richard MacDonald. Players: Dirk Bogarde, James Fox, Wendy Craig, Sarah Miles, Catherine Lacey, Richard Vernon, Ann Firbank, Patrick Magee. Production: Springbok-Elstree. (115 mins.)

Human frailty and the temptations that encourage devious behavior are the recurrent components of Joseph Losey's cinema. In *The Servant* he offers a characteristically sharp comment on the British class system. A struggle for power is waged in a Chelsea house between Tony (James Fox), the young monied man about town, and Barrett (Dirk Bogarde), a smooth, lynx-eyed servant from the North Country. It is a duel between Faust and Mephistopheles, a duel that each man seeks to disguise until Tony drifts into vice and Barrett's servility becomes dictatorship. The last phase of the film degenerates in a series of perverse interludes that underlines Losey's difficulty in handling dramatic situations. His direction excels instead in the ambiguous conversations within the narrow confines of the house. His camera finds untold areas of space in which to observe the conflict, and his use of mirrors is quite brilliant. At the start of the film, the house is bare and almost empty; by the end it is a shambles. It seems to grow horribly vulnerable and corrupt like the aggrieved Tony himself. The film teases because it lacks a motive. Barrett has no urge to dominate his master; he merely ministers to his proclivities. The growth of the homosexual attraction is mutual; each man needs the other for a brief space of time. One admires Losey's thoughtful, analytical approach, the immaculate craftsmanship that distinguishes script, photography, and music; and the extraordinary performance by Bogarde.

1963: James Fox and Sarah Miles in THE SERVANT.

Checklist of other important features

THE BIRDS. United States. Implications of guilt and fear predominate in Hitchcock's most horrific assault on his audience, as thousands of birds suddenly harry a Californian coastal town.

THE FIANCES (I Fidanzati). Italy. Director: Ermanno Olmi. A quiet, reflective film about a worker moved to Sicily, away from home and fiancée, related in a complex tangle of flashbacks and documentary vignettes of factory life.

HARAKIRI (Seppuku). Japan. Director: Masaki Kobayashi. As a samurai prepares to commit suicide in public ("harakiri"), he tells his life story. A brilliantly topical indictment of the samurai outlook and the concept of virtue through strength.

HUD. United States. Director: Martin Ritt. A battle of wills between father (Melvyn Douglas) and son (Paul Newman) on a ranch in the Texas Panhandle, treated with an admirable lack of sentimentality by Ritt and cameraman James Wong Howe.

THE LEOPARD (Il Gattopardo). Italy/France. Sicily at the time of the Garibaldi campaign, with Burt Lancaster as the weary aristocrat coming to terms with a new society; told in Visconti's sumptuous and operatic manner.

THE MAGNET OF DOOM (L'Aîné des Ferchaux). France/Italy. Director: Jean-Pierre Melville. A contemplation of loyalty between the generations as Charles Vanel (a ruined banker), and his companion Jean-Paul Belmondo (a failed boxer) scour America in search of security.

MURIEL (Muriel ou le temps d'un retour). France/Italy. A middle aged woman summons her old lover to Boulogne. Other characters congregate in her tiny apartment; and out of the trivia of daily life and its anxieties Alain Resnais makes a hermetic, provincial masterpiece.

DIE PARALLELSTRASSE. West Germany. Director: Ferdinand Khittl. This hallucinatory, enigmatic film won the Grand Prix at the Belgian experimental film festival. Five men are confronted with a series of apparently unrelated documents. They must find the key to them all—or die. One of the most persuasive avant-garde works of the sixties.

RAVEN'S END (Kvarteret korpen). Sweden. Director: Bo Widerberg. An ambitious young novelist tries to break free of his facetious family household in the depression of the thirties. Moving and evocative.

THIS SPORTING LIFE. Britain. Director: Lindsay Anderson. The most talented of "new" British films, with Richard Harris as the surly, forceful, and ultimately cruel rugby footballer in the North of England.

TOM JONES. Britain. Director: Tony Richardson. A coarse and vibrant adaptation of Fielding's picaresque novel of the eighteenth century, full of mischievous enthusiasm and robust caricature.

VOYAGE TO THE END OF THE UNIVERSE (Ikaria XB1). Czechoslovakia. Director: Jindrich Polák. A spaceship of the future encounters a dead craft from the twentieth century. An eerie and thoroughly plausible science-fiction film, well acted by its Czech cast.

Short films and Documentaries

AUTOMANIA 2000. Britain. Director: John Halas. A concentrated and disturbing cartoon parable about the dangers of car production—reaching a stage where people are compelled to live buried in their vehicles and to be fed by helicopter.

A VALPARAISO. France/Chile. Director: Joris Ivens. A dignified, muted glance at a city cramped almost to death against the hills, with a remarkable commentary by Chris Marker.

THE CRITIC. United States. Director: Ernest Pintoff. The cynical, spare monologue by Mel Brooks is the best element in this satirical cartoon.

GALLINA VOGELBIRDAE. Czechoslovakia. The winner of the year's animation festival at Annecy (France). A delicate, delightfully colored whimsey by Jiri Brdecka.

INSOMNIA (Insomnie). France. Director: Pierre Etaix. A very amusing parody of the horror film and its effects.

LABYRINTH. Poland. Jan Lenica's terrifying tale of an innocent roaming through a deserted city. Animated with steel engravings and cut-out figures.

SAILING (Zeilen). Netherlands. Director: Hattum Hoving. The sense of freedom, the exultation of the yachtsman as he combats the winds and the waves, are conveyed here with a discreet lyricism that raises the film to the level of an ode to the sport.

1963: Facts of Interest

Death of Jean Cocteau.
Foundation of the Swedish Film Institute, revolutionary in its system of awards to quality pictures.
Higher box-office receipts *and* attendances in the U.S.A. are heartening signs of a stabilization in cinema fortunes.

1964

THE RED DESERT (Deserto Rosso). Italy/France. Script: Michelangelo Antonioni and Tonino Guerra. Direction: Antonioni. Photography: Carlo Di Palma (Eastmancolor). Editing: Eraldo Da Roma. Music: Giovanni Fusco. Art Direction: Piero Poletto. Players: Monica Vitti, Richard Harris, Carlo Chionetti, Xenia Valderi, Rita Renoir, Aldo Grotti, Valerio Bartoleschi. Production: Film Duemila/Cinematografica Federiz (Rome)/Francoriz (Paris). (116 mins.)

Antonioni's style is not just formally attractive and supple, but it respects the duration of real time on the screen and attempts to catch the reflection of the characters' inner thoughts and feelings, without forcing them to explain themselves through intellectual conversation. *The Red Desert* is another masterly, pessimistic study of a neurotic woman. Whereas Antonioni's previous heroines have been seemingly frustrated by their sterility, Giuliana's child only makes her life more difficult. Unable to draw understanding from her dispassionate husband, she turns hopefully to a newcomer, Corrado (Richard Harris). But he, like Giovanni in *La Notte* (see *1961*), can offer merely physical love. Giuliana's malaise is ostensibly the aftermath of a car accident, but the film shows, in a series of remarkably imaginative scenes among the complex of factories and marshland outside Ravenna, that it stems in truth from her failure to yield to a scientific age. She has visions of drowning in quicksands: her longing is for a wall of loving people to shield her from the inscrutable machines that are invading modern life.

Antonioni balances the mental turmoil with a piercing style. The soundtrack consists of strange electronic whines and hums. The colors are at once unprecedentedly *real* and consciously artificial. The yellow of the poison gas and of the quarantine flag would lose its disturbing symbolism in monochrome. Grey ships drift like preternatural monsters through the misty estuaries; even the gum trees in a hotel foyer are whitened for clinical effect. Antonioni's world has become a ravaged, mineral landscape, where human

1964: Monica Vitti at the beginning of THE RED DESERT.

beings must either adjust and be drained of dreams and emotions, or, like Giuliana, wander distraught in search of love and sympathy.

THE UMBRELLAS OF CHERBOURG (Les Parapluies de Cherbourg). France/West Germany. Script and Direction: Jacques Demy. Photography: Jean Rabier (Eastmancolor). Editing: Anne-Marie Cotret. Music: Michel Legrand. Art Direction: Bernard Evein. Players: Catherine Deneuve, Nino Castelnuovo, Anne Vernon, Ellen Farner, Marc Michel, Mireille Perrey. Production: Parc Film/Madeleine Films (Paris)/Beta Film (Munich). (92 mins.)

Jacques Demy is a young French director free of the severe, discordant attitudes of his contemporaries. In *The Umbrellas of Cherbourg*, he is preoccupied with the subtleties, transfigurations, and deceptions of time. The film has a fast narrative pace, like a ballad, and is at its most successful when most romantic. The dialogue is sung throughout, from a

1964: "The fragile beauty" of THE UMBRELLAS OF CHERBOURG.

casual phrase to an ardent expression of love or despair. But it is in the tradition neither of filmed opera nor of the American musical. Michel Legrand's music is based on five essential phrases and links people, places, and situations in an entirely original way. The central threnody underscores the grief of Geneviève (Catherine Deneuve) and—later—that of her lover, Guy (Nino Castelnuovo). The charm of each theme is counterpointed visually by the colors: indigo, saffron, olive, aquamarine. (Certain streets in Cherbourg were painted so as to achieve additional harmony.)

Absence is the cruellest adversary in Demy's world. All his films, like Prévert's, abound in tender farewells. "The sun and death go together—how strange," muses Guy, and but for the sheer intensity of the sentiment it would sound old-fashioned and faintly ridiculous. The film is sustained by such moments of gravity and poignance as well as by the unblemished honesty of its characters. Its fragile beauty is unique among the films of 1964.

DOCTOR STRANGELOVE, Or How I learned to stop worrying and love the Bomb. Britain. Script: Stanley Kubrick, Terry Southern, and Peter George, based on the latter's novel, "Red Alert." Direction: Kubrick. Photography: Gilbert Taylor. Editing: Anthony Harvey. Music: Laurie Johnson. Art Direction: Ken Adam. Players: Peter Sellers, George C. Scott, Sterling Hayden, Keenan Wynn, Slim Pickens, Peter Bull. Production: Hawk Films/Columbia. (94 mins.)

Black comedy in the cinema has never been more appreciated than in the last decade. *Doctor Strangelove* is a dazzlingly wrought, Carrollian vision of nuclear doomsday. An insane American general (frustrated because war is becoming more and more the prerogative of politicians) sends his wing of B-52 bombers beyond their "fail-safe" point. He seals off his base, and radio contact with the aircraft is broken. One zealous pilot eventually bombs his target: thus a single "slip-up" has plunged the world into a century of radioactivity.

Kubrick grasps this hideous conception by cleverly mixing two styles—the satirical encounters between Peter Sellers and Sterling Hayden, and the earnest combat routine that proceeds relentlessly aboard the B-52. These twin approaches fuse in a stunning climax as Doctor Strangelove rants in the Pentagon war room and the Texan pilot rides his warhead to destruction like a rodeo steer. *Doctor Strangelove* can safely be numbered among the most intelligent American films of its time. Kubrick has worked outside the Hollywood system for much of his career (*Paths of Glory* was shot in Germany; *Lolita* and *2001: A Space Odyssey* in Britain). Only in this way can he express his bitter vision of our mechanistic age.

DIAMONDS OF THE NIGHT (Démanty Noci). Czechoslovakia. Script: Arnost Lustig and Jan Nemec, from the novel, *Darkness has no Shadows,* by Lustig. Direction: Nemec. Photography: Jaroslav Kucera. Editing: Miroslav Hájek. Music: none. Art Direction: Oldrich Bosák. Players: Ladislav Jansky, Antonín Kumbera, Ilse Bischofová. Production: Filmstudio Barrandov. (64 mins.)

It is towards the end of the war in the Sudetenland on the borders of Czechoslovakia. Two boys escape from a Nazi "transport," and plunge through a forest trying to shake off pursuit. Gradually they become animalistic in their gestures and outlook. Their minds

1964: DOCTOR STRANGELOVE—panic in the Pentagon war room.

259

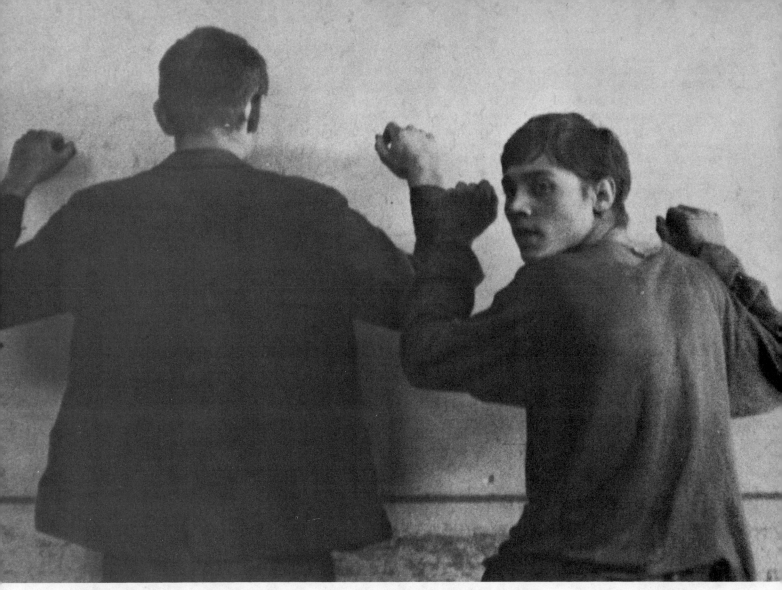

1964: The two captives in DIAMONDS OF THE NIGHT.

start to wander; memories, hallucinations, and desires rise and die away like the knelling of the bell behind the credits. They imagine trees falling on top of them, ants swarming over their hands and face, and summon up distorted visions of wartime Prague, with strange elongated trams, and a woman who gazes impassively down from a first floor window like some figure from a Goya portrait. At length they are hunted down and arrested by a Home Guard composed of weird old men who celebrate the capture with beer and grinding songs. The film is an episode, the experience of days condensed into one hour. Arnost Lustig, the author, has used the flashback technique in the script to match the panic-stricken flight from the train. The memories are like a stabbing pain; they are literally *injected* into the spectator's psyche. At first they are ambivalent and illogical. Then, as they recur, they slowly bloom into tangible recollections and realizations. Kucera's hand-held camera clings obsessively to the fugitives, registering the slightest change in ex-

pression on their faces. When they stagger away from the Home Guard, they are little more than automata, caught up in a flight from captivity that implies a flight from reality. *Diamonds of the Night* is horribly disquieting in its suggestion that the human mind is so much clay, molded by events and contingencies and infinitely impressionable. Nemec is a superb stylist, a master of the chiaroscuro effect, and capable of ordering the soundtrack so that silence becomes as haunting as the mastications of a toothless old man as he tears at a cooked chicken in front of the boys.

THE GOSPEL ACCORDING TO ST. MATTHEW (Il Vangelo Secondo Matteo). Italy/France. Script and Direction: Pier Paolo Pasolini, from the Gospel according to St. Matthew (Assisi text). Photography: Tonino Delli Colli. Editing: Nino Baragli. Music: Bach, Mozart, Prokofiev, Webern, and the Congolese Mass "Misa Luba"; also original music by Luis E. Bacalov. Art Direction: Luigi Scaccianoce. Players:

Enrique Irazoqui, Margherita Caruso, Susanna Pasolini, Marcello Morante, Mario Socrate, Settimio Di Porto, Otello Sestili. Production: Arco Film (Rome) /Lux (Paris). (142 mins.)

Pier Paolo Pasolini, the Marxist writer and film theorist, had already levelled a hefty blow at Biblical epics in the final episode of *Rogopag* (1962) before tackling *The Gospel according to St. Matthew*. Like all milestones in religious art this comprehensive version of the life of Christ is both self-confident and full of humility. Enrique Irazoqui's Jesus suggests purposefulness, deliberation and, finally, resignation. His career is set rigorously in its historical context; the authorities regard him as a meddlesome agitator, all too well versed in the Law. This Jesus, like the film as a whole, is free of the effete glamor attaching to most of Hollywood's New Testament spectaculars.

Pasolini looks unflinchingly at the Agony in the Garden and the Journey to the Crucifixion; and at Pilate's mock trial the camera peers over shoulders and between heads like a shocked witness. The high priests call to mind Renaissance princes, shrewd and fleshy, with hats shaped like baskets as in Rembrandt's religious paintings. But most of the cast consists of simple, unadorned folk who gape and smile and somehow sense the importance of this Prophet's unequivocal demand for faith. Although the locations are in Italy, with Jerusalem a straggling hill town, one never questions the film's historical authenticity. *The Gospel according to St. Matthew* is a masterpiece of its kind, ascending at times to the serene heights of Bach, whose music is suitably linked to many scenes.

Checklist of other important features

THE DIARY OF A CHAMBERMAID (Le Journal d'une Femme de Chambre). France/Italy. Some devastating, lightning-fast jabs at the sacred cows of bourgeois society, illuminate Buñuel's version of the Mirbeau novel (see *1946* for Renoir's film of the same name.) Jeanne Moreau is a far from delightful heroine and bears a fatal resemblance to the valet who plagues her life in the country.

GERTRUD. Denmark. Carl Dreyer's first film in ten years, based on the Hjalmar Söderberg play about the opera singer who finds three men unable to satisfy her idealistic conception of love. Austere, uncompromising, and penetrating in its observation.

HAMLET. U.S.S.R. Director: Grigori Kozintsev. A screen treatment of the play that is rich in powerful imagery and personal interpretation, and dominated by the arrogant crescendos of Shostakovitch's score.

LIFE UPSIDE DOWN (La Vie à l'envers). France.

1964: THE GOSPEL ACCORDING TO ST. MATTHEW.

Alain Jessua's astute hero relishes the idea of retreating into his private world, free of the mechanized puppetry and inane conventions of modern life. Witty and bizarre.

THE PEACH THIEF (Kradezat na Praskovi). Bulgaria. Director: Veulo Radev. The first film of importance from Bulgaria, a melancholy backward glance at World War I and a plaintive love affair between a Serbian POW and the wife of the Commandant at Turnovo.

THE SARAGOSSA MANUSCRIPT (Rekopis Znaleziony w Saragossie). Poland. Director: Wojciech J. Has. A subtle fable that contrives to parody the historical spectacle film, with Zbigniew Cybulski as the Guards officer who enters a half-real, half-fantasy world during the Napoleonic wars in Spain.

SILKEN SKIN (La Peau Douce). France. A seriously underrated study of frustration by François Truffaut. One believes instinctively in Jean Desailly's sensitive portrayal of the middle-aged lecturer falling desperately in love with an air hostess (the late Françoise Dorléac).

THOMAS THE IMPOSTER (Thomas l'Imposteur). France. Director: Georges Franju. From a novel about World War I by Cocteau, with a Polish princess whose enigmatic and scintillating personality is utterly deceived by the young Thomas, with his pretended relationship to a great general.

261

WOMAN IN THE DUNES (Suna no Onna). Japan. Director: Hiroshi Teshigahara. An entomologist is lured into a deep pit in the sands. His efforts to escape and his final complaisant behavior give the film its haunting ambiguity and a restless sense of frustration.

Short films and Documentaries

THE PIER (La Jetée). France. Director: Chris Marker. Science fiction is a genre often essayed by the cinema, but not often with the massive intelligence and sophistication of *The Pier*. After "World War III" has devastated Paris, a man is subjected to experiments by German scientists in the catacombs beneath the city. As a child he has foreseen his own death and only now, impelled by the curious drugs of the enemy, can he travel back through time to achieve this ghastly rendezvous on the pier at Orly Airport. All this is told with still photographs, blending elliptically into each other like fragments of a story rescued from some archive: the arrested postures seem to radiate more life than the movements themselves. Men's faces become craggy and filled with shadow like petrified stones. This bold style gives *The Pier* much dignity and also a degree of *elongated* emotion that makes the romance at the film's center appear excruciating in its doomed beauty, and the idea of a voyage through time appear horrific and unfair.

A. West Germany. Jan Lenica is a major graphic artist in the tradition of Munch and Lautrec, with a squat style of his own that combines ruthless and nostalgic elements. *A* is a beguiling tale of a man irritated and then attacked by a monstrous letter A.

ALF BILL AND FRED. Britain. A hilarious morality story flaunting, like all Bob Godfrey's cartoons and "live action" shorts, a ripe sense of humor and a fondness for the Edwardian world of veiled naughtiness.

HELP! MY SNOWMAN'S BURNING DOWN. United States. A surrealist comedy by Carson Davidson that starts with the hero typing away in a bathtub of water in New York harbor.

LES JEUX DES ANGES. France. Director: Walerian Borowczyk. An abstract and nightmarish masterpiece by one of the world's foremost artists in the field of animation. An overwhelming atmosphere of desolation and anguish emerges from these weird tableaux.

PEACHES. Britain. Director: Michael Gill. Unusual fantasy about a girl whose cleverness and fondness for peaches lead her into all kinds of diverting situations.

1964: Facts of Interest

Sir Michael Balcon wins a much publicized battle for control of British Lion, long associated with enterprising film production in England.
Death of Robert Hamer, Peter Lorre, Alan Ladd, and Harpo Marx.

1964: THE PIER—The "ghastly rendezvous . . . at Orly Airport."

1965

TOKYO OLYMPIAD 1964. Japan. Script: Natto Wada, Yoshio Shirasaka, Shuntaro Tanikawa, Kon Ichikawa. Direction: Ichikawa. Photography: Shigeo Hayashida, Kazuo Miyagawa, Juichi Nagano, Kinji Nakamura, Tadashi Tanaka (Eastmancolor). Music: Toshiro Mayuzumi. Art Direction: Yusaku Kamekura. Production: Organising Committee of the Games of the 18th Olympiad/Toho (Suketaru Taguchi). (130 mins.)

Grace was the keynote of Leni Riefenstahl's *Olympia* (see *1938*). Strength and guts, "blood, sweat, and tears," are the vital qualities that pervade *Tokyo Olympiad*. Without the competition the Games would be a ludicrous parade. Ichikawa claims, "I have attempted to capture the solemnity of the moment when man defies his limits. And to express the solitude of the man who, to succeed, fights against himself." Whereas for Riefenstahl the athletes formed part of a larger conception, every competitor has his idiosyncrasies caught by Ichikawa. Away from the brash commentary, and the din of the stadium, he retreats into some intriguing limbo beyond his mere physical

1965:   TOKYO OLYMPIAD 1964—"a common tension and intoxication."

presence, the slow-motion film registering the slightest flutter of a nerve or, as in the instance of Ann Packer, a fleeting smile of relief. The conciseness of the film reaches its ultimate degree in the rifle shooting. Ichikawa studies one marksman in formidable close-up. The man's jowl sags over the butt of his rifle in readiness, then unfolds again as something disturbs the target area. Concentration is all. Because he can observe these competitors in such minute detail, Ichikawa can contribute that humor which is essentially an ingredient of his own work (*Alone on the Pacific*, for example). The walkers strut and wriggle in frustration along a soaked track; a Russian tosses the shot around like a cricket ball, rubbing his vest unceasingly.

More than 160 cameramen and 500 technicians were involved in the production and 1,600 mm and 2,000 mm telephoto lenses were frequently in operation. But *Tokyo Olympiad* is no brightly-colored newsreel. Despite its artificial nature, the film gives one a shared pleasure, a common tension and intoxication. It is a paean to human energy.

THE LOVES OF A BLONDE (Lásky jedné plavovlásky). Czechoslovakia. Script: Miloš Forman, Jaroslav Papousek, Ivan Passer. Direction: Forman. Photography: Miroslav Ondricek. Music: Evcen Hilin. Art Direction: Karel Cerný. Players: Hana Brejchová, Vladimír Pucholt, Vladimir Mensík, Antonin Blazejovsky, Milada Jezková, Josef Sebanek. Production: Sebor-Bor, Barrandov Studio. (82 mins.)

Miloš Forman's gift for describing young people without rancor or self-consciousness makes his comedies indicative of a fresh movement in Czech cinema. Forman is not preoccupied with the last war, like most of his countrymen. There is no glamor in his cinema; nor is there squalor and depression. Instead, Forman studies people in their daily surroundings. *The Loves of a Blonde* is his third picture, and probably his most agile. The heroine is a shy, watchful blonde called Andula. She works in a factory and

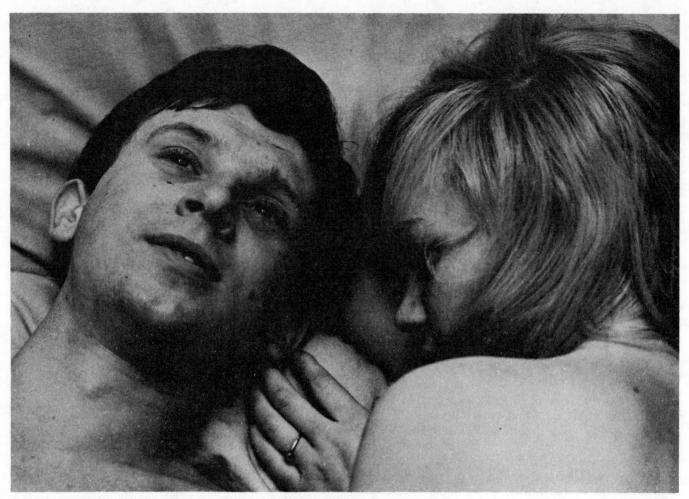

1965: From THE LOVES OF A BLONDE.

sleeps in a hostel with a group of girls. When she decides to trust a lover, a young dance musician (played with antic mournfulness by Vladimír Pucholt), she discovers that life only brings tears if one takes it too seriously. The film contains two brilliant anthology scenes: the first at a local dance, where three soldiers try to pick up some girls (Andula among them) until the fundamental differences in personality pull apart the evening's plans; the second at the boy's home, when Andula arrives unexpectedly with her belongings and stubbornly endures the parents' suspicious reaction. The tug of emotion at the close of a Forman sequence is not artificially engendered; nor does it pretend to be high tragedy. Andula will recover and laugh again. Her troubles teach her tolerance, and Forman's mischievous camera communicates this growth of understanding with a keenness born of candor and sincerity.

BETWEEN TWO WORLDS (I Pugni in Tasca). Italy. Script and Direction: Marco Bellocchio. Photography: Alberto Marrama. Editing: Aurelio Mangia-

rotti. Music: Ennio Morricone. Art Direction: Gisella Longo. Players: Lou Castel, Paola Pitagora, Marino Masè, Liliana Gerace, Pier Luigi Troglio, Jean Mc-Neil, Irene Agnelli, Sandra Bergamini. Production: Doria. (113 mins.)

No documentary about epilepsy could be quite as alarming and unforgettable as *Between Two Worlds*, a fiction film directed by a 26 year old student of cinema outside the normal production system in Italy. A blind widow lives in a villa near Piacenza with her four children. Three of them are epileptics; only Augusto is normal. Sandro claims to have been free of fits for over a year. But in Lou Castel's defensive performance he oscillates disconcertingly between rational behavior and snarling, convulsive outbursts. He wants to relieve Augusto of responsibility by driving his mother and the others over a precipice. But his resolution fails, and though he does murder the helpless woman and drowns his younger brother, he cannot act against his sister, to whom he finds himself more and more attracted. Sandro is a peculiarly complex character, struggling constantly between his egotism and his sympathy for Augusto. He is spilling over with unexploited energy; he is anxious to earn recognition from normal society; and the climactic fit which strikes him as he mimes gleefully to a Verdi aria is, in its ironic way, both a consummation and a solution to his life. The two extremes in his emotional make-up—agony and rapture—have fused. Bellocchio observes all this with such intensity and sensitivity that the film throws off a kind of electric tension. Even the aggravated editing, with sequences jerking spasmodically from one to another, is like the manifestation of epilepsy itself, while a sense of isolation creeps up from the wintry Po Valley to penetrate the loves of Sandro and his family.

Keaton and his contemporaries are exciting fresh admiration. Etaix is primarily a silent comedian, and when, in *Yoyo*, the "talkies" arrive, the film loses much of its inventiveness and intrinsic humor. The appeal of this minor masterpiece lies in the strength of feeling Etaix has for his characters, for their surroundings, and for a personal paradise reminiscent of Fellini's nostalgic settings. In 1925, a bored millionaire invites a circus to perform in his château, and recognizes an equestrienne as one of his former mistresses. The son he fathered so long ago is now an energetic little clown named Yoyo. The millionaire renounces his wealth and adopts the gypsy life with alacrity. As the years pass, Yoyo matures and hankers increasingly after the life of his father in the

1965: BETWEEN TWO WORLDS—"a kind of electric tension."

YOYO. France. Script: Pierre Etaix, Jean-Claude Carrière. Direction: Etaix. Photography: Jean Boffety. Editing: Henri Lanoë. Music: Jean Paillaud. Art Direction: Raymond Tournon, Raymond Gabutti. Players: Pierre Etaix, Claudine Auger, Luce Klein, Philippe Dionnet. Production: C.A.P.A.C. (Paul Claudon). (97 mins.)

It is hardly surprising that Pierre Etaix should prove so popular a comedian at a time when Buster

château. He devotes his earnings to reconstruction work, and eventually returns and holds a vast party in the ancestral home. But the pleasure is alloyed. The guests are insufferably boring and acquisitive. When his parents refuse to enter, Yoyo realizes his mistake and departs, astride his favorite elephant.

The story is faultless, graceful and overflowing with charm. The first forty minutes especially teem with those short, sharp movements followed by sudden moments of immobility that are symptomatic of Etaix's

1965: Pierre Etaix as YOYO.

tern of spectacle. Unforgettable images pile one upon another for, in Serandrei and Di Venanzo, Rosi had the finest technicians in Italy. The film is steeped in blood and yet—despite the cruelty—the swirling colors and the balletic, contemptuous movements of the matador express the archetypal dignity of the bull ring. The church ceremonies that clip the film together, and the majestic music score by Piccioni, make this ritualistic element even plainer.

There are hints of Hemingway's vision in the pregnant shots of the arena just before a fight. The expectancy grips like a claw. When Miguelin is mortally wounded, Rosi's telephoto lens enlarges the tragedy. Outside the ring, the direction is less astute. An expert at communicating the emotions of a crowd, Rosi is reluctant to let his audience share a private experience, and he is clearly uncomfortable during the love scene between Miguelin and Linda Christian. But one treasures the sequence in which the matador, now famous and wealthy, returns to watch his family laboring in the fields. He quietly relishes his freedom at the same time as his curiosity perceives the inevitable order of life. This, indeed, is a moment of truth.

Checklist of other important features

ALPHAVILLE (Alphaville, Une étrange aventure de Lemmy Caution). France/Italy. Paris in the future, ruled by a harsh computer which outlaws love and sentiment. Told with uncharacteristic discipline and allusiveness by Jean-Luc Godard.

THE EAVESDROPPER (El Oja de la Cerradura). Argentina/United States. Director: Leopoldo Torre Nilsson. A curious film that, through the antics of its central character, a smoldering patriot in an unnamed South American state, sheds much light on politics and its flotsam.

THE KNACK. Britain. Director: Richard Lester. Sprightly if rough-textured comedy about London life which won the Grand Prix at Cannes this year.

KWAIDAN. Japan. Director: Masaki Kobayashi. Deceptively formal horror film that makes brilliant use of color and fantasy.

ONIBABA. Japan. Director: Kaneto Shindo. An amalgam of lust, jealousy, and slaughter in the middle ages, justified by Shindo's handling of the locations (a field of reeds and pampas grass), and his appreciation of the superstitious elements in this tale.

RED BEARD (Akahige). Japan. A long and underrated period film from Akira Kurosawa, with Toshiro Mifune as the famous head of a clinic.

style. The behavior of the millionaire's bibulous retainers, the chorus girls who tease off his shoes and socks to the accompaniment of sweet music, and the silence punctuated by screeches from mincing feet or closing doors—all indicate a highly individual and controlled talent. Behind the severe face and the punctilious behavior one senses the wise and mellow sadness of the authentic clown.

THE MOMENT OF TRUTH (Il Momento della Verità). Italy/Spain. Script: Francesco Rosi, Pedro Portabella, Ricardo Munoz Suay, Pedro Beltrantis. Direction: Rosi. Photography: Gianni Di Venanzo, Ajace Parolin, Pasquale De Santis (Technicolor). Editing: Mario Serandrei. Music: Piero Piccioni. Players: Miguel Mateo Miguelin, José Gomez Sevillano, Pedro Basauri Pedrucho, Linda Christian. Production: Federiz (Rome)/A.S. Film (Madrid). (110 mins.)

From the many films that have been devoted to bull fighting, one admires most Francesco Rosi's *The Moment of Truth*. Miguel Mateo Miguelin enjoyed his years as a brilliant fighter, and Rosi uses his rise to fame as a thread around which to weave a fierce pat-

1965: Miguel Mateo Miguelin in THE MOMENT OF TRUTH.

SHAKESPEARE-WALLAH. India. Director: James Ivory. The declining fortunes of a troupe of players in modern India are treated with gentle wit, affection, and romanticism.

A SHOP ON MAIN STREET (Obchod na Korze). Czechoslovakia. Director: Jan Kadar and Elmar Klos. One of the most effective anti-Fascist films of recent years, a quiet, tragicomic account of life in a provincial town in occupied Czechoslovakia. An Oscar winner.

WAR AND PEACE (Wojna i Mir). U.S.S.R. Director: Sergei Bondarchuk. The massive Soviet version of Tolstoy's novel, filmed in four parts, with Bondarchuk's genius finding moments of contemplation and intimacy within the landscape of battle.

Short films and Documentaries

LA BRULURE DE MILLE SOLEILS. France. Pierre Kast's surprisingly successful science fiction fantasy, employing melancholy figures that could have been drawn by Henry Moore. Not quite cartoon, not quite "live action," but bewitching all the same.

THE KOUMIKO MYSTERY (Le Mystère Koumiko). France. Made while Chris Marker was in Tokyo for the Olympic Games, this fifty-minute film is a picturesque study of a girl, Koumiko, whom Marker met during his stay, and also an impression of a country where, unlike 1940, Emperors bow and transistors are manufactured by the million.

THE TIMEPIECE. U.S.A. Director: Jim Henson. A surreal comedy featuring a man in hospital, and his all-important pulse. A prize winner at many festivals.

1965: Facts of Interest

Death of Clara Bow, Jeanette MacDonald, Stan Laurel, and the producer David O. Selznick.

1966

PERSONA. Sweden. Script and Direction: Ingmar Bergman. Photography: Sven Nykvist. Editing: Ulla Ryghe. Music: Lars Johan Werle. Art Direction: Bibi Lindström. Players: Bibi Andersson, Liv Ullmann, Gunnar Björnstrand, Margaretha Krook. Production: Svensk Filmindustri. (81 mins.)

With *Persona*, Bergman takes a great leap forward in his attempt to suggest the communion of souls. The two women in the film, Sister Alma (Bibi Andersson), and Elisabeth Vogler (Liv Ullmann) are alone on an island in the Baltic, like the family in *Through a Glass Darkly* (see *1961*). Alma is eager to unburden the secrets and the fantasies of her past; Elisabeth merely listens impassively, and gradually consumes her companion's personality. This is "chamber cinema" at its most sophisticated pitch. Some of the avant garde affectations are not immediately successful—the burning of the film in the projector, the TV newsreel of a Buddhist monk's blazing to death in Saigon. But Bergman's talent for fastening on visual metaphors grows more and more remarkable. Desperation, for example, is distilled into the beating of fists on a hospital table. Reticence and mystery lie in the visors of shadow cast by the girls' wide sun-hats as

they sit together by the sea. Lars Johan Werle's music, with its abstract chords, is fitted miraculously to certain key passages, and Sven Nykvist's photography achieves uncanny extremes of clarity and translucency. Bergman expunges familiar reality in *Persona*: his heroines exist in a limbo reminiscent of Timoka in *The Silence* (see *1963*) or of Strindberg's walled town. He obeys no rigorous dramatic structure, adheres to no logical continuity; and yet by virtue of its respect for human problems, his *Persona* is the masterpiece of 1966.

CHIMES AT MIDNIGHT (Campanadas a Medianoche). Spain/Switzerland. Script and Direction: Orson Welles, from plays by William Shakespeare. Photography: Edmond Richard. Editing: Fritz Mueller. Music: Angelo Francesco Lavagnino. Art Direction: José Antonio de la Guerra, Mariano Erdorza. Players: Orson Welles, John Gielgud, Keith Baxter, Margaret Rutherford, Jeanne Moreau, Norman Rodway, Marina Vlady, Alan Webb, Tony Beckley. Production: Internacional Films Española (Madrid) / Alpine (Basle). (119 mins.)

By weaving together passages from *Richard II*, *Henry IV (Pts. I and II)*, *Henry V*, and *The Merry Wives of Windsor*, Welles has created a rotund and lifesize Falstaff in *Chimes at Midnight*. He regards Falstaff as "virtue, honesty, goodness, the spirit of Merrie England"; when first Hotspur and then Falstaff died, there passed away an entire age. Falstaff is—beneath his rumbustiousness—one of Shakespeare's most tragic figures, and Welles's performance is geared to the wounding climax when he staggers ingenuously into the train of his beloved Prince Hal, freshly crowned King of England. "I know thee not, old man: fall to thy prayers; How ill white hairs become a fool and jester!" responds Hal scornfully. Falstaff's weakness for living off others has betrayed him at last, while the Prince's determination to become "a famous English hero" has compelled him to abandon

1966: *PERSONA, Bergman's "attempt to suggest the communion of souls."*

his former friends. Like so many figures in Welles's cinema, Hal has lost his innocence. The somber tones of this rejection arrive in contrast to the brightly limned tableaux of the Battle of Shrewsbury. The clash of armies is a masterly evocation of medieval war. The sweeping cavalry charges degenerate into a heavy, panting violence as men and horses tire and the battlefield becomes a quagmire. It is, ultimately, the richness and the innate rhythm of Welles's imagery that give his films such stature.

THE WAR IS OVER (La Guerre est Finie). France/Sweden. Script: Jorge Semprun. Direction: Alain Resnais. Photography: Sacha Vierny. Editing: Eric Pluet. Music: Giovanni Fusco. Art Direction: Jacques Saulnier. Players: Yves Montand, Ingrid Thulin, Michel Piccoli, Geneviève Bujold, Dominique Rozan, Françoise Bertin. Production: Sofracima (Paris) / Europa Film (Stockholm). (122 mins.)

The more closely one studies Resnais's films, the more one realizes that in spite of their almost mechanical structure, they are deeply and sympathetically concerned with their characters: the woman in *Hiroshima Mon Amour,* or Hélène Aughain in *Muriel.* Diego Mora (Yves Montand), the Spanish hero of *The War is Over,* is a tired revolutionary who still has to make decisions every minute of his life. He dis-

1966: Orson Welles and Jeanne Moreau in CHIMES AT MIDNIGHT

1966: Ingrid Thulin and Yves Montand in THE WAR IS OVER.

likes his elders who fought in the Civil War as much as he despises the impatient young "Leninists" who will resort to any kind of violence to oust Franco. The film is related on the level of a political thriller, with Diego pursued by the ever-present fear of the police and of betrayal by inquisitive friends. His love for Marianne (Ingrid Thulin) consists of one long effort to shield her from the painful truth of his dedication, and their single love scene is among the most beautiful sequences in modern cinema, at once a compensation and a fulfillment for Diego. The intensity of *The War is Over* stems from Resnais's much copied but still unequalled combination of past, present, and future. Diego's mind strays from the here and now, experiencing memories and premonitions like the people in Sartre's novels. The commentary resembles a lament or a speech of resignation, while the music offers an escape into delirium, and Sacha Vierny's images of Paris and the car journeys through the countryside somehow characterize the grey futility of Diego's career.

CUL-DE-SAC. Britain. Script: Roman Polanski and Gerard Brach. Direction: Polanski. Photography: Gilbert Taylor. Editing: Alistair McIntyre. Music: Komeda. Art Direction: Voytek. Players: Donald Pleasence, Lionel Stander, Françoise Dorléac, Jack Mac-

1966: CUL-DE-SAC—"A gangster and his dying accomplice are on the run."

Gowran, William Franklyn, Robert Dorning. Production: Compton-Tekli. (111 mins.)

No English director of recent years has used a location so well as Roman Polanski uses the Northumberland coast in *Cul-de-Sac*, his second feature shot outside Poland. A gangster and his dying accomplice are on the run. They shelter on a castle at Lindisfarne, separated from the shore by a slender causeway, and dispense gravelly orders to the husband and wife who live there. Like the boat in *The Knife in the Water* (see *1962*), the castle becomes a trap in the surrounding sea. It is fowl-infested by day and owlridden by night, decaying in rhyme with its occupants, whom it only releases after violence—that cauterizing element in Polanski's world. The breakdown of rational behavior is the theme of *Cul-de-Sac:* those perversions and proclivities of the human soul that emerge under pressure. Teresa veers in her allegiance between her husband's ineffectual clowning and the insensitive arrogance of the gangster. George, bald-headed and a transvestite, flits around like some terrified Roman emperor, deriving unacknowledged pleasure from the situation. And beneath his ambivalence, Polanski proves as usual to be the most moral of directors. The bloody, fiery climax crowns all the previous grotesqueries of the film and gives it the durability of a nightmare. Circumstances and personalities interlock with horrible perfection.

SECOND BREATH (Le Deuxième Souffle). France. Script and Direction: Jean-Pierre Melville, from the novel by José Giovanni. Photography: Marcel Combes. Editing: Michel Bohème. Music: Bernard Gérard. Art Direction: Jean-Jacques Fabre. Players: Lino Ventura, Paul Meurisse, Raymond Pellegrin, Christine Fabrega, Pierre Zimmer, Michel Constantin, Marcel Bozzufi. Production: Les Productions Montaigne (Charles Lumbroso, André Labay). (150 mins.)

The French *film policier*, drawing its elegance of execution and its deadpan style of acting from the American thriller, has, at its best, touched on points of moral loyalty ignored by Hollywood. *Le Trou* (see *1960*) was a classic of its kind; Melville's *Second Breath* is another, a meticulously premeditated film that never appears purely functional in its progression towards final slaughter and redemption. Melville asserts in a prologue that a man has only one choice when he is born—the choice of his death, and his hero Gus Minda (Lino Ventura) clings to this uncompromising standpoint. He is an obstinate rock of a gangster who reaches, like so many of his predecessors in the genre, for the final snatch, the big, two-million-franc job, and plays into the clutches of his sarcastic enemy at police headquarters, Blot. His reputation in the underworld means everything to him; and

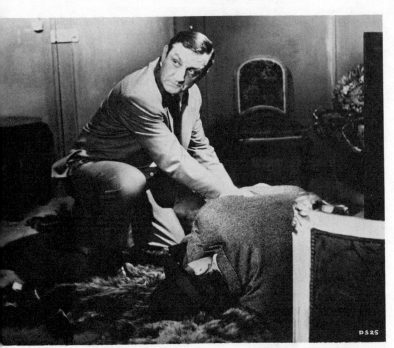

Lino Ventura as the aging mobster in SECOND BREATH.

though the final twenty minutes assume an arbitrary tinge as Gus takes fatal risks to restore his good name, this is in part excused by Melville's brave, unwavering stare at the relationship between police and criminal in France. Besides, *Second Breath* is intriguing because, despite Melville's sober, purposeful style (which embraces images of a telling beauty), it still contains an ambiguous flavor. There are incidents of fantasy mingled so cleverly in the factual narrative that, by portraying a man's physical actions, they simultaneously reveal his mental state. Melville does not condemn or condone the gangster's *métier;* he insists only that a man behaves according to a basic moral code—that he chooses how to die.

YESTERDAY GIRL (Abschied von gestern). West Germany. Script and Direction: Alexander Kluge, based partly on his book *Lebensläufe.* Photography: Edgar Reitz, Thomas Mauch. Editing: Beate Mainka. Players: Alexandra Kluge, Günther Mack, Eva Marie Meineke, Peter Staimmer, Hans Korte, Edith Kuntze,

1966: Alexandra Kluge in YESTERDAY GIRL.

Josef Kreindl. Production: Kairos Film Alexander Kluge/Independent Film. (90 mins.)

This is in a sense the year of the German cinema. *Es* (directed by Ulrich Schamoni), *Schonzeit für Fuchse* (directed by Peter Schamoni), and *Der Junge Törless* (directed by Volker Schlöndorff) are fresh and adventurous. Alexander Kluge's *Yesterday Girl* is more sophisticated than these films. Anita G. (played by Dr. Kluge's sister), is the face of the sixties, typical of a generation that has grown up since the war, hovering on the edge of delinquency and frustrated by the pettiness of bourgeois society. Then men and women who enter her life talk with maddening irrelevance—the teacher who babbles of Max Weber's theory of popular sovereignty, the civil servant who feeds her on Kafka and Verdi. Anita's knowledge of the past is masked by fairy tales and convenient historical fallacies, and yet she is reluctant to become part of society's design, to submit to the languorous violin music that fills the huge stuffy lounges of German hotels. She wanders instead along the autobahns, dragging her suitcase like a badge of incongruity, and eventually returns to prison for a term . . .

Kluge's elliptical film has none of the dry gravity of a postmortem, even though most of the characters are real-life professors, lawyers, and social workers. There is considerable satire in the mosaic of associations, usually at the expense of an ageing country's blinkered approach to life, and of the abstract phrases in which its intellectuals entangle themselves. There is one improvised scene, when a dog training demonstration drifts into farce in the rain, that justifies Anita's distrust of order, and belongs unmistakably to the anti-heroics of Godard, Skolimowski, Pasolini, and Bertolucci.

Checklist of other important features

ASHES (Popioly). Poland. Andrzej Wajda's salute to the brave resistance of a lost generation to change and—questionably—to progress, as the Poles side with Napoleon in Spain and Russia.

AU HASARD BALTHAZAR. France. Director: Robert Bresson. A wise and graceful tale of a donkey that embraces pastoral love and vicious beatniks without ever being ridiculous.

THE CHASE. United States. Director: Arthur Penn. An oddly dated but riveting tale of Deep South lawlessness, with Marlon Brando as the growling, much-punished sheriff.

FAHRENHEIT 451. Britain. François Truffaut's quaint but all too timid adaptation of Ray Bradbury's novel about a world where books are illegal.

HERE'S YOUR LIFE (Här har du ditt liv). Sweden. An extraordinary saga of a young man's coming to terms with life between 1914 and 1918, directed, photographed and edited by Jan Troell with a rare appreciation of character and an anecdotal charm.

A MAN FOR ALL SEASONS. Britain. Director: Fred Zinnemann. The story of Thomas More's struggle with Henry VIII, transferred from stage to screen with resplendent success. Winner of six Oscars; staring Paul Scofield as More.

A MAN AND A WOMAN (Un Homme et une Femme). France. Claude Lelouch won the Grand Prix at Cannes, two Oscars, and a multi-million dollar gross for this zestful but rather too sugary love film.

THE ROUND-UP (Szegénylegények). Hungary. Director: Miklós Jancsó. The most impressive postwar film from Hungary, full of psychological pressures as a group of brigands is herded together for interrogation in a huge plain after the failure of Kossuth's 1848 revolution.

SECONDS. United States. An implausible plot—a man's being "reborn" through elaborate surgery—given an hallucinating aura of tension by Frankenheimer's direction and the "fish eye" photography of James Wong Howe.

THE SPY WHO CAME IN FROM THE COLD. Britain. Director: Martin Ritt. A wintry, enthralling version of the novel by John Le Carré, with Richard Burton as the dragged-down cynic of a spy, forced to betray his girl and himself.

VIVA MARIA. France/Italy. Director: Louis Malle. A frothy, picaresque extravaganza as Jeanne Moreau and Brigitte Bardot cause havoc in early-twentieth-century Mexico.

WHO'S AFRAID OF VIRGINIA WOOLF? United States. Director: Mike Nichols. Edward Albee's scalding look at the sex war is translated with power and conviction to the screen. With Richard Burton and Elizabeth Taylor as the university lecturer and his virulent wife.

Short films and Documentaries

AU FOU. Japan. Director: Yoji Kuri. A characteristic cluster of jokes by the East's greatest and most grotesque cartoonist.

THE WAR GAME. Britain. Director: Peter Watkins.

The BBC television documentary about nuclear war and its aftermath that was banned from the small screen and subsequently acquired—with success—for cinema showing.

1966: Facts of Interest

Death of Buster Keaton, Walt Disney, Robert Rossen, Montgomery Clift, Clifton Webb, Nikolai Cherkassov, and Gianni Di Venanzo (the great Italian director of photography).

1967: *Vanessa Redgrave and David Hemmings meet in the park in* BLOW-UP.

Michelangelo Antonioni.

274

1967

BLOW-UP. Britain. Script: Michelangelo Antonioni, Tonino Guerra, from a short story by Julio Cortazar. Direction: Antonioni. Photography: Carlo Di Palma (Eastmancolor). Editing: Frank Clarke. Music: Herbert Hancock. Art Direction: Assheton Gorton. Players: David Hemmings, Vanessa Redgrave, Sarah Miles, Peter Bowles. Production: Bridge Films / M-G-M. (111 mins.)

In *Blow-Up,* Thomas (David Hemmings), the loutish and successful young photographer, is confronted by the clashing colors and tempi of the mid-sixties. He is as aggressive as he is unstable, his grasshopper mind endowing him with a superficial brilliance. The murder he apparently witnesses in a London park is never explained. Antonioni is interested in characters, not in causes, and Thomas's abandonment of moral responsibility is all that matters. His laxity is illustrated through the orgies and the parties in which he participates. Antonioni has commented: "All these people who amuse themselves at parties are smiling cynics. Young people who are against order because they want a greater emotional happiness than in the past—who try to live a freer life than before and are therefore against everything, even against love." At the end of *Blow-Up,* Thomas has learned that contemporary life is closed to interpretation; only the spontaneous reaction or "happening" (like the beat concert) can be accounted a genuine experience. Yet Antonioni makes this shameless surrender appear meaningful. Perspectives and colors seem unpredictable, like Thomas's spurts of movement, or the flour-faced students' drive through an urban dawn. In *Blow-Up* the symbols do not intrude. They are invariably linked to the pattern of the film, a pattern of abstract suspense.

BONNIE AND CLYDE. United States. Script: David Newman and Robert Benton. Direction: Arthur Penn. Photography: Burnett Guffey (Technicolor). Editing: Dede Allen. Music: Charles Strouse. Art Direction: Dean Tavoularis. Players: Warren Beatty, Faye Dunaway, Michael J. Pollard, Gene Hackman, Estelle Parsons, Denver Pyle. Production: Warren Beatty / Seven Arts-Warner Bros. (111 mins.)

The free-wheeling moral attitudes of the decade have yielded some curious films. *Bonnie and Clyde* glances wickedly back at the Depression years. Bonnie and Clyde are two southerners who try to muster a dangerous gaiety out of the period. She is a frustrated blonde; he is just out of the state penitentiary and about to steal her mother's car when she intercepts him. So begins one of the most notorious partnerships in thirties' crime. When they are joined by Clyde's brother and his wife, and by a laconic garage hand named C. W. Moss, they constitute a formidable gang. They take outrageous risks; they kill clumsily as if from a guilty conscience. Bystanders seem to envy their escape from the grey idleness that has engulfed the South. A series of blazing altercations with the police only serves to addict them the more to violence. Bonnie sends doggerel verses to the 'papers, recounting the gang's exploits. If, the film appears to say, life is nothing much to lose, then crime pays: it produces a peculiar intoxication that makes the world appear crass and slow-thinking. Arthur Penn directs the film with unflinching zeal, charting the gang's progress like a ballad and bringing the thirties acutely to life.

BELLE DE JOUR. France/Italy. Script: Luis Buñuel and Jean-Claude Carrière, from the novel by Joseph Kessel. Direction: Buñuel. Photography: Sacha Vierny (Eastmancolor). Editing: Walter Spohr. Music: none. Art Direction: Robert Clavel. Players: Catherine Deneuve, Jean Sorel, Michel Piccoli, Geneviève Page, Francisco Rabal, Pierre Clémenti, Georges Marchal. Production: Paris Film (Paris) / Five Films (Rome). (100 mins.)

For Buñuel, purity is a virtue incompatible with honesty, and the heroine of *Belle de Jour* is punished, like Viridiana, for the demure innocence of her exterior. Séverine (Catherine Deneuve) has been mar-

1967: *Faye Dunaway and Warren Beatty in* BONNIE AND CLYDE.

1967: *BELLE DE JOUR—"feelings mingled of disgust and pleasure."*

ried for a year or so to a rich and successful young surgeon (Jean Sorel), but she is obsessed by sexual fantasies and masochistic desires. Her psyche longs for degradation and *la manière forte*. She starts working in a high-class brothel in the afternoons and endures, with feelings mingled of disgust and pleasure, all kinds of humiliation. It is not long before this furtive indulgence encroaches on her married life, with disastrous results, and it is a measure of Buñuel's candor that one feels sympathy for both Séverine and her husband. The observation is piercingly accurate, and concentrates on the unacknowledged sexual deviations which lurk in every wealthy society. The brothel is a fitting symbol of all the taboos that Séverine seeks to escape, a place where reputations are put at stake and disguises adopted. Séverine and her husband live in surroundings of stylized luxury, giving the film the tone of a fable floating free of any one period in

276

time. For all its flashes of imaginary experience, *Belle de Jour* is as seamless and lucid a film as any in the Buñuel canon. It won the Golden Lion at the Venice Film Festival in 1967.

ELVIRA MADIGAN. Sweden. Script, Direction, and Editing: Bo Widerberg. Photography: Jörgen Persson (color). Music: "Piano concerto No. 21" by Mozart; also Vivaldi's Violin Concerti. Players: Pia Degermark, Thommy Berggren, Lennart Malmer, Cleo Jansen, Nina Widerberg. Production: Europa Film. (95 mins.)

In his short career, Bo Widerberg has mixed wild comedy with social complaint, and period frolics with love scenes of quite overwhelming emotion. He is probably the leading film *auteur* of a generation that has tried anxiously to escape the shadow and preoccupations of Ingmar Bergman, and in *Elvira Madigan* he achieves a uniform density of tone that hints at maturity after only five feature films. Elvira and Sixten are doomed lovers at the turn of the century. She is a tightrope artiste, he a Swedish count who has deserted from the army. They are afraid of

their own identity; they feel betrayed by an anonymous society. While they hide from his family and from her step-parents, they undergo a short interval of pastoral bliss. Then, their money exhausted, they commit suicide. The film is essentially a communication of their ecstasy, and Widerberg uses colors like a painter, his affection for natural light and objects giving the affair a charm that lingers rather than palls. *Elvira Madigan* is a tranquil and elegiac film; its textural grace is tinctured with Scandinavian premonitions of death—the wild strawberries suggesting an intimate but evanescent happiness, and the spilled wine signalling the fatal loss of blood and vitality.

THE START (Le Départ). Belgium. Script: Jerzy Skolimowski and Andrzej Kostenko. Director: Skolimowski. Photography: Willy Kurant. Editing: Bob Wade. Music: K. T. Komeda. Players: Jean-Pierre Léaud, Catherine Duport, Jacqueline Bir, Paul Roland, Léon Dony. Production: Elisabeth Films. (89 mins.)

Like his compatriot Polanski, Jerzy Skolimowski

1967: ELVIRA MADIGAN, an "interval of pastoral bliss."

1967: THE START—"a vein of wild humour."

has made a successful attempt to film in a foreign language. His work in Poland is dour and sharply reminiscent of Jean-Luc Godard's style. *The Start,* which won the top award at the Berlin Festival, is set in and around Brussels. It reveals a hitherto untapped vein of wild humor in the Polish director, so that only in the past few shots, as nineteen-year-old Marc realizes that his dream of racing success is irrelevant, does the grey introspection of the Warsaw films return. *The Start* has no story to speak of; it is founded on Marc's obsessive desire to patent his personality, an eagerness translated here into his almost physical love of fast cars. The race for which he trains so urgently remains a chimera, but his efforts to succeed are eloquent clues to his personality and to contemporary youth. His response to violence suggests more curiosity than cynicism. His own cheekiness is infectious, and provides a mordant contrast to the universal happiness preached by posters in the streets. His approach to life derives from convention, but, like Skolimowski's direction, his frustrated behavior not only ridicules each cliché but endows it with fresh currency. The musical score by Komeda matches to perfection the vagaries of the film, and Kurant's agile camerawork clings brilliantly to the action.

Checklist of other important features

ACCIDENT. Britain. Director: Joseph Losey. An understated, haunting piece about English university life, and its undercurrents of hostility and passion. With Dirk Bogarde and Stanley Baker.

DUTCHMAN. Britain. Director: Anthony Harvey. A 55-minute version of the play by LeRoi Jones, with the conversation between Shirley Knight (the white girl) and Al Freeman Jr. (her Negro "victim") aboard the New York subway gripping from start to hideous finish.

EL DORADO. United States. Director: Howard Hawks. John Wayne and Robert Mitchum join forces in a leisurely, genial Western that recalls the best days of Hollywood.

LOVE AFFAIR or The Case of the Missing Switch-board Operator (Ljubavni slucaj). Yugoslavia. Director: Dušan Makavejev. An extraordinarily advanced film from Yugoslavia, fertile with idiosyncratic ideas and black comedy as a man and a girl fall in love and progress exuberantly towards disaster.

MOUCHETTE. France. Director: Robert Bresson. A young peasant girl in the French countryside finds life too bleak and hopeless for anything but suicide to be a salve. As concentrated as anything Bresson has done in the cinema.

PLAYTIME. France. Jacques Tati's first comedy for nearly ten years: slow, reflective, and—cumulatively —very funny. Shot in 70mm in a city where bureaucracy and internationalism run mad.

ULYSSES. Britain. Director: Joseph Strick. A sincere and uncompromising, if understandably abridged, film of the Joyce novel. Quaint, ribald, and, in Barbara Jefford's performance, revealing an undertow of sensuality and suggestiveness.

Short films and Documentaries

BREATH. United States. Director: Jimmy Murakami. An exciting four-minute cartoon on the theme that breath not only sustains life but also registers emotions. Grand Prix winner at the Annecy festival of animation.

CALANDA. France. Director: Juan-Luis Buñuel. Buñuel's son has his father's eye for human intensity as he records the twenty-four hours of drum beating in a Spanish town, with its subtle variations in tone and hysteria.

THE FLY (Muha). Yugoslavia. Directors: Aleksandar Marks and Vladimir Jutriša. Excellently drawn cartoon which observes a man who stamps on a fly being haunted and chastized for his arrogance.

MOTHER AND SON (Mutter und Sohn). West

Germany/Netherlands. Director: Jan Nemec. A hard gem of a short that slices through the traditional view of family love and shows how a mother's adored son is a sadistic torturer convulsed by his past.

TAMER OF WILD HORSES (Krotitelj divljih Konja). Yugoslavia. Director: Nedeljko Dragić. A prodigious, animated paradigm on misguided oppression, all flowing movement and twilight colors.

1967: Facts of Interest

Death of Spencer Tracy, Anthony Mann, G. W. Pabst, Claude Rains, Martine Carol, Julien Duvivier, Paul Muni, Vivien Leigh, Anton Walbrook, Charles Bickford.

The Sound of Music becomes the highest grossing picture in film history.

Seven Arts acquires control of Warner Brothers.

Index to Films Reviewed or Listed
Those accompanied by illustrations appear in Italics.

Illustrations of Directors and Personalities